A
WILD DEER
AMID
SOARING
PHOENIXES

A
WILD DEER
AMID
SOARING
PHOENIXES

The Opposition Poetics of Wang Ji

❀

Ding Xiang Warner

UNIVERSITY OF HAWAI'I PRESS
HONOLULU

Publication has been supported in part
by a grant from the Hull Memorial Publication
Fund of Cornell University.

Library of Congress Cataloging-in-Publication Data
Warner, Ding Xiang.
A wild deer amid soaring phoenixes : the opposition poetics of Wang Ji
/ Ding Xiang Warner.
p.   cm.
Includes bibliographical references and index.
ISBN 0-8248-2669-8 (alk. paper)
1. Wang, Ji, 585–644—Criticism and interpretation.   I. Title:
Opposition poetics of Wang Ji.   II. Title.
PL2677.W265 Z95 2003
895.1'124—dc21
2003005066

Designed by Santos Barbasa Jr.
Printed by The Maple-Vail Book Manufacturing Group

Contents

❀

Acknowledgments

❀

DURING THE LONG course of preparing this book, I have received generous support and encouragement from good friends, nurturing teachers, and kindhearted colleagues. To all of them I wish to express my deep gratitude. I especially thank the following for their major roles in helping me to shape and complete this study of Wang Ji's poetry: Professors David R. Knechtges, William G. Boltz, and Jerry Norman of the University of Washington for the invaluable training they provided me during my graduate school years as well as their comments on the initial stage of this project represented by my Ph.D. dissertation; the late Professor Jack L. Dull, also of the University of Washington, for his remarks during one of our conversations which assisted me in conceiving of my approach to interpreting Wang Ji's poetry; Professor Alvin P. Cohen of the University of Massachusetts, Amherst, for his input on an earlier version of the manuscript and for his encouragement since; and Professor Daniel Boucher of Cornell University for his timely assistance with several of Wang Ji's obscure allusions to Buddhist texts. I am also greatly indebted to Professor Paul W. Kroll of the University of Colorado, Boulder, both for his unflagging support of my work on Wang Ji over the years and for his meticulous reading of the manuscript in its penultimate form. His scrupulous detail and accuracy saved me from potential embarrassments and his insightful suggestions for revision (or requests for clarification) helped to improve my argument in many places. I am likewise grateful to an anonymous reader for the University of Hawai'i Press for many useful comments and recommendations; to Mr. Don Yoder for his careful copyediting of the final manuscript; and to Ms. Pamela Kelley, whose efforts made the entire process of this book's evaluation and preparation for the University of

Hawai'i Press a genuine pleasure. For any errors of fact or interpretation that remain in its pages, however, I am of course solely responsible.

Members of the American Oriental Society, Western Branch, gave me several opportunities to present portions of my work on the life and poetry of Wang Ji at their annual meetings, and their feedback helped me to develop a number of ideas presented in this study. Some material included in Chapters 4 and 5 of this book was previously published in an earlier form. I thank Paul W. Kroll and the American Oriental Society for permission to reprint a revised version of my essay "Mr. Five Dippers of Drunkenville: The Representation of Enlightenment in Wang Ji's Drinking Poems," which appeared in the *Journal of the American Oriental Society* 118(3) (1998): 347–355. I thank Ge Yun and China's Jiangsu Education Press for permission to use "Shi lun Wang Ji de 'You Beishan fu'" (Inquiry into the Reading of Wang Ji's "*Fu* on Roaming the Northern Mountains"), in *Cifu wenxue lunji* (Essays on *cifu* literature), ed. Chinese Department of Nanjing University (Nanjing: Jiangsu jiaoyu chubanshe, 1999), pp. 426–439.

I am, as well, profoundly grateful to the Hull Memorial Publication Fund review committee at Cornell University. A generous grant from this fund met the extra production costs of including Chinese characters in the text and notes of this book.

Finally, I wish to express my most sincere thanks to my husband, J. Christopher Warner, an accomplished scholar in the field of English Renaissance literature. Throughout my work on this project he was my most avid supporter, always taking time from his teaching and research schedule to listen to my ideas, ask probing questions, and critique my drafts. I learned as much from his critical insights as the manuscript benefits from them. Chris, this book is for you.

A Note on Transliteration

❃

ALL TRANSLITERATIONS of Chinese in this study are in pinyin. When quoting English translations and studies that employ the Wade-Giles system, I have silently changed their spellings to pinyin for the sake of uniformity. I have not, however, altered in any way the titles of these works.

Introduction
Reading Wang Ji

❀

IF THERE IS ONE achievement for which late-twentieth-century critical theory congratulates itself, it is for disabusing literary criticism of the notion that the text can be a vehicle for the author's unmediated self-expression. But in the West, it was only a relatively late and romantic belief that poetry could convey the essence of the poet—or that readers might consider it a primary aim to grasp the poet's essence through his text. In the history of Chinese literature, in contrast, there is a great body of late-classical and early-medieval Chinese poetry that takes the apparent form of direct expressions of the poet's inner thoughts and feelings. And in the history of commentary and criticism on this verse, so pervasive is the habit of reading it as a mirror of the inner man that modern scholarship has found it difficult to relinquish traditional interpretive assumptions and practices.

Recent studies on the Sui and early Tang dynasty poet Wang Ji 王績 (590–644) offer a case in point. On the one hand, Wang Ji is generally praised in histories of Chinese literature for being a transitional figure whose direct, unpolished style stood in refreshing contrast to the ornate, courtly lyrics of his time; for his reviving of scholar-recluse and country-living themes from the earlier Wei-Jin period (third–fourth centuries); and for anticipating the rise of the regulated verse forms that made the Tang dynasty a golden era in the history of Chinese poetry. On the other hand, the confessional or self-expressive style of Wang Ji's poetry has continued to invite, in studies published recently in China, Taiwan, and Japan, efforts to define Wang Ji's "true identity" through the evidence of his poetry. In particular, the predominant issue has been the extent to which Wang Ji's moral character lives up to his primary literary models of the Wei-Jin period: the "eccentric scholar" Ruan Ji 阮籍 (210–263) and the "recluse poet" Tao Qian 陶潛 (365–427). As a result, we have as yet no analytical studies of Wang Ji's poetry—no efforts to articulate how the textual features of his poetry convey meaning and experience—and, therefore, have only a very imperfect understanding of Wang Ji as a transitional figure in Chinese literary history.

It is this book's aim to demonstrate that Wang Ji's central "transitional" achievement is to be located precisely in the function of his poetic "I." Through analysis that is resolutely literary and historical, rather than quasi-psychoanalytical, we are able to perceive that Wang Ji was not attempting to communicate his "true recluse identity" fashioned after the characters of past recluses. Instead (in a manner that critics recognize is characteristic of certain poets from later periods in China's history),[1] he is personifying in his literary self-image a set of philosophical concepts rooted in the Taoist texts *Laozi* 老子 and *Zhuangzi* 莊子.

Chapter 1 examines the revived interest in these ideas during the medieval period and outlines the historical circumstances that, in my view, prompted Wang Ji to construct his literary persona as he did. But it is not our apprehension of a set of Lao-Zhuang concepts, for their own sake, that I am arguing constitutes the reward of analyzing Wang Ji's poetry or qualifies him for a higher place in some canonical hierarchy of China's poets. I mean to avoid the tendency, which we see in Chinese literary studies published both in the East and in the West, to assume that interpretive scholarship should also confirm the canonical status of a master or to argue that more attention should be paid to a neglected genius. Either course invariably leaves interpretation behind, eliciting instead vague generalizations in praise of a poet's great artistry and his supposedly profound insights into the nature of the universe. The philosophical ideas that Wang Ji personifies in his poetry, like the ideas to be found in Ruan Ji, Tao Qian, and indeed in Chinese poetry generally, are hardly deep or difficult to grasp: they were commonplaces in China's literate culture well before they made their way from philosophical to literary discourse. My aim, therefore, is to reveal that Wang Ji's poetry achieves effects that are profoundly interesting—conveying the experience of Lao-Zhuang ideas once they are taken, in the person of Wang Ji's poetic "I," to their logical conclusions.

This interpretation of Wang Ji's method furthermore resolves the interpretive cruxes that have proved to be most puzzling to Wang Ji's readers. In the remainder of this introduction, therefore, I summarize these cruxes and show how they have shaped the peculiar reception of Wang Ji's poetry, including the ideologically motivated textual transmission of his corpus. At the heart of readers' concerns is the perplexing nature of Wang Ji's supposed personal emulation of the two writers he most often alludes to in his works: Ruan Ji and Tao Qian. Wang Ji's eccentric manner, both as represented in his own writings and as reported by other writers, his somber philosophical musings, and the simplicity of his style clearly are modeled on Ruan Ji's writings and Ruan Ji's character as it had come to be romanticized over the years. Moreover, Wang Ji's idyllic depictions of his own life as a self-sufficient farmer, his attitude of complete detachment from worldly affairs, and his celebration of this personal freedom mimic Tao Qian's poetic self-representation and chronicled lifestyle. As this bare summary reveals, the historical images of Ruan Ji and Tao Qian were very different from each other. This difference, however, did not seem to bother Wang Ji. He echoes in his own writing their contrasting attitudes and poetic themes, and thus readers have found the resulting image of his character problematic. Wang Ji variously portrays himself as a melancholy scholar whose timely withdrawal from the political world saves him from its dangers but who still hopes to gain recognition one day for his merits; at another time he seems an eccentric intellectual who detaches himself from the profane world's values and ritual constraints to live in lofty oblivion; at another time he presents himself as a self-sufficient farmer-scholar who isolates himself from the world of the court in favor of preserving his personal freedom and reveling in the virtues of a simple life.

In Wang Ji's best-known characterization, as a drunkard-poet, he often claims a spiritual kinship with the whole range of famous drunkard-poets of the past—from Ruan Ji, Xi Kang 嵇康 (223–262), and Liu Ling 劉伶 (d. after 265) to Tao Qian. But readers have been troubled by the fact that these men are thought to have had different reasons for drinking. Ruan Ji and Xi Kang are reputed to have deliberately kept themselves in a drunken stupor in order to avoid both emotional involvement and official engagement in times of fallen morals; Liu Ling for his part had an innate love of wine and drank constantly whatever the circumstances; for Tao Qian leisurely drinking and the celebration of simple wine with simple fare was an integral part of the carefree man's rustic lifestyle. How can it be, critics ask, that Wang Ji can blithely ascribe to himself all of the apparently incompatible motives and drinking habits of his different models?

The same critics have been troubled by apparent contradictions between Wang Ji's poetic persona and what they know of his life and times. It has often been argued that there was a vast difference between the disordered and perilous political climate of the Wei-Jin period, when intellectuals had good reason to seek peace in distant isolation, and the later, more prosperous period in which Wang Ji lived, when a drive to reestablish social order and patronize scholars at court attended the consolidation of the empire. Critics have therefore been inspired to defend or to question the sincerity of Wang Ji's self-representation, and they regularly resolve on one of three opinions. The first is that the political and moral condition of the times did not influence Wang Ji; he had a thorough understanding of the writings of Laozi and Zhuangzi and should be admired for his detached and carefree attitude toward life. The second starts from the argument that Wang Ji's time was indeed one of great political turmoil and danger (as a period of transition, it must have been chaotic, so the reasoning goes), and it defends his conduct either as an astute strategy for self-preservation or as ethical protest. The third stresses the difference between the chaos of the Wei-Jin era and the relative prosperity of the Sui and early Tang and hence denies Wang Ji ethical or philosophical justification for his conduct. On this basis he is criticized for being egoistic and for avoiding responsibilities in life, and his emulation of Ruan Ji and Tao Qian is dismissed as a disreputable attempt to ennoble his failure as a court official.

The overriding concern with the identification of Wang Ji's character and motives can partly be ascribed to the fragmentary nature of his literary corpus. Until the 1980s, no reader since the end of the Song dynasty had recorded seeing the original five-*juan* collection of Wang Ji's works, which was compiled shortly before his death by a close associate, Lü Cai 呂才 (600–665).[2] The standard collection until then, the *Donggaozi ji* 東皋子集 compiled by Lu Chun 陸淳 (d. 805?) in three *juan*, represents slightly less than half of the works included in the five-*juan* collection.[3] In his postface, Lu Chun explains that he extracted from Lü Cai's compilation the works that he regarded as best representing Wang Ji's recluse image, and he expresses his admiration for Wang Ji by calling him a second Zhuangzi and more of an exemplar of complete detachment from worldly affairs than either Tao Qian or Ruan Ji. Furthermore, Lu Chun claims that his own tacit understanding of Wang Ji's character qualifies him to make this abridgment, for he has endeavored to "edit out [Wang Ji's] expressions of desire for accomplishments" in order to "keep intact his resolution to hang up his official's cap and untie his official's tassel."[4] In sum, Lu Chun made it his mission to capture and transmit to us what he took to be the essence of Wang Ji's character.

Lu Chun furthermore trimmed Lü Cai's original preface by about a thousand characters.[5] The omitted passages contain what Lu Chun likely perceived as further indications of Wang Ji's "ambition" for success, as well as details that appear to complicate the image of Wang Ji as a completely detached and lofty-minded recluse. These include the passages describing Wang Ji's childhood study of the classics in preparation for eventual official service; a story about his impressive debut in the capital when influential ministers and statesmen exclaimed at his perspicuity; anecdotes of his reputed prescience, which tend to suggest a discerning and politically astute Wang Ji rather than an aloof recluse; and, finally, references to Wang Ji's close friendship with Xue Shou 薛收 (592–624) and Dong Heng 董恆,[6] disciples of Wang Ji's brother, the Confucian master Wang Tong 王通 (ca. 584–617).

When we read Lü Cai's preface in its entirety, we get the impression that he is intent on portraying Wang Ji as the unorthodox individual he knew him to be but admired all the same. One senses a hint of apology in Lü Cai's tone, perhaps reflecting his desire to defend Wang Ji's character in anticipation of others' puzzlement or even condemnation. In Lu Chun's abridgment and his own postface, by contrast, Wang Ji is represented pursuing his natural course but never transgressing the Confucian moral code. Lu Chun categorizes worthy men into three types: gentlemen engaged in worldly affairs who nonetheless maintain their moral standards; gentlemen "of the yonder realm" living in reclusion without ambition or regard for arbitrary measures and practices of virtue; and lastly the ancient sages. Wang Ji, says Lu Chun, is a paragon of the second group:

> In cases of those of the yonder realm, no one is able to fathom them. Can it be that it is easy to tread in others' tracks but difficult to comprehend the principle of neglecting speech?[7] Or is it that they mingle in the world of men but find contentment within themselves? There have been very few men who could achieve this in the thousands of years since the time of Old Man Zhuang. But I found the model in Mr. Wang![8]

What Lu Chun specifically found in Wang Ji is a man whose

> mind was intuitive of natural things; his inner capacity was not displayed on the outside. He adjusted himself to changes, content with his lot. He was oblivious of his environment, but his conduct was not detrimental to the teachings [of sages]. He discarded burdens [of the profane world], yet his

Way did not cut himself off from it. This is why he withdrew from office like Mr. Tao [Qian] yet did not speak in complaint against his time; he was unrestrained in manner like Mr. Ruan [Ji] yet did not violate principles of conduct. How untrammeled! How profound! He is truly a man whom we can call a naturally happy gentleman.[9]

Of course, this image is as much Lu Chun's creation—a product of his effort to "preserve intact Wang Ji's resolve in detachment"—as it is Wang Ji's. By attempting to edit out Wang Ji's expressions of human desire, his worldly concerns and ordinary emotions, Lu Chun hopes to make Wang Ji's tenure in office look involuntary, accepted out of a necessity to earn a livelihood. This was the fabled justification for Zhuangzi's and Laozi's acceptance of official posts and, as well, the justification for Tao Qian's taking office.

In fact, Lu Chun was unable to eliminate entirely Wang Ji's variety of conflicting self-representations, which remains even in his abridged edition and belies Lu Chun's claim to having established a single, consistent image of Wang Ji. Yet this failure, if we can call it that, did not discourage later readers from following in Lu Chun's footsteps and (though their conclusions varied greatly) trying to define once and for all the real Wang Ji. Xin Wenfang 辛文房 (fl. ca. 1300) of the Yuan dynasty, for example, in his *Tang caizi zhuan* 唐才子傳, praised Wang Ji for having the insight and moral strength to withdraw from the hostile environment of the early Tang period, when "orderly days were few and chaotic days were many":

> Beginning with Mr. Wang onward, there were frequent cases of hidden men, and all were gentlemen who leaped into the distance and departed forever. They were upright in conduct and unassuming in words. Time and again they avoided potential calamity. Official ranks and honors were husk and chaff in their eyes; they hung up their caps, withdrew and retired.... Yet, even so, some of them could not escape gleaming blades and ill-fated death.... Had they been living in the glorious era of the Three Lords and Five Rulers, even if they were cowards, they would have known to take on an active role. But today they abandon the pursuit for fame and benefit, turning to "nest-dwelling" instead.[10]

In contrast to Lu Chun, then, Xin interprets the reclusion of Wang Ji and other Tang recluses not as philosophical detachment but as the preservation of their lives and integrity—the proper course of action according to

the Confucian code of conduct regarding a worthy man's timely with-
drawal from worldly affairs.[11]

Others are skeptical of this image of Wang Ji as a worthy Confucian.
After all, Wang Ji more than once challenges and belittles Confucian values,
at times even mocking Confucius himself. These readers recognize the
contradictions in Wang Ji's self-representation, but they are inclined to be
apologetic about them. A representative of this view is Cao Quan 曹荃 (six-
teenth century) of the Ming dynasty.[12] In the preface to his printed edition
of Wang Ji's three-*juan* collection, Cao admits that his initial impression of
the poet was not positive; he thought Wang Ji's language "absurd, unconven-
tional, and unorthodox" and his person "dispirited and self-indulgent."[13]
But he goes on to say that after reading through Wang Ji's complete collec-
tion (though, to be sure, Cao is speaking of Lu Chun's three-*juan* abridg-
ment), he began to feel that Wang Ji's behavior was justified and deserved
sympathy, because circumstances forced him to behave the way he did.
Wang Ji's conduct, in Cao's final assessment, was indeed unconventional
but did not violate any moral principle:

> I do not know his person, but I can see his deeds. He was unceremonious yet
> in conformity, untrammeled yet respectful, carefree yet composed. He
> roamed about on the potency of wine and his literary mind. He is truly a gen-
> tleman of the Way. Pushing one step further, is he not on a par with the
> worthy man in Li Village?[14] ... As to the gentlemen of the bamboo grove,[15]
> who indulged themselves with their own desires, violated the code of rites,
> and abandoned moral principles, they ought to concede themselves inferior to
> Mr. Wang.[16]

The pairs of somewhat contrasting traits at the beginning of this pas-
sage signal Cao Quan's awareness of the many sides of Wang Ji's self-
representation, but ultimately he chooses to emphasize only those qualities
that he finds most admirable in order to praise the poet as a lofty-minded
recluse.[17]

During the Qing dynasty readers were less inclined to overlook or
explain away the inconsistencies in Wang Ji's recluse image. In his sum-
mary of Wang Ji's collection, the chief editor of *Siku quanshu zongmu
tiyao* 四庫全書總目提要, Ji Yun 紀昀 (1724–1805), criticizes historians
in the Song dynasty for including Wang Ji in the "Yinyi zhuan" 隱逸傳
chapter (Biographies of recluses and disengaged gentlemen) of *Xin Tang
shu*:

Wang Ji ... served in the courts of two dynasties [Sui and Tang] but was
unsuccessful with his official career in both. So he retired, unbridled and
adrift in mountains and woods. *Xin Tang shu* lists his biography in the
"Biographies of Recluses and Disengaged Gentlemen"; that was because they
did not fully comprehend [the nature of his retirement].... He is the younger
brother of Wang Tong, and his resolve is haughty and his interest refined ...
[but] in character he does not measure up to his brother.[18]

In the twentieth century, when scholars aspired to more analytical
approaches to literature than in the past, Wang Ji's critics were still pre-
occupied with the issue of his character and continued to fall into the two
basic categories of apologists and debunkers. In an article published in
1990, for example, Zhang Daxin 張大新 and Zhang Bai'ang 張百昂 argue
that Wang Ji's reclusion cannot be justified by the condition of his times.
In their view, it was a careful calculation on his part to achieve official
recognition through an insincere presentation of himself as a morally lofty
man, and they regard Wang Ji's frustration in politics as the result of his
own political miscalculations and missed opportunities:

An officer from the former court who lacked clear vision in politics, who put
his reputation on the line fishing for fame but was also overly cautious, who
was impractical, boastful, and very capricious—how could [Wang Ji] be appre-
ciated and trusted by the Tang court? Even though he did all he could to pose
as an exceptional lofty man in an attempt to obtain fame and prosperity in
officialdom, it was all in vain in the end. In other words, this eccentric charac-
ter, whose mind was complicated and who regarded himself as highly tal-
ented, desired to be accomplished in this period of change of dynasties from
the Sui to the Tang, yet did not take action; he designed a totally imaginary
and illusory career path for himself and lost his credibility again and again
before the newly empowered Tang court. So after several setbacks, he had no
better way to turn except to retire to his hut in the country.[19]

Once Zhang Daxin and Zhang Bai'ang judge Wang Ji's reclusion as a delib-
erate strategy to obtain recognition in court, they consistently read those of
his works that seem to express an aspiration for achievement as mere "self-
promotion," while those representing Wang Ji's resolve to live in retire-
ment they view as vehicles for self-justification and self-consolation. The
rest of the collection they ignore.[20]

In a study published at about the same time, Jia Jinhua 賈晉華 comes to Wang Ji's defense. She suggests that Wang Ji's three short tenures in office betray a deep conflict between his personal values and his consciousness of an individual's duty to society, and this conflict manifests itself in his poetry. Despite Wang Ji's attraction to Wei-Jin recluses as models for his own conduct and philosophy, says Jia, Wang Ji at least in his early days aspired to an official career. But unlike Zhang Daxin and Zhang Bai'ang, Jia argues that Wang Ji did not turn to reclusion merely as a way to advertise his abilities or justify his unemployment. She suggests instead that Wang Ji realized that his chances for advancement in office were hurt by his incidental association at the start of his career with a contender in the power struggle to overthrow the Sui court, Dou Jiande 竇建德, who was himself defeated by the Tang. Though Wang Ji's encounter with Dou was accidental and brief, Jia surmises that it must have damaged his standing with the new rulers. She also gives credence to a report that Wang Ji and his brothers were denied official posts after one of the brothers offended certain court favorites.[21] It was then, says Jia, that Wang Ji turned to embrace Wei-Jin eremitic attitudes and practices, maintaining his personal integrity to counterbalance his frustrated expectations in life. Jia also argues that Wang Ji did not indiscriminately embrace Wei-Jin eremitic ideas and literary themes but adapted them to suit his particular situation and feelings—and that unlike his idols Ruan Ji and Tao Qian, who used poetry to express their emotions and thoughts about life, Wang Ji employed literature as a means to create an idealized self-image that would be admired both by his contemporaries and by future generations. Thus Wang Ji resolved to acquire through literature what he could not attain in political life: an immortal reputation as a worthy man. Jia concludes with a note of regret that, though Wang Ji's choice of lifestyle and self-image was noble, it was unfashionable at the time, and thus he remained unrecognized and isolated during his life.[22]

Jia Jinhua's observation on the function of Wang Ji's poetic persona makes an important distinction between the person and the text. Even so, her study starts from the premise that Wang Ji's literature is primarily to be used to illuminate his character. We have not progressed past the assumption that the goal of literary analysis is to discover the poet's true identity and real motives. This concern stems ultimately from an impulse to judge the moral qualities of writers—hence the propensity to apologize or condemn—as well as a simplistic conception of the truth value of fiction. While a few critics have attempted to describe Wang Ji's literary merits, without fail they repeat the vague generalities about his "refreshing and simple" style and observe the Wei-Jin inspiration of his writing, urging our admiration of Wang Ji as an important figure in the development of Chinese literature but not undertaking the close scrutiny of his works that would justify such admiration.[23] More helpfully, Stephen Owen has discussed Wang Ji within the larger context of the development of early Tang poetics. He notes that Wang Ji's fascination with recluses and the ethos of the Wei-Jin era is consistent with the trend of intellectual and literary thought of his time, in which there was a general, shared romantic fascination with the past. But like Jia Jinhua, Owen also rightly asserts that Wang Ji's poetic "I" is not serving the self-expressive function that critics have assumed we encounter in the poetry of Ruan Ji and Tao Qian. Rather, he says, Wang Ji is interested in "capturing the mood or manner of a historical period and making it live in the present."[24] In this sense, Owen likens Wang Ji's style and method to the "opposition poetics" of some of his contemporaries: "Wang Ji's poetry is essentially negative," he argues, "a counterstatement to the aristocratic and worldly glory of court poetry," which may take the form of "drunkenness, pastoralism, or Taoist nihilism, but all these responses may be defined in negative relation to court poetry and the aristocratic society that produced it."[25]

From this assessment we see Owen's characteristically productive foregrounding of questions of literary technique and literary history; but because they come within the broad scope of a survey of early Tang poets, his observations on Wang Ji are not pursued further. His association of Wang Ji with an "opposition poetics," however, is a key concept that I purpose to elaborate in this study. It is one that underlies much of the praise, blame, and bafflement in the history of Wang Ji's reception—including the admiring assertion of the Qing scholar Weng Fanggang 翁方綱 (1733–1818) that confronting "the pure, direct, unembellished style" of Wang Ji, after reading the palace-style poetry of his contemporaries, is "like suddenly encountering a wild deer amid a crowd of soaring phoenixes and simurghs."[26] This is an image, we shall see, that appropriately emblematizes Wang Ji's poetry in several respects, not just in terms of his unembellished style or even in its symbolizing Wang Ji's philosophical opposition to the court-sanctioned, intellectual trends of his times. It serves, as well, to symbolize the reader's experience of the personified Taoist ideas in Wang Ji's poetry—the experience of constant change in an illusive world—which can be likened to the movements of a wild deer that is out of its element, skittish and darting now this way and that.

In sum, then, this book aims to supply the in-depth study of Wang Ji's poetry that is needed to define his "opposition poetics" fully and bridge our understanding of the transition from Wei-Jin to Tang and Song literary practice. It begins with the claim that Wang Ji's poetic self-representation is foremost a personification of concepts central to Lao-Zhuang thought— namely, that the enlightened man follows "the natural way" (ziran 自然) by means of "nonaction" (wuwei 無為) because he recognizes that reality is ever-changing or "inconstant" (wuchang 無常). Thus he perceives that the phenomenal world—and our knowledge of things in the world—is illusory. Again, I am not saying that these commonplace ideas are the "lessons" that Wang Ji's poems inevitably teach or that the reason for reading him is to discover his repeated statements of precepts that he found in *Laozi* and *Zhuangzi*. Much more rewarding, and more challenging, is the discovery and articulation of the many different ways that the precepts are manifested in the textual features of Wang Ji's poetry—and how they shape the experience of reading it.

Toward this goal, Chapter 1 surveys what we know of Wang Ji's life and times. But more important, it places an interpretation of his poetic method within the context of intellectual, literary, and political developments in Sui and early Tang China against which Wang Ji's "oppositional poetics" can be contrasted. In Chapters 2, 3, and 4, I extend Owen's remarks on Wang Ji's shift away from the self-expressive function of poetry to show that in Wang Ji's works we see the introduction of a deliberate distancing between the poet and the poetic "I" for the purposes of dramatizing an idea or proposition. In each of these chapters I examine a different dimension of Wang Ji's literary persona—the recluse as philosopher, as country farmer, and as drunkard—first surveying the range of self-representational styles that comprise each of these facets of Wang Ji's persona and then explicating the manner by which this persona manifests the conception of an ever-changing world and, in some of the most obscure and interesting of his poems, compels readers to experience with their speaker the illusoriness of perceived reality. The most elaborate example of this latter type is the subject of Chapter 5, Wang Ji's "*Fu* on Roaming the Northern Mountains" (You Beishan fu 遊北山賦), in which the speaker exhibits a series of perspective shifts and transformations of purpose that deny any confident apprehension of his character and his world. In conclusion I return to the issue of Wang Ji's historical reception—first to reveal how the critical commonplaces attached to Wang Ji have shaped editorial decisions concerning the textual and attribution problems in his literary corpus and, second, to consider the implications of this study's methodology and conclusions to the practice of Chinese literary studies generally. For, as we shall note, the history of Wang Ji criticism has contributed to a history of misreadings and missed opportunities in scholarship on later Chinese literary history—most of all in critical studies of the major Tang and Song poets who explicitly imitated Wang Ji.

1
Wang Ji and Sui-Tang Literati Culture

❀

FOR INFORMATION ON Wang Ji's life, we have only one biographical document of any length that is reliable: the preface by Lü Cai 呂才 attached to his compilation of Wang Ji's collected works, the *Wang Wugong wenji* 王無功文集[1] Lü Cai, according to this account, had been a close friend of Wang Ji's since his youth, so he is able to share with his readers anecdotes that he believes to illustrate Wang Ji's character and talents.

Much shorter biographies of Wang Ji are included in the "Biographies of Recluses and Disengaged Gentlemen" 隱逸傳 chapters in the two official histories of the Tang. Both of these, as one would expect, emphasize Wang Ji's reputation as a recluse. The entry in the *Jiu Tang shu* depicts him in a highly romanticized manner as a detached and carefree farmer-scholar lacking in ambition for fame or official accomplishment. Readers of this account are immediately reminded of other famous farmer-scholars who are praised for their lofty minds and carefree spirits, men such as Wang Ba 王霸 (fl. first century), Zhongchang Tong 仲長統 (180–220), and Tao Qian. Wang Ji's longer biography in *Xin Tang shu*, by contrast, portrays him as a wine-loving eccentric who openly defied ritual and social expectations, an image resembling that of Xi Kang, Ruan Ji, and other notorious nonconformist intellectuals of the third century.[2] These two different entries, in other words, emphasize two different dimensions of Wang Ji's own idealized self-representation, an image built on his identifications with various recluses and eccentric scholars from the past. For this reason I do not rely on the two Tang histories as sources of biographical record. Instead I draw carefully from Lü Cai's preface and, even more tentatively, from Wang Ji's personal writings and some poems.[3]

"Bright and Intelligent, with an Unusual Mind ..."

Wang Ji was born some time around 590 into a family that claimed deep roots in the local aristocracy.[4] Descendants of a branch of the illustrious Taiyuan Wang clan, the family traced its origin back to the House of Zhou in antiquity, a distinction in which Wang Ji and his siblings confidently believed and claimed pride.[5] For many generations, men in Wang Ji's family had held prominent positions in court. Two of his forefathers in particular—his great-great-grandfather, Wang Qiu 王虯, and his great-grandfather, Wang Yan 王彥—were revered by the members of the Wang clan for their lofty principles and conduct. In the preface to his "Fu on Roaming the Northern Mountains," for example, Wang Ji begins by proclaiming his noble descent:

> We are the people of Zhou. Our original home was in Qi. During the Yong-jia era [307–312], my ancestor accompanied the Jin emperor to the south. Our land truly nurtures learned men; many of our people are exalted and prominent. Duke Mu was mortified by the Jianyuan affair and returned to Luoyang. Tongzhou was saddened by the Yongan events and retired to the river bend.[6]

"Duke Mu" in this passage is the posthumous title of Wang Qiu, who at the start of his official career served in the Song court (420–479) in the south. During the time of his service, Xiao Daocheng 蕭道成 (427–482), a general in the Song army who would later be remembered in history as the founding emperor of the Qi dynasty (480–502), took control of the court and coerced the Song emperor to relinquish to him all but the imperial title. Several Song ministers plotted to revolt against Xiao, but their plan was exposed and Xiao Daocheng had the plotters put to death. He then conducted a purge, and one of the casualties was the minister of education, Yuan Can 袁粲 (420–477), purportedly a close associate of Wang Qiu's. This presumably is the "Jianyuan affair" that Wang Ji alludes to, Jianyuan 建元 being the reign title of Xiao Daocheng.[7] Wang Qiu was said to have left the south in 478 to avoid submission to the usurper, returning to his ancestral home in the north which, at the time, was under the rule of the Toba house of the Northern Wei (386–534). There he was welcomed with an appointment to the position of inspector of Bingzhou 并州刺史. As Wang Qiu was reaching the end of his career, the court awarded him the honorary title Duke Mu of Jinyang 晉陽穆公. Ever afterward, Wang Qiu was held by his progeny as a model of one who adhered to moral principles in times of crisis.[8]

Wang Qiu's son, Wang Yan, reinforced the Wang family's reputation for maintaining high moral standards. The "Yongan events" to which Wang Ji refers were a series of bloody incidents that took place during the Yongan 永安 reign period of Emperor Xiaozhuang of Wei 孝莊帝 (r. 528–530). In 528, the emperor plotted with his minister Wen Zisheng 溫子昇 to kill Erzhu Rong 尒朱容 (491–528), a powerful general whom he perceived to be a threat. As a consequence the Erzhu clan revolted. It set up a puppet emperor in Jinyang and imprisoned Emperor Xiaozhuang, who eventually died in confinement.[9] Once this turmoil began, Wang Yan resigned in disgust from his position as inspector of Tongzhou 同州刺史 and returned to his ancestral land in Longmen 龍門 of Jiang commandery 絳州 in southwestern Shanxi, where he remained in retirement for the rest of his life.[10]

The Wang clan also boasted a long tradition of Confucian learning. Many of Wang Ji's ancestors purportedly were experts in the Confucian classics, nearly all of them beginning their official service as professors in the Imperial University (國子監博士). Wang Ji's father, Wang Long 王隆, and his second brother, Wang Tong, made careers teaching the Confucian classics at their own private academies.[11] Wang Ji himself began his formal education under the tutelage of his father, as Lü Cai recounts in an apostrophe to his friend: "When you were young, you were bright and intelligent with an unusual mind. At age eight, you studied the *Spring and Autumn Annals with the Zuo Commentary*, reciting ten pages a day."[12] At one point in his youth Wang Ji also studied with his elder brother, Wang Tong, if not as one of his full-fledged disciples then at least as a member of the intellectual circle that was associated with his brother's school.[13] Even while he was preparing himself in this way for an official career, however, the young Wang Ji pursued other interests that were outside the orthodox Confucian curriculum, studying yin-yang theories, calendrical science, and numerology, so that he is said to have become an expert in the methods of divination and prognostication.[14] In one of his late poems,[15] Wang Ji romanticizes this busy time in his life:

At a tender age, I favored uncommon tunes;	弱齡慕奇調
There was nothing that I did not study.	無事不兼修
To watch the rising ethers I climbed up the tiered loft;	望氣登重閣
To divine astral movements I ascended the small tower.	占星上小樓

Explicating the classics, I hoped for the emperor's summons;	明經思待詔
Studying swordsmanship, I sought ennoblement.	學劍覓封侯
Tossing aside the silken passport, I traveled north many times;	棄繻頻北上
Tucking a calling card in my bosom, I journeyed west more than once.	懷刺幾西遊

Here we see Wang Ji representing himself in youth as a multitalented student with great ambitions in life, using two historical allusions to illustrate the point. The silken passport refers to a warrant written on a piece of silk that was then split into two halves. When a traveler from inland passed through Hangu Pass 函谷關, gateway to the capital region, he was issued one half; when he returned, he had to match his half with the one retained by the official at the pass. One story has it that the Han official Zhong Jun 終軍, when he was eighteen years old, was summoned to the capital for an official appointment. But when at the pass to the capital he was handed a silken certificate allowing his return home, he said to the official: "When a great man goes west, he is never going to turn back." He then threw away his half of the passport and continued onward.[16] By this allusion Wang Ji claims for himself the same determination to succeed in a career at court. The calling card in the last line quoted earlier is a reference to Mi Heng 禰衡 of the Later Han, who on a visit to Xuxia 許下, the capital during the Jian'an 建安 period (196–220), is said to have refused to call on any but men of the highest worth. Because he felt he had never met any, so the story goes, the card he carried with him in his robe was worn to illegibility before he had once used it.[17] Wang Ji's evocation of Mi Heng's story thus claims that not only were his ambitions high but he too would maintain the highest of moral standards.[18]

Wang Ji had his first opportunity to prove himself sometime after 610, when Emperor Yang of the Sui 隋煬帝 issued an edict requesting each commandery in the empire to recommend ten candidates worthy to be recognized as "Filial and Brotherly, Incorrupt and Pure" 孝悌廉潔 to take the placement examination for office.[19] Wang Ji was selected as one of the candidates representing his commandery, and he placed very highly. To his disappointment, however, he was assigned to a low-ranking position in the palace library, copying and editing documents and texts.[20] Wang Ji reportedly found the daily routine of his duties stifling and dull,[21] so he asked to be released from the palace library on grounds of illness. He requested a transfer to an office outside the capital and was appointed as an assistant to the Luhe 六合 district magistrate of Yangzhou prefecture, near Jiangdu 江都 (in modern Jiangsu province), the southern capital of the Sui. While Wang Ji was serving in Luhe his drinking became so reckless that he was frequently cited for negligence of duty and eventually he resigned, again pleading illness.[22] On the night of his departure, says Lü Cai, Wang Ji left behind all his salary in a pile outside the city gate.[23]

It was not, it seems, a very long time from the date Wang Ji first entered service to his departure from Luhe.[24] For many the shortness of his tenure attests to the sincerity of his recluse image: it reveals the perspicacious withdrawal of a moral hero from the political tumult of the time— a perception that is supposed to derive support from the fact that the Sui ruling house collapsed only two years after Wang Ji's retirement and, moreover, from a presumption that his story should follow the same trajectory as his forefathers'. Proponents of this interpretation of Wang Ji's first retirement claim to find warrant for it, too, in Lü Cai's preface. In reporting the problems Wang Ji encountered in office, Lü Cai remarks, "At the time, the empire was on the verge of turmoil" (時天下將亂), and he quotes Wang Ji's lament: "The snares and nets are hanging high. I am leaving, but where will I go?" (網羅高懸, 去將安所?).[25] The "snares and nets" have always been interpreted as a reference to the looming political dangers that Wang Ji sensed around him. Thus the statement that he is leaving has been taken as his announcement to withdraw in a time of fallen morals. But if we read this evidence in the context of its original passage, we see that such an interpretation is quite off the mark. As Lü Cai recalls:

> [While taking office in Luhe,] you [Wang Ji] were hopelessly indulgent in drinking, regarding that as your virtue. It greatly interfered with your performance in office. At the time, the empire was on the verge of turmoil, and the local Administration Commission was very strictly enforcing the law. For that reason, you were repeatedly cited [for your negligence of duty]. You sighed and said, "The snares and nets are hanging high. I am leaving, but where will I go?" Whereupon you took out the salary you received and left it in a pile outside the gate of the prefecture. Using the excuse of suffering from rheumatism, you boarded a light boat and ran away under cover of night.[26]

In short, Lü Cai hardly testifies to Wang Ji's being an upright moral hero. Rather the question seems to be whether Wang Ji's drunkenness, or his apparent conviction that drunkenness was his primary virtue, contributed most to his dereliction of duties and eventual departure from service. Thus the "snares and nets" would seem to refer to the increasingly strict official rules and regulations that Wang Ji likely found too constraining, rather than to political intrigues. In any case, the eccentric-drinker explanation is the one we get from Wang Ji himself in his poem titled "Returning Home After Resigning from Office in Luhe" (Jie Luhe chen huan 解六合丞還):[27]

	My home is over by the vast sea of the white clouds;	我家滄海白雲邊
	Let me return to my country home, to the woods and the streams.	還將別業對林泉
	I don't need merit and fame to boast about my life;	不用功名喧一世
4	I'll simply send off my remaining years in mist and clouds.	直取煙霞送百年
	The Magistrate of Pengze had land, but he only planted glutinous millet;[28]	彭澤有田惟種黍
	The Infantry Commandant took office, but did he care about the salary?[29]	步兵從宦豈論錢
	I only wish to wake up in perpetual drunkenness morning after morning,[30]	但願朝朝長得醉
8	So why would I decline to sleep among wine jugs night after night?	何辭夜夜甕間眠

Here we perceive no feelings of frustrated ambition or trepidation at a crumbling political world. Instead Wang Ji speaks simply of his desire to abandon the meaningless pursuit of fame and official honors for a peaceful life in the country where he can drink to his heart's content.

Nor does Wang Ji's failure to obtain a prestigious position at court necessarily explain his subsequent devotion to a life of reclusion. As early as his late teens, even as he prepared for an official career, he was already revealing an attraction to recluse themes. This we see in the prefatory note to an early piece composed on the occasion of the Lustration Festival, "*Fu on the Third Day of the Third Month*" (Sanyue sanri fu 三月三日賦):[31]

In the fourth year of the Daye era I had a chance to visit the capital. It was at the end of spring, in the third month. I took this opportunity to enjoy excursions to the fullest. Having just docked my recluse boat, I immediately rushed to join the gatherings of assembled gentlemen. Relaxed and jubilant, we roamed about side by side and with our chariots running abreast.

The fourth year of the Daye reign period corresponds to 608 in the Western calendar, so Wang Ji was probably no older than eighteen years of age at the time of this visit. It would be at least another two years before he received his first official appointment. Yet already we see that he is characterizing himself, if not as a genuine recluse, then at least as the kind of literatus who has the personality and values of the recluse (as his reference to his "recluse boat" 隱士船 suggests). Indeed Wang Ji sustains the preface's expression of a free-spirited, carefree philosophical attitude—counter to our expectations of a young candidate's frame of mind at the very outset of a promising official career—into and completely through to the *fu*'s final lines where he muses:

Thinking of the merrymaking on this day,	念此日之嬉戲
We give ourselves to endless enjoyment.	亦無窮之賞託
All about the ford, there is nothing but drifting boats;	但是津傍悉泛舟
Of the hills all around, on which are there not tents pitched?	若箇山頭不投幕
As banquets and feasts follow in turns,	俎席交時
Mists and clouds mingle and blend.	煙霞綺錯
Which town, which district,	何縣何州
Does not have groves or gullies?	無林無壑
It is not just a custom for the regions of the Zhen and Wei,[32]	俗非溱洧
But also a practice in the capitals of Ye and Luo.[33]	風成鄴洛
Year after year at this time,	年年歲歲
Whole cities and whole towns empty out.	傾城傾郭
It is all because the sights and sounds of spring stir our mood,	祇為春光動性靈
Making us wish that this fun and joy might never stop for even a moment.	剩使娛樂不暫停
By Nandu Bridge, countless people are drunk;[34]	南度橋邊無數醉
On the waters flowing east, how many are still sober?	東流水上幾人醒
The recluse kept to his herbs on the boat;[35]	隱士船中藥
King Zhao of Qin found inscriptions on the sword.[36]	秦王劍裡銘
If we find Peach Blossom Bay of Zheng unsatisfying,[37]	若嫌鄭國桃花浦
Then we just turn to Magnolia Leaf Pavilion in Shanyin.[38]	為向山陰蘭葉亭

Such an early expression of Wang Ji's detached, carefree attitude indicates that his imitation of famous recluses was not just a consequence of his troubled official career. Later, in a poem that Wang Ji wrote to a childhood friend on the occasion of their reunion,[39] he would also assert his long attraction to recluse culture:

Fond of Tao Yuanming, we used to	嘗愛陶淵明
Pour each other wine while roasting dry fish.[40]	酌醴焚枯魚
We used to imitate Gongsun Hong,[41]	嘗學公孫弘
Staff in hand, out herding pigs.	策杖牧群豬

Accepting this scene not as a literal memory of past experience but as an accurate indication of Wang Ji's long-held personal ideals and literary and intellectual tastes, we may be more inclined to understand how he so readily turned away from official life to retirement, with or without the prompting of political "snares and nets."

Nonetheless, with the founding of the Tang dynasty Wang Ji was summoned to office. And judging from the poem he wrote shortly before traveling to the capital,[42] he was quite pleased with this new career opportunity and proud of having been so honored:

	August brilliance shines on all regions;	皇明照區域
	The emperor's mind turns its attention to men of prominence.	帝思屬風雲
	Setting fire to the mountain, he flushes out recluses;	燒山出隱士
4	Putting the Way in order, he sends off the summoned gentleman.	治道送徵君
	I am only the shadow of a mugwort bush,	自惟蓬艾影
	Lacking the true fragrance of osmanthus and orchid.	叨名桂蘭芬
	Yet the royal messenger left me the white jade disk;	使君留白璧
8	The Son of Heaven bestowed on me dark and crimson silk.[43]	天子降玄纁
	The pheasant will be disappointed after all;	山雞終失望
	The wild deer takes leave from its herd for now.	野鹿暫辭群
	Mist in the valley envelops the vermilion sun;	川氣含丹日
12	Smoke from the village blends with the white clouds.	鄉煙間白雲
	Stopping the carriage, I have nothing to leave you;	停驂無以贈
	So I grab a brush and compose this piece.	握管遂成文

Wang Ji opens this poem by hailing the awe-inspiring majesty of the new emperor, whose power affects everything in, above, and below his realm. The allusion in line 3 to Jie Zitui 介子推, a nobleman of the Spring and Autumn period, is remarkable for its revision of a commonplace exemplum of an official who resists service to the court in order to maintain his integrity. According to several records, Jie Zitui faithfully accompanied his lord Chong'er 重耳 (a.k.a. Duke Wen of Jin) during his long exile and was extremely devoted to him. When Chong'er eventually returned to his home state and became duke, he rewarded everyone that followed him in exile but neglected to recognize Jie Zitui for his loyal service, whereupon Jie withdrew and went into hiding on a mountain. The duke later realized his mistake and sent for Jie with the offer of an appointment, but Jie evaded the duke's envoy and refused to come down from the mountain. The duke finally ordered his men to set the mountain on fire to force Jie out, but he clung to a tree and was burned to death.[44] In Wang Ji's poem, the allusion to Jie evokes his recluse persona and implies, as well, that Wang Ji's emergence from retirement comes at a time of such high virtue at court that even a Jie Zitui would heed the emperor's call. Six lines later, Wang Ji makes a similar announcement in referring to the pheasant. In literary lore, pheasants had difficulty forming pairs because of their absorption in their own beauty, preferring to gaze at their own reflections rather than find a mate.[45] By asserting that "the pheasant will be disappointed after all," Wang Ji declares an intention to reject his own brand of "self-absorption" in solitude and to grab this opportunity now that it has come. Lines 11 and 12 at first seem merely to describe the poet's last look at his home village, but Wang Ji is cleverly symbolizing the union of recluse and court. Misty air in the mountain valley and chimney smoke from the village are conventional poetic images for representing the peaceful and isolated life away from court and society, while the vermilion color of the sun and the whiteness of the clouds are often associated with the imperial court.[46] The manner in which Wang Ji conjoins these images—the way the valley mist *envelops* the sun and the smoke *blends* with the white clouds—highlights a great sense of harmony in the union of the recluses (talents in hiding) and the central court. The poem concludes, therefore, with the excited poet halting the carriage to write this hurried farewell message just before rushing off to his new duties.[47]

When Wang Ji arrived in Chang'an he was awarded the status of officer-waiting-for-appointment 待詔, which turned out to be the beginning of a long wait for an appointment that never came. He stayed in the capital for over six years, during which period rule passed from the founding emperor Gaozu 高祖 (r. 618–626) to his son Li Shimin 李世民, posthumously Taizong 太宗. In a poem that presumably indicates his feelings during this time, Wang Ji reveals his disappointment and homesickness:[48]

	I have moored here on a sojourn for many years,	旅泊多年歲
	Turning old, I have no idea when I can go home.[49]	老去不知回
	Suddenly I see a guest at the door	忽逢門外客
4	Just coming from my native land.	道發故鄉來
	With our brows knitted, we clasp hands,	斂眉俱握手
	Through tears, we raise wine cups together.	破涕共銜杯
	Eagerly I inquire after my old acquaintances;	殷勤訪朋舊
8	One by one, I ask about all the children:	屈曲問童孩
	My waning clan has many cousins and nephews;	衰宗多弟侄
	Which are still playing by the terrace near the pond?	若箇賞池臺
	Is our old garden still there?	舊園今在否
12	There must have been new trees planted, too.	新樹也應栽
	How densely are our willow trees spreading?	柳行疏密布
	How wide is the thatched hut they built?	茅齋寬窄裁
	The bamboo along the path, whence was it transferred?	經移何處竹
16	How many more apricot trees did they plant?[50]	別種幾株梅
	I assume that water never runs dry in the ditch;	渠當無絕水
	I suppose there are always lichens on the rocks.	石計總生苔
	Which fruit in the courtyard ripens first?	院果誰先熟
20	Which flower in the grove blooms last?	林花那後開
	All this sojourner can think of are the questions to ask;	羈心祇欲問
	Please answer me, do not hesitate.	為報不須猜
	I really should hurry my carriage through the marsh,[51]	行當驅下澤
24	And return to my old garden to clip pigweed.[52]	去剪故園萊

Shortly after this poem was composed Wang Ji withdrew his name from candidacy for office and for the second time retired to the country, though he stayed in retirement for only a few years before seeking office again. This time, according to Lü Cai, he was driven by financial difficulties at home. It is apparent, in any case, that Wang Ji cared little about whether his official appointment matched his qualifications, for he asked to serve as an assistant in the Grand Music Bureau, even though the Department of Appointments regarded this as inappropriate for his scholar-official status.[53] According to Lü Cai, Wang Ji insisted on being assigned to the bureau for one reason: the director, Jiao Ge 焦革, was well known for making excellent wine. Eventually Wang Ji persuaded the Department of Appointments to grant him his request, and Jiao Ge gratified his new assistant with a steady supply of his home-made specialty. To Wang Ji's grief, Jiao Ge died just a few months later. Although his widow continued supplying Wang Ji with wine, she too passed away at the end of that year. Lamenting his loss, Wang Ji resigned a third time, this time for good. Afterward his poetry becomes increasingly focused on the pleasures of country living and his resolve to remain detached from society. Now in permanent retirement, Wang Ji lived off the land he inherited from his family near the juncture of the Yellow River and the Fen River, and he styled himself Donggaozi 東皋子 (Master of the Eastern Embankment), his famous sobriquet.

By Lü Cai's account, Wang Ji's heavy drinking was the main reason he did not succeed in an official career. "You held several positions," he writes, "but none was carried to the full term, all because of your love for wine."[54] Subsequent readers, however, have noted Wang Ji's fashioning of his literary practice after earlier Wei and Jin poets who lived in a time of fallen morals and political turmoil. These readers assume that Wang Ji's several resignations from office were either the response of a moral man to tumultuous times or merely a means to excuse his failure to obtain positions of prestige. Although I too have cited a number of Wang Ji's poems as clues to his life and interests, I have largely avoided addressing the main points of contention for these readers: was Wang Ji sincere in embracing the life and philosophy of reclusion, and did the political situation of the time justify it? To my mind, we learn far less about Wang Ji's literary practice when we view it in the context of his career, or in the context of political upheaval, than we do when we examine it in the light of Sui and early Tang intellectual history, the subject of the next section.

Unification and Codification in the Sui and early Tang

In his lifetime, Wang Ji experienced the decline of the Sui dynasty (581–618)—which only three decades earlier had reestablished China as a united empire after three hundred years of disunion—and witnessed the spectacular rise of the Tang dynasty (618–907). While acknowledging its various accomplishments, historians have generally characterized the Sui era as a period of weakness and turmoil, a time of high taxes and peasant revolt, directly resulting from the court's ambitious military campaigns and expensive civil projects, such as the repeatedly failed attempts to conquer the Koguryŏ kingdom (modern Korea) and the monumental construction of the Grand Canal. In contrast the Sui's successor, the Tang, has conventionally been admired for its astute policies to consolidate China's political, military, and economic power bases and for quickly securing authority over the realm. The Zhenguan 貞觀 period (627–649) under the reign of Taizong is remembered in particular as a golden age in Chinese history. And Wang Ji, we should bear in mind, lived until just five years before Taizong himself passed away.[55]

The political changes that Wang Ji saw during his lifetime impinged on society at all levels. Though social and political unrest did from time to time threaten and even interrupt the consolidation of the empire, the success of the Sui and early Tang, in the words of Denis Twitchett and Arthur Wright, initiated "a time of unprecedented material prosperity, of institutional growth, of new departures in thought and religion, of creativity in all arts."[56] The court was also eager to institute standard political and moral codes as a means to legitimate its rule—and the intellectual community, as Twitchett describes, rose to meet its needs:

> The Sui and early T'ang were not periods of radical institutional change or innovation.... It was a period of rationalization, simplification and streamlining of procedures.... It was also a period of codification and formalization of practice, when confidence in the permanence of strong central government inclined statesmen to think in terms of uniform institutions applicable to the whole empire, and of everlasting norms of social behavior, rather than to deal empirically with specific issues as they rose.[57]

Scholars during this period generally followed one of two trends in undertaking this "codification and formalization of practice," normally termed the northern and southern styles of scholarship. Broadly speaking, southern learning was characterized by its development out of the third-century intellectual movement associated with "the learning of the mysterious" (xuanxue 玄學), which took the form of syntheses of diverse philosophical systems and the application of sophistical reasoning in interpreting classical texts. The northern style, by contrast, was more conventional in its aims and methods, closer in its ties to the tradition of Han-dynasty scholarship, and rarely extended beyond textual commentary in the treatment of the Confucian canon.[58] Scholars were aware of the differences between the northern and southern learning before the Sui, of course, and made efforts toward standardizing their various practices. But with reunification and the gathering of scholars from throughout the empire at one capital the differences between them became more pronounced and their labors toward "codification and formalization" took on official purpose.

Among the earliest of these scholars was Lu Deming 陸德明 (ca. 550–630), a renowned expert on the Confucian classics who was also well versed in *Laozi* and *Zhuangzi* and the *xuanxue* school of learning.[59] Lu held high-ranking positions first in the southern court of Chen (558–589) and later in the Sui and Tang courts. Observing the loss of standards for the exegetical treatment of classical texts in his time, Lu Deming feared that future generations would not be able to comprehend their true meaning. He insisted that the proper understanding of Confucian ideas could only be obtained through correct recitation of texts. The existing glossaries, however, were vastly different from one another due to differences between each compiler's dialect and style of scholarly training. Thus Lu Deming set out to write the definitive guide to the interpretation of the classics. The result was his *Jingdian shiwen* 經典釋文, containing phonetic glosses and annotations to fourteen classical texts. Lu considered his project in line with the Confucian principle of "the rectification of names" (正名),[60] though claiming he was only "transmitting, not creating" (述而不作) the standard.[61] His work is one of the earliest instances of the consultation of multiple sources—over 230 texts written in the preceding four centuries—for the purpose of establishing an authoritative commentary.

Lu Deming's alarm at the lack of a standardized recitation for the reading of texts was shared by many others, and in 581, the founding year of the Sui dynasty, a group of eight prominent scholars met in Chang'an to discuss "the rights and the wrongs of the northern and southern pronunciation, the permissible and the impermissible of [readings in] the ancient and the present day." Such is the report of Lu Fayan 陸法言 in his preface to the *Qieyun* 切韻, the dictionary that he eventually compiled as a consequence of that meeting in which an outline of the basic discrepancies between northern and southern pronunciation was produced.[62] The *Qieyun* is a full-scale dictionary designed to be nothing less than the definitive handbook for future scholars' composition and recitation of literature— one of the earliest products of a collective effort on the part of northern and southern scholars to reconcile their different practices and establish a single standard. Lu Fayan recounts that one of them, Wei Yanyuan 魏彦淵, said to him midway through their first meeting: "Up to this point we have been discussing these problems, and we have identified all the questionable points. Why don't you write down [our discussion] as we speak? What has been settled by those of us here will then be settled once and for all."[63]

This impulse to evaluate, define, and standardize not only guided the state-sponsored scholarship of the Sui and early Tang. It is evident, as well, in projects of self-evaluation and self-definition carried out by scholars of the time who were eager to reaffirm their role in society and clarify their relationship with the new dynasty. In particular, many were intent to maintain their inherited, elite social status besides their privileged position as China's cultural caretakers. One result of this concern was the composition of the *Family Instructions for the Yan Clan* 顏氏家訓 by Yan Zhitui 顏之推 (531–591). Yan was the descendant of a prominent southern clan and a respected scholar; in fact, he was one of the eight scholars involved in outlining the phonetic system of Lu Fayan's *Qieyun*. As the title of his work indicates, Yan Zhitui's aim in his *Family Instructions* was to teach the younger generations of his family the manner of conduct deemed fitting for the status of a scholar-official. He constantly contrasts the proper "manner and behavior of a scholar-official" (士大夫風操) with that of a commoner (凡人)—betraying his fear, it seems, that his descendants might relinquish their elite status by losing touch with the codes of cultivated living that define one as a member of the official class. As Peter Bol remarks, Yan "brings a 'cultural' perspective to bear on almost everything he discusses, from remarriage and the family to learning and literary composition."[64] And indeed his prescriptions cover the whole range of an individual's behavior and responsibilities, social customs and ritual practices, religious beliefs, miscellaneous arts and skills, and most importantly one's courses of study, including phonology, philology, and literary composition: "If one is able to obtain [knowledge of] several hundred scrolls of books," he says, "then he would not become a petty person even in a thousand years."[65] In other words: learning is the most important step toward the gentleman's ultimate goal of making himself respectable in society and valuable to the ruler.

These projects exemplify the tendency toward codification and formalization that, Twitchett and Wright observe, accompanied the reunification of the empire. As they and other scholars have documented, however, this trend during the early Tang became increasingly varied and complex.[66] Although the Sui and Tang courts were both anxious about the stability of the newly established empire—and both hoped that a restored Confucian ideological system would bring uniformity and conformity—the Sui court's overt stimulation of intellectual work did not compare to the Tang's. The Sui did set many examples for the Tang court's policies, it is true. For as Twitchett and Wright point out, the Tang inherited from the Sui the mechanisms of government without having to make "striking innovations."[67] Yet a major difference between the two dynasties was the Tang's remarkable openness to a variety of scholarly pursuits and unsolicited political consultation. The Tang showed little concern for blood lineage or past political or intellectual affiliations.[68] Taizong, in particular, took an active role in sanctioning scholarly projects, and he welcomed the submission of manuscripts from persons outside the court. His promotion of intellectual study and debate, not only on canonical texts but on unorthodox philosophical ideas and religion, created a climate for an unprecedented variety of intellectual concerns, which in return immortalized his administration among later scholars as one of China's most enlightened.

David McMullen has observed that the sudden increase in scholarly activity during the early Tang was made possible first of all by a complementary relationship between the court and the intellectual community. As he puts it, the Tang ruling house recognized that Confucian scholars were "indispensable" to them—in the sense that their knowledge of literary tradition, Confucian ideology, and institutional and ritual directives sanctioned by the Confucian canon would need to be tapped in order to "legitimize and strengthen the entire edifice of dynastic government." Furthermore, their expertise in such practical fields as law, calendrical science, yin-yang theory, and astrology "provided essential sanctions for dynastic power."[69] Thus the ruling house opened the central court to scholars, established permanent academic institutions within the state bureaucracy, and called on intellectuals to formulate canonically sanctioned ritual programs and government procedures.

As McMullen points out, it was a mutually beneficial relationship that went beyond the matter of conducting state business. By encouraging scholars in their pursuits, the court gave its "sign of approval for scholars, a recognition [that] their activities were dignified and worthwhile."[70] Although scholars rarely held positions so powerful in their political influence as those occupied by the military class from the northwest, their visibility and status in court were the subject of sincere high praise for the emperor. This praise in turn propagandized the wisdom and benevolence of the court. Hence the dynasty took measures to ensure that scholars felt a sense of direct involvement in court policymaking. Taizong, for example, is said regularly to have called in his learned councillors "to listen to their lectures and discussions on scriptural interpretation or to discuss with them administrative matters."[71] Scholars were encouraged to express their dissent and offer competing recommendations to the throne. And this attitude of open-mindedness, McMullen argues, had both the psychological and propagandistic advantage for the ruling house of validating its legitimacy, because the presence of "well qualified scholars willing to speak their minds to the emperor and his court was in itself a sign of achievement, an indication that the dynasty was politically successful."[72]

But McMullen also notes that the Tang's relaxed attitudes toward a diversity of competing opinions greatly affected the period's "codifying and formalizing" intellectual activity. Though still very much utilitarian in their goals, scholars felt encouraged to take an eclectic approach in their scholarship, drawing widely from the plural cultural strands of the remote Han as well as the preceding period of disunion. Their aim was not to establish rigid systems of governance or scholarship. The process of standardizing canonical texts and commentaries, for example, was meant to introduce an efficient means for administering the examination system. Beyond that, McMullen comments, "the state had no other interest in enforcing a narrow Confucian orthodoxy, nor was the scholar community committed to define one."[73] The result, McMullen admits, was almost paradoxical: on the one hand, scholars produced compilations of diverse material from all the centuries past, holding to an ideal of "comprehensiveness"; on the other hand, these works "were intended to have definitive status in the official world to which they were addressed."[74]

We may recognize this eclecticism, I would point out, as one of the characteristics of Lu Deming's *Jingdian shiwen*. The title of the collection announces that it is composed of the canonical classics. But Lu did not restrict his selection of texts to the Confucian classics that defined the orthodox canon in the Han; instead, after the practice of scholars in the southern dynasties, he included the *Laozi* and *Zhuangzi*. Yet the *Jingdian shiwen* was much admired in the early Tang: it is reported that Taizong prized it so highly that he encouraged its circulation among the scholars in the imperial academies and sent copies to his sons. He furthermore granted Lu Deming's family a hundred bolts of silk and cloth as a reward for their presenting the collection to the throne.[75]

The intellectual climate resulting from the Tang's sponsoring of scholarship extended beyond the court, and we see a like impulse in the works of independent intellectuals to survey and evaluate the past in order to formulate comprehensive but definitive models suitable for present and future utility. In line with this trend was renewed interest in literary theory and in compiling compendia of literary commonplaces as aids to composition. Among the earliest of these works is the *Beitang shuchao* 北堂書鈔 compiled by Yu Shinan 虞世南 (558–638) during the Sui. Primarily occupied in its content with topics related to government, the *Beitang shuchao* emphasizes the utilitarian function of literature, assuming its value is to assist in the efficient administration of the state. This focus is consistent with the official policy of the Sui court, in which Yu Shinan served as a secretary for a time. With the unification of the empire, the differences between northern and southern attitudes toward literature confronted both court and scholars and already, at the court of the Sui's founding emperor Yang Jian 楊堅 (r. 581–604), we learn of a campaign of criticism against what many considered the south's decadent literary subjects—typically the sentiments of palace ladies and the celebration of courtly pleasures—and its ostentatious, ornate literary style, which in fact had long been imitated by many among the northern literati, as well as by members of the ruling classes. Throughout the northern dynasties, members of the non-Chinese elite or interracial aristocrats, including those of the royal Sui family, perceived southern culture to be more sophisticated than their own and made conscious efforts to become sinicized through the emulation of the cultural, including the literary, legacy of their neighboring states to the south. Yang Jian feared that the literary ostentation and decadent morals which many believed had characterized this emulation would weaken the government's effectiveness. And so, in 585, he issued an edict requesting his subjects to abandon frivolous literary styles both for government matters and in their private compositions. He urged them to strive instead for factual representations and truthful opinions in their writing. Yu Shinan's *Beitang shuchao* offers a range of model passages to guide officials and literati who aspired to write according to this edict's prescriptions.[76]

Tang writers were similarly anxious to define the proper function of literature, but their interests were not so rigidly orthodox. Most characteristically, they strove to define the proper balance between the ethical value of literature and its aesthetic qualities. This wider concern is reflected in the purpose and structure of the literary compendia produced during the early Tang, such as the *Yiwen leiju* 藝文類聚. This work, completed in 624 and containing far more categories of topics than the *Beitang shuchao*, was compiled under imperial auspices by a group of scholars directed by

Ouyang Xun 歐陽詢 (557–641), whose principles of selection were both didactic utility and stylistic excellence. For each entry, citations are provided from the classics, historical documents, philosophical works, and other forms of nonliterary writings, presenting the background of each topic, followed by excerpts from various literary genres demonstrating the artful ways to treat the topic. By so modeling alternative literary models for the poetic communication of ethical ideas, the *Yiwen leiju*, we should note, at the same time set limits on variation. The examples the compilers selected were intended to be definitive. As the director Ouyang Xun states, the work "provides those who read it an easy way to improve [their own writing] and a reference source for those who write, so that they can choose from [models of] the present and the past and regulate their writing with the [standard of the] classics and the canon."[77] The compilation of such compendia can thus be regarded as another manifestation of the effort toward codification and formalization that characterized intellectual endeavor in the period, governed too by the impulse to identify the permissible and the impermissible in the culture's intellectual heritage.

The question foremost in these scholars' minds, then, was how to define a style proper to the new dynasty's needs. Historians in the Tang and ever since in China have maintained a critical view of southern-style literature, considering its refined and ornate style to be decadent and a contributing factor in the general decline in morals that led to the southern states' collapse. Wei Zheng 魏徵 (580–643), chief compiler of the *Sui shu*, was a particularly avid critic of the southern style. In his introduction to the "Biographies of Learned Men," he draws a parallel between the increasing sophistication of poetics and the gradual decay of morality throughout the Southern Dynasties period, and he is much alarmed at the prospect of the southern style's corruption of traditional orthodox northern practice. Describing such corruption among authors of the state of Liang, Wei laments:

> Since the Datong 大同 era [535–546] of the Liang, the way of *ya* 雅 has gone into all but oblivion.[78] The writers increasingly defied canonical principles, contending and striving only for novelty and artifice.... Their ideas were shallow yet overelaborately expressed; their style was obscure yet embellished with ornamentation; their language was frivolous and startling; the sentiment [in their writings] was mostly melancholy and brooding. If we judge by Yanling's 延陵 standards,[79] is it not the music of a fallen state? After [Northern] Zhou conquered the Liang and Jing, this trend spread east of the pass. The ambitious

and impetuous style suddenly became the vogue; writers strayed and forgot to return to the orthodox; they no longer conformed to the proper standard.[80]

The idea of *ya* in the early Tang connoted such ethical concepts of elegance as "uprightness," "loftiness," and "propriety."[81] Other historian-writers of the time, such as Li Boyao 李百藥 (565–648) and Linghu Defen 令狐德棻 (583–666), likewise appealed to this concept in echoing Wei's criticism of the ostentatious literary style of southern authors.[82] Even Taizong denounced this style, when he declared that "to forgo substance for ornament is to allow oneself to pursue his [licentious] desire. It brings disorder to the Great Way. A true gentleman regards such conduct as shameful."[83]

And yet Emperor Taizong was himself an admirer and composer of southern-style court poetry, and neither he nor his ministers completely rejected the poetry and poetics of the Six Dynasties period. Rather, they held that certain of the ornate qualities of southern literature could be combined with the best characteristics of the orthodox northern style to produce new literary forms suited to this new age in history. As Wei Zheng argues:

> West of the Yangzi River, the poetic sounds of *gong* 宮 and *shang* 商 sprang and flowed,[84] the lucid and the ornate were esteemed. North of the Yellow River, the meaning of the words was candid and bold, vigor and substance were valued. But with vigor and substance, argument (*li* 理) will outweigh eloquence (*ci* 辭); with a pure and refined style, ornament will override meaning. Profound argument is helpful for dealing with issues of the time. Ornate style is appropriate for versification. This is the approximate comparison of the merits and faults of northern and southern literary styles. If we can adopt the quality of purity on the one hand and simplify the prolix reasoning on the other, discard the defective qualities and combine their good qualities, then we will have a literature with both form and content. That would be the acme of perfection![85]

This enthusiasm for combining the "best" qualities of northern and southern literature was tied to Wei Zheng's commitment to heightening the utilitarian function of literature without sacrificing the pleasures of its ornamentation. Similarly, Wei's contemporary Linghu Defen, in his discussion of literary writers in the *Zhou shu*, integrated past theories of literature to promote not only ethical content but self-expression that makes full use of rhetorical forms, poetic diction, and prosody. As for the various literary genres, Linghu observes:

> None is as good as relying on one's qi 氣 as the guiding factor and relying on refined writing to transfer ideas.... It is noble that the tune is lofty; it is desirable that the purport is profound; it is valuable that the argument is appropriate; and it is commendable that the diction is ingenious. After that, we polish it with the luster of bronze and jade, adorn it with the fragrance of thoroughwort. Form and content adjust to suit each other; the prolix and the terse alter to compromise one another. Balancing the light and the weighty, judging the ancient and the present, it is harmonious yet powerful; it is splendid yet restrained. Glamorous, it is like the composition of five colors; compounded, it is like the convergence of eight sounds.[86]

In short, scholars paid increasing attention during the early Tang to the features and purposes of literature, striving to reassert its utilitarian function and to standardize literary practice, in an attempt to merge northern and southern models and the alternative poetics of the previous centuries with orthodox Confucian ideology. These efforts were part of a drive to establish a literary legitimacy to complement and affirm the legitimacy of the new court. There is, perhaps, no better indication of this perceived relation between a new form of literature expressing moral ideas in a refined style, on the one hand, and the new dynasty unifying diverse cultures, on the other, than the writing of Taizong himself. In a ten-poem sequence titled "The Imperial Capital" (Dijing pian 帝京篇), Taizong disseminated an idealized image of himself as an eminently moral emperor in traditional Confucian terms but in the style of southern court poetry.[87]

This is the historical era and the intellectual climate within which Wang Ji lived and wrote, and it is clear he shared his contemporaries' desire to reassert literature's utilitarian purpose to communicate one's moral and philosophical ideas. In his preface to "Fu on Roaming the Northern Mountains," for example, he invokes two classic statements of this view when he asserts: "One's intent of mind (zhi 志) goes into poetry," and "fu is one branch of poetry."[88] The source of the first statement is the "Great Preface" to the Mao commentary of the Book of Songs,[89] a canonical pronouncement on the utilitarian function of poetry that had been repeated for centuries. The second is from the moralist historian Ban Gu 班固 (32–92), who first asserted the derivative relationship between fu and the classical poetry of the *Book of Songs*, thereby claiming *fu*'s legitimacy as a genre with the authority and moral efficacy of the Confucian canon.[90]

Elsewhere Wang Ji writes that "the apprehension of ideas is the only merit" in "the composition of poetry,"[91] a conviction that is evident also in Wang Ji's literary practice. Attention to this feature will enable us to interpret Wang Ji's poems appropriately and to understand his distinctness from other poets and intellectuals of his time—more so, certainly, than readings based simply on the assumption that his poetic persona and themes reflect his misfortunes and frustration in a time of political instability or as a consequence of his failures in office. Although Wang Ji shared his contemporaries' utilitarian view of literature and strove as they did to emphasize the philosophical and moral content of his writing, we shall find that the very ideas he embraced made his work atypical because these ideas stood in philosophical opposition to the impulse toward codification and formalization which characterized the intellectual activity of the period. In general, that activity was based on Confucian ideology—as exemplified by Wei Zheng's political admonitions, Li Boyao's orthodox contemplations of the past, and Taizong's self-representation as a sage-ruler—and it presumed the attainability of permanent empire by means of consolidating and institutionalizing ritual practices and learning. Wang Ji, by contrast, found attractive a philosophy of "naturalness" and "inaction" grounded in the texts of *Laozi* and *Zhuangzi,* and he shared their rejection of the notion that anything can be permanent in human affairs. Furthermore, he was drawn to the Wei-Jin tradition of inquiry into this philosophy known as *xuanxue,* "the learning of the mysterious." The influence of this tradition on the development of Six Dynasties poetry generally, and on Wang Ji's specifically, is the subject of the next section.

Xuanxue and Its Significance to Reading Wang Ji

Historians of Chinese political thought have observed that a philosophy based on the texts of *Laozi* and *Zhuangzi* emerged as a popular alternative to Confucianism following the collapse of the Han empire—and this philosophy especially flourished during the Zhengshi 正始 period (240–249) of the Wei dynasty as a consequence of the constant political upheaval and bloodshed that accompanied the competition for the throne between powerful military clans in those years. As explained by K. C. Hsiao (Xiao Gongquan 蕭公權), disillusioned intellectuals after the fall of the Han questioned the efficacy of Confucian values and looked for alternative political and religious ideas:

> The thought of the Lao-Zhuang school of learning originally had centered on forgetting about the world in egocentric concern for the individual, and its somewhat decadent way of life was, furthermore, a phenomenon regularly accompanying ages of decline and disorder. That Lao-Zhuang thought should have become widely current during the Wei-Jin period is therefore a most natural development.[92]

Charles Holcombe reminds us, however, that "the tone pervading much of what is recorded of third-century thought is one of liberation rather than despair" and contends that post-Han "Lao-Zhuang thought" actually represents the continuation of Han intellectual trends toward metaphysical speculation.[93] Citing such writers as Dong Zhongshu 董仲舒 (ca. 179–104 B.C.), Yang Xiong 揚雄 (53 B.C.–A.D. 18), Huan Tan 桓譚 (43 B.C.–A.D. 28), and Wang Chong 王充 (29–97), Holcombe asserts that it was their "rational, materialistic outlook" and their denial of "an anthropomorphic moralistic heaven" that "formed the intellectual foundation for what is often described as third-century Neo-Taoist 'nihilism.'"[94] The more accurate term for this "Neo-Taoism" is *xuanxue*, variously called "abstruse learning" or "the learning of the mysterious." While it may not have been quite "a new metaphysics," as Richard Mather calls it, the term is associated with an intellectual movement "based on *Laozi* and *Zhuangzi* and the 'Book of Changes.'"[95] Wang Bi 王弼 (226–249) and He Yan 何晏 (d. 249) were the most notable "high priests" of this movement. In their writings we see their shared interest in determining the two meanings of *ziran* 自然 (naturalness and spontaneity) and the nature of *you* 有 and *wu* 無 (conventionally translated as "being" and "nonbeing" or "the actual" and "the nonactual"). For illustration, Mather cites He Yan's statement in *Wuming lun* 無名論—that "Heaven and Earth revolve by naturalness (*ziran*); the sage functions by naturalness, [which] is the Tao, and the Tao is basically nameless (*wuming*)"—and Wang Bi's commentary on *Laozi* 5 that "Heaven and Earth comply with the Naturally-so; they are non-active and non-creative. The ten thousand things control and order each other by themselves."[96]

He Yan and Wang Bi may appear to be sinking into "some kind of 'nihilism' or 'mystical escapism,'" as Mather concedes, but their ideas had a very practical "political viability in the Zhengshi era because such expressions as 'beginning from the Non-actual'" were really "another way of saying 'starting from scratch,'" a sentiment that accorded well with the desire of Cao Cao 曹操 (155–220; posthumously known as Emperor Wu of Wei) to "break with the past and with the stranglehold of tradition"—to conduct his state affairs according to "what each situation calls for" rather than "what is prescribed in the 'Analects' or the 'Record of the Rites.'"[97] After the fall of the Wei, *xuanxue* continued to have political significance—but as an indication of ideological resistance to the new court. The ruling Sima 司馬 clan that founded the Western Jin established a rigid Confucianism in reaction to Wei innovations, and one way intellectuals such as Xi Kang and Ruan Ji could register their opposition to the new regime was by advocating naturalness and inaction. As Xi Kang observes in his "Discourse on Release from Self-interest" (Shi si lun 釋私論):

> The mind of one who claims the name of gentleman is not involved with "right and wrong," nor do his acts violate the Tao.... Moreover, in the mind of one whose vital force is quiescent and whose spirit is empty, there resides no pride or arrogance, and the feelings of one whose body is luminous and whose mind is untrammeled are not fettered by what he desires. Because pride and arrogance do not reside in his mind, he is able to transcend the Teaching of Names [Confucian doctrine] and let himself free in Naturalness.[98]

Xi Kang's execution by Sima Zhao, in 262, marked the decline of serious political opposition to the Sima clan and the end of *xuanxue*'s association with resistance. Scholars in Xi Kang's circle (in later years known as the "Seven Worthies of the Bamboo Grove") and others endeavored "to reconcile the opposing claims of activism and quietism" by discovering points of similarity between the ideas of *Laozi* and *Zhuangzi* and Confucian orthodoxy. And in Mather's view the earliest and most self-conscious effort toward such a "rationalization" was the "amalgamated" *Zhuangzi* commentary of Xiang Xiu 向秀 (ca. 221–300) and Guo Xiang 郭象 (d. 312). "Non-action," in the view of these exegetes, does not require withdrawal from politics, as Mather recounts, for one may possess an "inward naturalness" while maintaining an "outward conformity" and an emperor may actually "practice 'non-action' *while fulfilling his duties as a ruler*."[99]

This process of reconciliation eased the assimilation of *xuanxue* ideas and terminology into an increasingly inclusive (or fractured) orthodoxy during the years of disunion following the decline of the Western Jin. Indeed as Mather observes it was not long until "the idea of the Non-actual had been accepted as a sort of ground of existence, with Non-action its mode of operation," so that "it became de rigueur to pay at least lip service to these values." At the same time, this tendency toward the integration of philosophical systems facilitated the accommodation of Buddhist religious ideas, Mather continues, for "the *xuanxue* concept of Nonactuality could easily be identified with the Buddhist concept of emptiness, or Relativity (śūnyatā), and Non-action with Nirvāṇa."[100]

For Six Dynasties poets—and, as I will show, for Wang Ji—not only the ideas of the *xuanxue* movement but the forms of its discursive practice were influential. Right at its beginning, *xuanxue* inquiry was associated with a form of oral discourse known as *qingtan* 清談, or "pure discourse," which first emerged in the Later Han dynasty. But whereas *qingtan* originally was used for itemizing a person's talents and moral character, by the Wei-Jin period it had evolved into a sophisticated mode of debate employed not only to expound upon the central *xuanxue* notions of naturalness and inaction but a wide range of topics including philosophical propositions, "names and principles" (*mingli* 名理), the methods and aims of scholarship, and the aesthetic criteria of the various arts. Wing-tsit Chan explains that the practice of "pure discourse" gave scholars an opportunity to communicate their ideals, to stimulate their thinking and sharpen their imagination, as well as to display their wit and eloquence.[101] And this is exactly how it is represented in numerous places in *Shishuo xinyu* 世說新語, including an account of a "bout" between Wang Bi and He Yan:

> Since Yan had heard of Bi's reputation, he culled some of the best arguments from past conversations and said to Bi, "These arguments I consider to be ultimate. Do you care to raise any objections?"
>
> Bi proceeded to raise objections, and after he was finished the whole company considered that Yan had been defeated. Bi then went on, himself acting as both "host" and "guest" for several bouts.[102]

It is a commonplace generalization that *xuanxue* and the practice of pure discourse influenced the formation of a new poetics in the Wei-Jin period, but even full-length studies ostensibly devoted to the subject are extremely vague about the nature of this influence.[103] I would start by observing that intellectual activity associated with *xuanxue* was in some ways paralleled by literary activity: the poetry of Ruan Ji, Xi Kang, and such later figures as Tao Qian, for instance, synthesizes imaginatively the metaphysical dimensions of *Laozi* and *Zhuangzi* with traditional Confucian ideology. Donald Holzman, in his study of Ruan Ji, remarks that this inclination toward the combining of diverse ideas represented an attempt to "re-animate post-Han Confucianism." Holzman points out that Ruan Ji's poetry and prose betray a strong desire "for some kind of 'wholeness' and 'unity' in which all mankind would work together in a single, integrated organism." For Ruan Ji, Holzman concludes, Lao-Zhuang philosophy was a method for discovering the means to such unity, because it provided "a superior way of looking at the world from a more sophisticated, metaphysical plane."[104] With the same motive, the poet Sun Chuo 孫綽 (ca. 310–397), who "equated Buddha with Confucius," says Mather, merges Buddhist with Confucian and Taoist ideas and imagery in his "*Fu* on Roaming in the Tiantai Mountains" (You Tiantai shan fu 遊天台山賦).[105]

As for the influence of pure discourse on literature, we need to focus on the significance of its form. The metaphysics of *xuanxue* prompted philosophical debate over esoteric ideas such as the meaning of "following the natural way" and "living a life of inaction." By engaging in this debate, in the form of "bouts" of pure discourse, the disputant took a stand on a selected topic, advanced a thesis, and "culled the best arguments from past conversations" (as He Yan was said to have done in the passage from *Shishuo xinyu* cited earlier) in order to construct the "ultimate argument," which, all the same, one expected to have answered by the objections of a "guest" (as He Yan's was met by Wang Bi's). Participation in pure discourse was an important intellectual and social activity in the life of Wei-Jin literati, and its practice seems to have influenced the writing of poetry in that there occurred a general shift away from moral didacticism and the expression of feelings toward the imaginative proposition of philosophical and religious ideas.

We find the most obvious evidence of pure discourse's influence on this shift in the few extant *xuanyan* 玄言 poems ("words of the abstruse") by Sun Chuo and Xu Xun 許詢 (fl. ca. 358), which seem to incorporate wholesale *qingtan* themes and terminology and are characterized by mystical abstractions and a blending of concepts from the Confucian, Lao-Zhuang, and Buddhist traditions. Though commonly condemned for its obscurity, *xuanyan* poetry was admired for its metaphorical and metonymic treatment of natural scenes and objects, especially the elements of landscape scenery, for the purpose of advancing philosophical ideas. Thus the familiar literary mode of describing nature, which traditionally mirrored the poet's state of mind, in such later "landscape poets" as Xie Lingyun 謝靈運 (385–433) represents a seeking of the truth or order of the Way in the natural world.

Early in the history of the *xuanxue* movement and the development of pure discourse, other literary themes traditionally devoted to moral teaching and personal expression were employed to explore the implications of philosophical and religious ideas by representing or arguing the case for different life choices that might be made on the basis of these ideas. In He Shao's 何邵 (236–301) and Guo Pu's 郭璞 (276–324) "Poems of Wandering Immortals" (Youxian shi 遊仙詩), in Lu Ji's 陸機 (261–303) and Zuo Si's 左思 (ca. 250–ca. 305) "Poems Summoning the Recluse" (Zhaoyin shi 招隱詩), and in Wang Kangju's 王康琚 (fl. fourth century) "Rebuttal to 'Summoning the Recluse'" (Fan zhaoyin 反招隱), we encounter various arguments for and against fulfilling official obligations, escaping this world through the pursuit of immortality, and freeing oneself of worldly entanglements by choosing to live in the wilderness.

Wang Ji is always recognized as an imitator of Wei-Jin poets. But without exception modern scholars have taken his poems as sites of unmediated self-expression in the apparent "confessional style" of Ruan Ji, Xi Kang, and Tao Qian, in particular. No one seems to have noted how deeply Wang Ji's poetry is immersed in an intellectual tradition derived from the *xuanxue* movement and how much he is indebted to its literary influence —even though in his poetry and private communications we regularly encounter explicit references to his participation in activities associated with *xuanxue* thinkers. In one of his poems on the theme of "contemplating solitude,"[106] for example, he writes:

I ask you, aside from a jug of wine,	問君樽酒外
What more do I need when sitting alone?	獨坐更何須
I have visitors who will discuss Names and Principles with me,	有客談名理
But there is no one to bother me with land taxes.	無人索地租

"Names and Principles," in the third line, refers to a form of debate that involved matching terms with their corresponding realities—a popular theme of pure discourse among Wei-Jin era thinkers associated with the *xuanxue* movement. Elsewhere Wang Ji testifies again to his attraction to the ideas and practices of pure discourse when he describes in a letter a gathering of his like-minded friends:

Those who are in the same realm with me, they number no more than two or three. From time to time, we visit one another. Casting aside ceremonial rituals, we sit around with our legs stretched out, our hair loose, engaging in discussions of the mysterious and in discourse on the void. Oblivious, we drink together to a drunken stupor. Feeling content, we then go back home, not discerning wherefore we gather and disperse.[107]

This scene reads like a narrative description of a famous mural depicting the reputed gathering of the group of eccentric, antiritualist poets and thinkers known as the "Seven Worthies of the Bamboo Grove," which included Ruan Ji, Xi Kang, and Liu Ling. But just as significantly, Wang Ji asserts that he and his friends enter into "conversations about the mysterious" and "discussions of the void" (xuantan xulun 玄談虛論). Such phrases, which would have been immediately recognized as descriptive of pure discourse on xuanxue topics, do not in themselves indicate that Wang Ji would have counted himself a xuanxue devotee. But this is not what I intend to establish. Rather they are valuable for focusing our attention as readers of Wang Ji's poetry on his engagement in the discursive practices associated with xuanxue inquiry.

In fact, Wang Ji at times structured his prose compositions after the manner of Wei-Jin pure discourse. Though he is notorious for his cynical view of Confucianism, his mockery of the Buddha, and even his occasional criticism of Laozi and Zhuangzi, his writings often contain arguments based on the synthesis of ideas from all their teachings. The following excerpt from one of his letters demonstrates this rhetorical practice.[108] It was written in response to a friend who apparently criticized Wang Ji for his unconventional lifestyle or urged him to return to official service. Invoking the concept of shi 適 (naturalness), Wang Ji proceeds in the traditional manner of the xuanxue reasoner:

> In the past, Confucius said: "I have no preconceptions about the permissible and the impermissible";[109] and he wanted to settle among the nine barbarian tribes of the east.[110] Laozi said: "As for [the nameless and the named] being the same, we call it the Abstruse";[111] and he left the pass and headed out west.[112] Śākyamuni said: "Form is none other than Emptiness";[113] and so he laid down the principle for all things.[114] This is all because to sages the abstruse truth penetrates all and the mysterious storehouse extends far. The truth is that a placid-minded and perspicacious man looks out toward the yonder realm of the world, so how can one judge him by his words and conduct? Hence Confucius said that the way of a good man does not follow the tracks of others;[115] Laozi said that those who take no action leave nothing

unaccomplished;[116] and Śākyamuni said that when the three calamities completely pervade the world, one's karmic accumulation is still pure and clear.[117] The primal pneuma was first a congealed entity; the phenomenal movements blew it into myriads of things. Although the myriads of different things are distinct from one another, the Way penetrates through all of them and unites them into one.[118] Therefore if one has settled peacefully into his own destined lot, is there anything so different that it is not comprehensible? If one goes against what complies with his nature, then is there any undertaking that does not meet obstruction? Thus "sages" are nothing more than a name for those who comply with nature and are devoid of obstruction and for those who adhere to their destined lot and comprehend all things. Because they adhere to their destined lot and are thoroughly comprehending, they stand firm without changing their course.[119] Because they comply with their natures and are devoid of obstruction, they roam about unscrupulous of where they go. As for those who overstep their lot yet wish to obtain thorough comprehension, who are adverse to their nature but wish to meet no obstruction, even if they have the ability of the divine Yu, what can they possibly do about it? Someone once said: "Although a duck's legs are short, lengthening them will make the duck sad. Although a crane's legs are long, cutting them short will distress the crane."[120] This is saying that one's destined lot cannot be defied. And: "When dreaming about being a bird, I soar into the sky. When I dream about being a fish, I submerge into the spring."[121] This is saying that naturalness cannot be defied.

In explicating his determination to "hold to the natural order of things," as we see, Wang Ji's rhetorical procedure is to draw authority from the several philosophies available to him and to employ their different terminologies to argue his one position—on the premise common to *xuanxue* thinkers that these different philosophies are complementary rather than in opposition.

Turning to Wang Ji's poetry, we find three prominent themes that are typical of Wei-Jin era recluse poetry. Yet the extent to which *xuanxue* ideas are implicated in these themes has been entirely missed by modern readers. The first of these themes is represented in Wang Ji's poems on "Ancient Themes" (Guyi 古意) and "Expressions of Personal Thoughts" (alternatively Yanzhi 言志, Xuzhi 敘志, Yongsi 詠思, and Yanhuai 言懷), which invoke the style and mood that we associate with Ruan Ji's series of "Poems Expressing My Inner Thoughts" (Yonghuai shi 詠懷詩). Also in this group are the poems set to eremitic themes that were popular during

Jin times, such as "summoning recluses" and "wandering immortals." The second theme is represented by poems on country living, especially the simple farmer's life in seclusion, the model for which was Tao Qian. The third comprises poems on drinking, for which Wang Ji's person has since been likened to all the celebrated drinkers of the Wei-Jin period and his poems to those of Tao Qian on the same theme. But at this point we are in a position to observe one deeper similarity (and make important distinctions) between Wang Ji and his Wei-Jin recluse-poet models.

What is most striking about Ruan Ji's "Yonghuai" poems and Tao Qian's country poems is their different presentation of personal responses to natural scenes. As other readers have observed, a "tremendous gulf" exists between the two in their view of nature.[122] Ruan Ji's use of natural imagery is entirely symbolic, communicating his feelings of loneliness and creating a tone of solemnity and melancholy. Tao Qian's presentation of his responses to nature, by contrast, reveals genuine delight in what he beholds.[123] Lu Kanru 陸侃如 and Feng Yuanjun 馮沅君 point out that the one common thread which does connect Ruan Ji's and Tao Qian's poetry is their effort to comprehend a particular philosophical issue of vital concern to *xuanxue* thinkers—namely the inconstancy underlying every aspect of life: the realization that everything in the world is transient and that the constant changes and transformations are the Way of nature, beyond human control.[124]

Wang Ji shares this philosophical stance with Ruan Ji and Tao Qian, and at times we shall see that his attraction to the concept of permanence-in-change—the constancy of inconstancy—is explicitly stated as a thesis in such poems as those in his "Ancient Theme" sequence, in his "Poem on the Divine Tortoise" (Linggui 靈龜), and in a number of "presentation" poems that he wrote to acquaintances within and without official circles. But it is this book's project to show that Wang Ji takes this idea one step further than did his Wei-Jin models in that he manifests the concept of an ever-changing world in the imagery, allusions, and syntax of his poetry—including his own self-representation. By so doing, Wang Ji controverts the very notion of "personal self-expression" in literature. For as his poems repeatedly are devised to reveal, the poet's identity is as illusory as the phenomenal world in which the poet resides.

To summarize, then, Wang Ji's fashioning of a poetic persona and style after Wei-Jin models should be viewed within the context of Sui-Tang intellectual activity, not according to their presumed moral or personality likenesses. Unlike Ruan Ji and Tao Qian, Wang Ji did not withdraw himself from a chaotic or perilous political situation; nor was his self-advertised reclusion a protest against the corrupt ethos of the time. For as we have seen, his was a time of relative stability and prosperity, restored moral standards, and general optimism in the reunification of the empire. In fact, we cannot even say that Wang Ji's recluse poetry expresses, explicitly or implicitly, his personal frustration in his failed career or that his drinking poems drown that frustration. For as I will show in the following chapters, Wang Ji conveys neither the bitterness that inevitably surfaces in Ruan Ji's poetry nor the self-apology that is so evident in Tao Qian's. And while many of Wang Ji's readers have pointed to these differences as reasons to regard his character as morally inferior to his noble predecessors, this is not an illuminating judgment. We should rather be asking what Wang Ji is in fact doing in his poetry, if he so departs from his models.

Wang Ji, as we have seen, was very much interested in the intellectual issues that generally occupied scholars of his time—that is, the permanence of the empire and the codification of everything that supported it, from forms of ritual to language. But in contrast to most of his contemporaries Wang Ji was philosophically invested in the concept of the world's inherent and interminable change, of the impossibility of knowing or permanently codifying anything. His poetics was "oppositional," therefore, not because he was dissenting against the court, writing polemics against other scholars, or denouncing the decadent poetics of court poetry (as Owen uses the term "opposition poetics" to characterize the theory and practice of a number of poets of this period).[125] Rather, Wang Ji's poetry was oppositional in that his ideals were rooted in a philosophical perspective that kept him insisting—not dogmatically but through poetic demonstration, sometimes solemnly but more often comically—that the only constancy in the world is inconstancy and human knowledge is inherently illusory. The reward of apprehending Wang Ji's poetic method in such terms will become clear in the chapters that follow, for it enables us to account for features of Wang Ji's poetry that have thus far proved inexplicable to modern scholarship.

2
The Recluse as Philosopher

❀

IN MANY OF Wang Ji's poems we see the poet advancing himself as a philosopher-recluse, adopting the perspective of an enlightened, detached sage who reflects deeply on his own life and the ways of the cosmos. Some of these poems are addressed to acquaintances from court officials to fellow recluses; in others he addresses himself; still others seem spoken in abstraction and to the world in general. Often Wang Ji explicitly states what I contend was his philosophical position, and in this chapter I will first examine several such poems whose message is straightforward in this regard. But I then turn to consider the more interesting cases: the poems in which this philosophy is not (or not only) stated but rather enacted. That is, we shall see how Wang Ji's conception of "the permanence of impermanence," and thus the illusory nature of all knowledge, is not merely asserted or argued as a "thesis" but personified in his literary self-representation, a character formed from Wang Ji's unconventional, unpredictable selection and arrangement of familiar materials from the poetic and philosophical traditions. Critics who have not ignored this unpredictability ordinarily conclude that it betrays Wang Ji's fundamentally contradictory or insincere character. I say that we should greet it as a poetic method. By its nature, it is a method that resists its readers' confident, comfortable application of past knowledge to the act of interpretation because it forces us to experience recurring shifts in poetic perspective that in turn emblematize the ever-changing nature of the world.

The poems I refer to here can be categorized as contemplative or reflective. Some of these are in the conventional poetic modes of *guyi* 古意 (on an ancient theme) and *yonghuai* 詠懷 (expressing my innermost thoughts), the latter alternatively designated *yongsi* 詠思 or *yanhuai* 言懷, *xuzhi* 敘志, or *yanzhi* 言志 (expressing my intent). Others are written as presentation poems on social occasions indicated by terms such as *zeng* 贈 (presented to) or *shi* 示 (shown to) in the title. Still others are meant to be taken as introspective poems composed in solitude, such as those titled "Sitting in Solitude" (Du zuo 獨坐), "Contemplating in Solitude" (Du si 獨思), "Presented to Myself" (Zi zeng 自贈), and "Reply to Myself" (Zi da 自答). Despite the apparent differences in occasion and authorial stance in this range of poems, Wang Ji consistently invokes in them the contemplative mood that characterizes Ruan Ji's "Yonghuai shi" sequence—a series of eighty-two poems that writers since the Wei-Jin era had taken as a model for the personal, introspective expression of a scholar's feelings, ambitions, and ideals in poetry.

Several of Wang Ji's contemporaries, known for advocating an "opposition poetics" as described in the previous chapter, turned to the *yonghuai* tradition for poetic inspiration. An example is the poem "Expressing My Feelings" (Shu huai 述懷) by Wei Zheng,[1] a prominent statesman of the Sui and early Tang. As we can see, this poem is filled with straightforward statements of personal feelings and political concerns intermixed with only a few allusive historical references:

When the deer chase first began on the central plain,[2]	中原初逐鹿
I cast aside my brush to serve in the campaign.	投筆事戎軒
Although my strategies did not prevail,	縱橫計不就
4 Impassioned, my resolve remains firm.	慷慨志猶存
Staff in hand, I paid homage to the Son of Heaven,	杖策謁天子
Then spurred my horse and galloped out from the pass.[3]	驅馬出關門
I asked for a long rein to tie up the king of southern Yue;	請纓繫南粵
8 From the rail of my chariot, I subjugated the eastern state.[4]	憑軾下東藩
Trudging along the tortuous path, I ascend high peaks,	鬱紆陟高岫
Gazing at the plain appearing and disappearing beneath me.	出沒望平原
In the cold, a bird calls out on an ancient tree;	古木鳴寒鳥
12 At night, a gibbon wails on an empty mountain.	空山啼夜猿
It brings a twinge to my eyes that have been gazing into the distance a thousand *li* away,	既傷千里目

And startles my soul that flies home many a time.[5] 還驚九逝魂

How could I not quiver at such hardship and 豈不憚艱險
danger?

16 Yet I deeply cherish the honor His Majesty 深懷國士恩
bestowed on me.

Like Ji Bu, I do not make the same promise twice; 季布無二諾

Like Hou Ying, I honor my word once it is uttered.[6] 侯嬴重一言

In life one should act on a sense of honor and duty; 人生感意氣

20 Who cares only to think about merit and fame? 功名誰復論

In comparison to court poetry of his time, the language of Wei Zheng's poem is so direct that Owen says it is representative of a type of poetry that "successfully fulfilled the goals of the opposition poetics" because it expresses private feelings and serves a specific didactic or political purpose.[7] But while Wang Ji's contemporaries seemed eager to proclaim their personal desires and their political views and ambitions, Wang Ji was intent to invoke the *yonghuai* tradition to give voice to general philosophical musings, even when in certain cases his poems appear to begin with local political commentary.

We see an example of this in the poem "On an Ancient Theme: Composed in Haste and Presented to Xue Shou, the Secretarial Aide to the Prince, When He Stopped by My Village for a Visit," which Wang Ji wrote sometime in late 621 when he was still in his first retirement:[8]

Years ago, we were caught in turbulence; 伊昔遭喪亂

Intercalation interrupted the heavenly succession. 歷數閏當餘

Jackals and wolves blocked the thoroughfare; 豺狼塞衢路

4 Our homes were turned into ruins.[9] 桑梓成丘墟

You and I both fled; 余及爾皆亡

East and west, we settled in different places. 東西各異居

You became the great bird riding on the wind; 爾為培風鳥

8 I became the fish stranded in a carriage rut.[10] 我為涸轍魚

After the clouds and thunder had passed, 逮承雲雷後

To our delight heaven and earth opened anew. 欣逢天地初

By the eastern river, I while my time angling; 東川聊下釣

12 On southern acres, I try my hand at wielding the hoe. 南畝試揮鋤

Luckily taxes do not apply to me, 資稅幸不及

For summer and winter, I always have plenty of 伏臘常有儲
reserves.

Free and unrestrained, I frequently require wine; 散誕時須酒

16 Alone and idle, I lazily turn to my books. 蕭條嬾向書

I am a piece of rotten wood and cannnot be carved; 朽木不可雕

My wings unfledged, how can I soar? 短翮將焉攄

My dear old friend, from long time past, 故人有深契

20 Stopped by my thatched hut. 過我蓬蒿廬

With shoes half slipped on, I rushed out the door 曳履出門迎
to greet him;

Our hands clasped together, we climbed the front 握手登前除
steps.

Looking at each other, our faces are no longer 相看非舊顏
familiar

24 And our bodies seem those of strangers. 忽若形骸疎

Remembering events of the past, 追悼宿昔事

Earnest and sincere, we pour out our heart. 切切心相於

We recall our youthful years, 憶我少年時

28 When we roamed about the eastern canal hand 攜手遊東渠
in hand;

Apricot and plum lined the bank on either side, 梅李夾兩岸

Their branches in bloom, how luxuriant! 花枝何扶疏

Our like-minded companions numbered few, 同志亦不多

32 But there were Mr. Yao and Mr. Xu of West Village.[11] 西莊有姚徐

Fond of Tao Yuanming, we used to 嘗愛陶淵明

Pour each other wine and roast dry fish.[12] 酌醴焚枯魚

We used to imitate Gongsun Hong,[13] 嘗學公孫弘

36 Staff in hand, out herding pigs. 策杖牧群豬

Reminiscing on the past, it seems only yesterday, 追念甫如昨

Yet so quickly all becomes empty and void. 奄忽成空虛

How long does a man's life last? 人生詎能幾

40 Troubled and distressed, I often feel anxiety. 蹙迫常不舒

Luckily a monk in the Northern Mountains 賴有北山僧

Taught me about the Absolute Reality. 教我以真如

He made me abandon sight and hearing, 使我視聽遣

44 And willingly shed the burden of the world's dust. 自覺塵累袪

Why would one need traps and snares, 何事須筌蹄

When the fish and hare are now obtained? 今已得兔魚

If you, my old friend, have more leisure, 舊遊儻多暇

48 Join me and detach yourself from the world's 同此釋紛挐
entanglements.

Wang Ji opens this poem by recalling the tumultuous time in the past when "intercalation interrupted the heavenly succession" (that is, the collapse of the Sui) and power contenders ("jackals and wolves" [line 3]) destroyed homes and the lives of the people, which left him like a "fish stranded in a carriage rut" (line 8). In contrast to the disdain and distress betrayed in these opening lines, Wang Ji appears overjoyed with the new regime ("heaven and earth opened anew," he celebrates in line 10). What is unconventional about this poem is Wang Ji's conspicuous silence in expressing ambition to devote his service to the new court and establish himself by his accomplishments in this promising new era, as we saw in Wei Zheng's poem and indeed as was common in the poems of his contemporaries. Instead Wang Ji turns the final section of this poem on "an ancient theme"—after describing his joyful reunion with his old friend and recalling fondly the youthful days of innocence they shared together—into a declaration of his philosophical outlook on life (lines 37–48). Here he confesses that he was first "troubled and distressed" by the impermanence of mortal life (lines 37–40); but then he claims to have found deliverance from this worry in the Buddhist practice of purification of the mind. The term "Absolute Reality" (*zhenru* 真如; literally the "genuine thusness") in line 42 is the concept of *bhūtatathatā* in Buddhist teaching. Here the argument is that because all things in the world, including human knowledge and experience, are merely illusions of the mind based on sensual perceptions, we live in a state of mental disturbance so long as we depend on the senses and trust in our own feelings and thoughts. The goal, therefore, is to be free of this dependence— to clear the mind and reach a true realization of the eternal Absolute Reality that is nothingness. By this means one perceives, as Wang Ji asserts that he himself does, the impermanence of the mortal world and the truth of *zhenru*. Finally, in the poem's last lines, Wang Ji follows his declaration of Buddhist enlightenment with an allusion to a passage in chapter 26 of *Zhuangzi* on the unimportance of words in relation to ideas. Here Wang Ji's use of the metaphor repeats the idea that once the true reality of nothingness is realized, one finds no need for the illusions of the mind, just as traps and snares are useless after catching fish and rabbits.[14]

This coupling of the Buddhist concept of *bhūtatathatā* and the notion of the illusoriness of sensory and mental perception espoused in *Zhuangzi* was hardly unusual, of course. As Feng Youlan explains in his *History of Chinese Philosophy*:

In Buddhist thought there is the antithesis between the *bhūtatathatā* or Absolute *(zhenru)* on the one hand, and production-annihilation or the temporal on the other; between permanence and change; between nirvāna *(niepan* 涅槃*)* and the cycle of life and death. Thinkers of the Period of Disunity regarded the first contrast as equivalent to the Taoist one between non-being *(wu)* and being *(you)*, the second as equivalent to the Taoist contrast between quiescence *(jing* 靜*)* and movement *(dong* 動*)*, and the third as equivalent to the Taoist contrast between non-activity *(wuwei* 無為*)* and having-activity *(youwei* 有為*)*. Some Buddhist exponents, in fact, used all these Taoist concepts, for which reason their brand of "Buddhism" might really be described as a branch of the "Mysterious Learning" *[xuanxue]*, i.e., of Neo-Taoism.[15]

By the Six Dynasties period in China (Feng's "Period of Disunity"), in other words, intellectuals were drawing on Buddhist teachings and the texts of *Laozi* and *Zhuangzi* for discourse on similar concepts. This practice led naturally to a free intermingling of terminology from these different sources, which as we have seen continues in Wang Ji's writing. For in the poem cited here he invokes the antithetical ideas of "reality being an illusion," the "unchanging truth of impermanency," and the "emptiness of substantiality" by drawing on the vocabulary of Buddhism, *Laozi*, and *Zhuangzi*. In fact we frequently encounter in his poetry terms strongly associated with Buddhist and Laozi-Zhuangzi ideas, such as *kong* 空 (empty), *xu* 虛 (vacuous), and *wu* 無 (nonexistence, nothingness, or to lack), which connote the sense of void.

In "Expressing My Innermost Thoughts" (Yonghuai 詠懷),[16] we find another example of Wang Ji's unconventional adoption of a traditionally contemplative poetic mode, as well as an explicit statement of his philosophical perspective:

There are mulberry and elm on the north bank of the Fen River,	桑榆汾水北
And chimney smoke is rising from east of the Yellow River;	煙火濁河東
But feeling no need to search for the road to return,	未必尋歸路
4 The tumbleweed rests calmly.	居然息轉蓬
Home is wherever I go;	故鄉行處是
Sitting still in an empty chamber, it is all the same.	虛室坐間同

When the western hills fade into dusk after
the sun sets,   日落西山暮

8   Then you will realize that the world is a void.   方知天下空

The title of the poem specifies that it is of the *yonghuai* genre, which
immediately invites our association with Ruan Ji. But Ruan Ji's poems are
closely, if obscurely, linked to the politics of his time. They convey, through
dark allusions and what Donald Holzman calls "humorless satire," Ruan
Ji's anger toward men in court and his grave commitment to moral and
religious values.[17] Wang Ji's poem, like his others in the *yonghuai* style,
conveys no such gravity or outrage. The tone is serene, and his subject is
universal truth, not politics. It begins with a view of his home village as
seen from the distance. The mulberry and elm trees, forming the unmis-
takable outline of an estate or a settlement, and the chimney smoke signal-
ing an occupied residence, evoke a nostalgic feeling for home. Yet this
setting leads neither to a description of a joyous homecoming nor to a sor-
rowful separation from home, but to images of contented detachment: the
tumbleweed, which ordinarily mirrors the uncertain life of a melancholy
poet tossed about by fickle political currents,[18] here is proposed by Wang Ji
as a model for such detachment. "Feeling no need to search for the road to
return, / The tumbleweed rests calmly," he remarks with admiration,
because, as he says, "Home is wherever I go."

   In the last lines Wang Ji sums up the poem's theme: nothing is worth
concern because the world is a void only perceived as reality. He makes
the point by referring to a conversation reported in chapter 4 of *Zhuangzi*
in which Confucius cautions his favorite disciple, Yan Hui 顏回, about the
dangers of political ambition and advises him to cultivate a "fasting of the
heart." Confucius goes on:

> Look at the vacant ones: When the chamber is empty, the brightness grows.
> Blessings and fortune stay with the stilled. As for those who cannot be still, I
> call it "galloping while you sit." Suppose you can channel your eyes and ears
> inward and expel knowledge from the heart, then even ghosts and spirits will
> come to reside with you, not to mention humans. This is the transformation of
> the myriad things. This is the key joint between Shun and Yu. This is where
> Fuxi and Jiju end their journey. How much less so should it be for a lesser
> man?[19]

The word "chamber" (*shi* 室) in Confucius' speech and in Wang Ji's sixth
line refers metaphorically to one's heart (*xinshi* 心室); *xushi* 虛室 (empty

chamber) thus stands for a clear mind void of desire. But in Wang Ji's poem, the metaphor of the "empty chamber" signifies not only the abandonment of political desire but the abandonment of all desires. And the last couplet, "When the western hills fade into dusk after the sun sets, / Then you will realize that the world is a void," echoes the claim, seen in the "ancient theme" poem addressed to Xue Shou, that the poet had comprehended "the Absolute Reality." Although dependence on one's sight is not voluntarily forfeited, it is taken away with the fading daylight, so that then, and only then (*fang* 方), one is made to realize the emptiness (*kong* 空) of the world.

Even in a casual occasional poem, such as the following one that records a river outing, Wang Ji responds to his immediate natural surroundings with characteristically Buddhist and Taoist sentiments:

Drifting My Boat on the River
(Fanchuan heshang 泛船河上)[20]

	Right after rain, what shall I do to comfort myself?	初晴何以慰
	In the dusk, I paddle my light raft.	薄暮理輕舟
	The white clouds are nearly all dispersed,	白雲銷向盡
4	The Yellow River winds around and flows on.	黃河曲復流
	Going with the wind, I skirt along the northern bank;	隨風依北岸
	Following the waves, I head toward the southern isle.	逐浪向南洲
	The river flow stretches far into the distance;	波瀾浩淼淼
8	My mind drifts along and beyond.	懷抱直悠悠
	I become aware that life is like a sojourn,	自覺生如寄
	And come to realize that the world is as if floating.	方知世若浮
	Penglai Island, where is it?	蓬萊何處在
12	Sitting still, I'll let my life turn to its own autumn.	坐使百年秋

In the metaphors "sojourn" (*ji* 寄) to represent the course of life, and "floating" (*fu* 浮) to represent the way of the world (lines 9 and 10), Wang Ji conveys his view of the impermanent and illusory nature of all things (even Penglai, the sacred island of immortals), which consequently leads to his resolve to detach himself from every care.

Perhaps the most obvious example of Wang Ji's explicit philosophical treatment of the contrast between perceived reality and the void of reality can be found in the poem "Sitting in Solitude":[21]

I place myself a thousand years back into the past	託身千載下
To reflect for a while on the beginning of all things.	聊思萬物初
I try to make Nothing turn into Something,	欲令無作有
4 Only to turn around and discover reality has become vacuous.	翻覺實成虛
King Wen of Zhou had just formulated his stratagems,	周文方定策
But the emperor of Qin immediately burned all the books.	秦帝即焚書
I send word to the one who aspires to inaction—	寄語無為者
8 I know you are more than capable of understanding this.	知君晤有餘

Here Wang Ji asserts the illusory nature of the world by arranging a series of opposite but complementary pairs—stressing by this means the point that change is constant. In the first couplet, the speaker is transformed through time back to the beginning of all things (we might say that he is transformed from the time of *you* 有 back to the time of *wu* 無). But his attempt to outwit reality, "to make Nothing turn into Something" (line 3), is only to be negated by his realization that what he perceived as real (*shi* 實) is in fact still nothing (*xu* 虛; line 4). Then in lines 5 and 6, Wang Ji uses historical examples to argue his point, reminding his readers that King Wen of Zhou's effort to establish policies and stratagems for founding the dynasty was eventually negated when the Qin emperor burned all the books. Thus he shows that even if something looks permanent, the promise of permanence is ultimately empty and any human effort to maintain that illusion is inherently frivolous and vain. Inaction (*wuwei* 無為), then, is the only course if one is to avoid disappointment in reality.

In all of these poems, Wang Ji espouses a philosophy—a philosophy that runs counter, as I have noted, to the general tendency of intellectual activity in his time toward codification and formalization. But such poems, containing such arguments, are only part of the story. We turn now to consider the more complicated and interesting cases: those poems of Wang Ji's in which the philosophical precept of the impermanent, illusory nature of the world is not merely stated but, as I suggest, enacted or manifested. For an illustration of this method, we turn to the set of six poems titled "On Ancient Themes" (Guyi 古意).[22]

In all editions of Wang Ji's collected works, the "Guyi" poems appear together and in the same order.[23] Generally they are read as topical allegories expressing Wang Ji's moral and political criticism of his times. Some readers see the poems as a reflection of Wang Ji's feelings of ambivalence toward the fall of the old regime, the Sui, and his own political future under the Tang.[24] Others hold that these poems express Wang Ji's frustration and anger at his perilous situation after his brother Wang Ning offended certain powerful figures at court.[25] In either case, readers who presume Wang Ji's identity as a recluse agree that these poems express his genuine desire to withdraw from the world and from the political dangers that supposedly surrounded him. My view is different. I maintain that these poems are general allegories. They do not express Wang Ji's specific moral or political concerns or commentary on particular situations or personal dangers. They are only topical insofar as they express his philosophical opposition to the general intellectual activity of his times. In other words, they model a philosophy of life that stands in utter contrast to the contemporary impulse toward the codification or formalization of knowledge.

In this Wang Ji differs distinctly from his model for these poems, Ruan Ji. And while it is true that the style of Wang Ji's "Guyi" closely resemble that of Ruan Ji's "Yonghuai" poems, they are nonetheless free of the anger and bitter satire that Holzman observes in the earlier poet. These differences are evident in the very opening poem:

	Where is the secluded man?	幽人何所在
	Beneath the purple cliffs is his mysterious trace.	紫巖有仙躅
	I lay out my precious zither under the moonlight;	月夜橫寶琴
4	What more could I wish for?	此外將安欲
	This zither is made with the wood from Mount Yi;[26]	材抽嶧山幹
	Its markers are dotted with jade from Mount Kun.[27]	徽點崑丘玉
	Lacquer varnishes its wyvern lips;	漆抱蛟龍唇
8	Silk wraps its phoenix feet.[28]	絲纏鳳凰足
	First I play the Guangling tune,[29]	前彈廣陵罷
	Then follow it with the Mingguang song.[30]	後以明光續
	A hundred cash would buy you one note;	百金買一聲
12	A thousand cash can get you one tune.	千金傳一曲
	But the world has no Zhong Ziqi;[31]	世無鍾子期
	Who could know what lies in my heart?	誰知心所屬

Wang Ji in this poem is deliberately invoking Ruan Ji's "Yonghuai, no. 1,"[32] which we will need before us for comparison:

	Sleepless in the middle of the night,	夜中不能寐
	Sitting up, I strum my zither.	起坐彈鳴琴
	Upon my thin curtain beams the shining moon;	薄帷鑒明月
4	A pure breeze brushes my breast.	清風吹我襟
	A lone wild goose wails on the distant moors,	孤鴻號外野
	A swooping bird cries in the northern wood.	翔鳥鳴北林
	Pacing back and forth, but what is there to see?	徘徊將何見
8	Alone, sad thoughts grieve my heart.	憂思獨傷心

The speaker in each poem is solitary and awake at night, playing his zither under the moonlight. Although Ruan Ji's poem was written after the manner of the last of the anonymously written "Nineteen Ancient Poems" (Gushi shijiu shou 古詩十九首), it was his that defined for literary tradition the characteristics of what Donald Holzman calls the "midnight insomnia" theme. Holzman also suggests that this theme might better be termed "midnight anguish" because of its typical expression of the poet's distress at the moral and political corruption of his times.[33] After Ruan Ji's "Yonghuai Poems," any speaker awake at night has been at once assumed to convey such a message—and this has proved uniformly true in critics' interpretations of Wang Ji's first "Guyi" poem.

But ultimately, I would point out, this poem defies our expectations for the "midnight insomnia" theme. It opens by inquiring of the whereabouts of "the secluded man," or recluse, followed by the observation that signs of his activity by the purple cliff are visible. This opening couplet seems to invite us to envision the speaker, presumably Wang Ji, out in the wilderness searching for a like-minded companion he has barely missed. Such an image provides the evidence readers have sought to perceive an expression of deep frustration in the speaker's question, as he sits up with his zither, "What more could I wish for?" (line 4).[34]

In my view, Wang Ji's evocation of the "midnight insomnia" theme serves different purposes. Wang Ji's poem does not in fact end with the speaker either soaking his garment with sorrowful tears or striking his breast in frustration and anger. Hence, in its refusal to satisfy our expectations for these details, we are called upon to distinguish its speaker's philosophical perspective from Ruan Ji's political attitude. Despite the absence of even one explicit word conveying emotion, Wang Ji's readers have nevertheless been determined to see the expression of distress, and traditionally the closing statement that "the world has no Zhong Ziqi, / Who could know what lies in my heart?" has been taken to reveal deep regret. We may indeed perceive in this couplet a tinge of regret at the absence of one like Zhong Ziqi who can truly understand the speaker's mind, but the overall absence of emotion in this poem forces us to reconsider our interpretation of the question "Who could know what lies in my heart?" Is the speaker really voicing regret or simply posing a rhetorical question—one that declares the inscrutability of his heart?

To help us toward an answer, let us consider another poem by Wang Ji that invokes the "midnight insomnia" theme: "An Instant Record of My Thoughts on a Spring Morning" (春旦直疏).[35] Although this lesser-known poem is preserved only in the five-*juan* editions of Wang Ji's works and a missing line makes it unfortunately incomplete, it is nevertheless quite clear that here too Wang Ji betrays no feeling of "midnight anguish":

	The spring night is already long as it is;	春夜猶自長
	Through the high window shines the bright moon.	高窗來明月
	Tossing and turning, I cannot sleep,	耿耿不能寐
4	So throwing on my garment, I pace about at the front door.	振衣步前楹
	My heart, for the moment, is not disturbed,	懷抱暫無擾
	I feel that both my body and my mind are pure.	自覺形影清
	I muse on the events of the ancient past,	遐想太古事
8	And closely examine the matters of today—	俯察今世情
	Be they pure or defiling—what is the difference?	淳薄何不同
	It is all in the cycle of fate.	運數之所成
	Amid my ten thousand sighs,	嘆息萬重陳
12	Already I hear the morning rooster crow.	已聞晨雞鳴
	Turning around toward the southeastern nook,	迴首東南隅
	....	....
	Who will understand that the one who forsakes artifice	誰知忘機者
16	Preserves his quintessence in placidity?[36]	寂泊存其精

This poem follows the model of Ruan Ji even more closely than "Guyi, no. 1," introducing all the conventional elements that characteristically open a poem on the "midnight insomnia" theme in its first two couplets: the bright moon at night (lines 1–2); sleeplessness; and pacing out of doors (lines 3–4). But anticipating the readers' inclination immediately to assume the speaker's anguish, he declares in the very next lines that his sleeplessness is not in fact the consequence of disturbed thoughts. In musing over "the events of the ancient past" and "the matters of today"—"be they pure or defiling"—his only response is that it makes no difference. But just as this detached attitude is asserted, Wang Ji again invites readers to perceive distress in his "ten thousand sighs" at the coming "already" of morning. This appears to be a melancholy image indeed, but once more this reading is negated. The poem's last couplet—"Who will understand that the one who forsakes artifice / Preserves his quintessence in placidity?"—asserts again that the speaker's mind is undisturbed. Here, as well as in the first "Guyi" poem, Wang Ji is posing a challenge to his reader: despite your knowledge of the "midnight insomnia" theme, will you be the one "who will understand" that this poem is not such a poem?

To insist on seeing anguish, in other words, despite the explicit evidence to the contrary, is to misread the situation. But this only invites another question: why does Wang Ji provoke such a misreading by means of his obvious inclusion of familiar elements from the "midnight insomnia" tradition? The answer is that Wang Ji shows us how knowledge of a familiar poetic mode is ultimately misleading. It is illusory because that knowledge—recognition of familiar elements—encourages us to presume that we know what we are seeing. In accordance with Wang Ji's philosophical perspective, then, "Guyi, no. 1" invites us to catch ourselves making problematic judgments based on past experience. It also appropriately introduces Wang Ji's series of "Guyi" poems in that this experience of discovering the unreliability of previously trusted knowledge is repeated, as we shall now see, as one moves from poem to poem in the sequence.

The subject of the second poem is the legendary bamboo of Bactria.[37] According to literary lore, a minister in the court of the Yellow Lord (黃帝), Ling Lun 伶倫, made the first yellow-bell pitch pipes with bamboo he found in the valleys of Bactria and Mount Kunlun and thus established for the world the standard for music scales.[38] In Wang Ji's poem, written in the fashion of a *yongwu* 詠物 piece (poem on objects), the traditional attributes of this legendary bamboo are all cited:

	In the ravine of Bactria grew a bamboo,	竹生大夏溪
	Lushly green, imbued with rare quality.	蒼蒼富奇質
	Its verdant leaves sang in the wind; they were strong.	綠葉吟風勁
4	Its green stalks pierced the sky; they were dense.[39]	翠莖犯霄密
	Frost and sleet sealed off its limbs;	霜霰封其柯
	Phoenix and simurgh fed on its fruits.	鴛鸞食其實
	Who would have guessed that after Xuanyuan[40]	寧知軒轅後

8	There would have been a Ling Lun?	更有伶倫出
	Suddenly hatchets and axes sought it out,	刀斧俄見尋
	Its roots and stems all lost to the blades.	根株坐相失
	It was cut into twelve tubes	裁為十二管
12	To make the sound of male and female pipes.[41]	吹作雄雌律
	Being useful, it brought on itself harm;	有用雖自傷
	Inadvertently it solicited calamity.	無心復招疾
	It does not compare to the grass on the hill—	不如山上草
16	Luxuriant and abundant, it keeps its blessed life to the very end.	離離保終吉

In Stephen Owen's discussion of the courtly *yongwu* poems of the early Tang, he states that an "important technique of amplification [in poetry written in this style] was the use of historical, mythical, or intellectual associations of a given object. In the case of some common topics, a set of associations will be so strong that a poem which ignores them seems wanting. . . . These commonplace associations made up a body of literary 'lore,' which was set forth neatly in encyclopedias such as *Chuxue ji* [初學記]."[42] In the opening lines of "Guyi, no. 2," Wang Ji seems to follow this pattern just as expected: the first couplet introduces his topic, the lush and rare bamboo of Bactria, and the statement about the bamboo's "rare quality" in line 2 is amplified in the next two couplets. The bamboo endures the battering of the wind and snow (lines 3 and 5) and still stands tall and thrives (line 4), reminding us of its strength of survival. Its "rare quality" is further emphasized with an allusion to a well-known passage in *Zhuangzi*, where it is asserted that the phoenix and simurgh, emblems of nobility and honor, would eat nothing but the fruit of bamboo.[43]

With these exceptional qualities established in readers' minds, the poet turns to narrate the bamboo's fate of becoming the first, definitive set of pitch pipes. What is unconventional about this allusion is that instead of celebrating the recognition of the bamboo's value, Wang Ji focuses on the catastrophe of the bamboo's end: it was destroyed because men recognized its usefulness. The violent language describing the bamboo's fate— "the hatchets and axes" that "sought it out," its "roots and stems" that were "lost to the blades" and "cut"—emphasizes not the birth of music from a human perspective but brutal death from the bamboo's.

Yet the perspective of the poem shifts once again, for the speaker does not lament this tragedy for the bamboo. "Being useful, it brought on itself harm," he states plainly and unemotionally (line 13). "Inadvertently it solicited calamity" he matter-of-factly observes (line 14). The poem then closes by pointing to the insignificant grass that no one cares even to look at, noting its ability to live out its life free of danger. In these last four lines, readers will recognize an echo of a statement in *Zhuangzi*: "The mountain trees do themselves harm; the grease in the torch burns itself up. The cinnamon bark is edible, and so people chop down its tree; the lacquer is useful, and so people split the tree trunk. People all know the use of the useful, but none knows the use of the useless."[44] In sum, then, by means of these shifting perspectives and this final allusion, Wang Ji reminds readers again to be wary of what one takes as trustworthy knowledge. What we might take at first as a conventional celebration of Ling Lun's recognition of bamboo's value, and metaphorically a celebration of honorable service rendered to a sagacious ruler, is from another standpoint tragic loss and brutal death. Yet, from another standpoint still, in the eyes of the detached philosopher-recluse it is all just further evidence of the ultimate meaninglessness of these terms of value.

"Guyi, no. 2" thus sets up and then counters expectations raised by its evocation of a familiar story and poetic convention. But in so doing it sets up expectations for "Guyi, no. 3" that are in turn countered. This time the subject is a precious tortoise, the type used to make divination implements for fortune telling, and Wang Ji exploits the irony of this creature that stumbles into death despite its innate ability to foretell the future:

	The precious tortoise, one-foot-two long,	寶龜尺二寸
	Had always lived in deep waters.	由來宅深水
	He drifted about in the Five Lakes,	浮遊五湖內
4	Traveled between the Three Rivers.[45]	宛轉三江裏
	Why didn't he go even further?	何不深復深
	Why did he so rashly come to the Zhen and Wei Rivers?[46]	輕然至溱洧
	The courses of the Zhen and Wei are narrow;	溱洧源流狹
8	In spring and autumn, the water does not even dampen an axle.	春秋不濡軌
	An endless flow of fishermen traveled up and down;	漁人遞往還
	A net caught the tortoise, tangled and trapped.	網罟相縈�
	In just one morning, his fortune was gone,	一朝失運會
12	His innards scraped out, blood drained, and he died.	刳腸血流死
	His sumptuous shells are now offered in the temple hall,[47]	豐骨輸廟堂

His delicate flesh is displayed on the sacrificial vessels. 鮮腴籍簿篡

Discarded and forgotten, whom can he blame? 棄置誰怨尤

16 He brought upon himself this disaster, did he not? 自我招此否

His lingering spirit remains in the luminous divinations, 餘靈寄明卜

To honor us when we pray for blessings with sacrifices. 復來欽所履

Like the bamboo in the previous poem, this tortoise is extraordinary and precious, as indicated by its one-foot-two-inch length. (According to the "Guice zhuan" 龜策傳 in *Shi ji*, this would indicate the tortoise is at least a thousand years old—and thus destined for the exclusive sacrificial ceremonies and divinations performed for the Son of Heaven.)[48] The explicit, violent language describing the bamboo's death is echoed here as well, in the way the tortoise's "innards [are] scraped out" and "blood drained." Thus Wang Ji stresses once more that what is auspicious for humans is calamitous from the perspective of the poem's subject. But again we experience an unexpected shift in perspective. After the opening description of this "precious tortoise" as it drifts in its expansive and deep natural abode, the tortoise is faulted for entering the narrow and shallow waters of the Zhen and Wei, where fishermen ply up and down the currents.[49] It has acted foolishly by putting itself in danger. The observation that the tortoise lost its fortune when caught in a net is almost sardonic, given its imminent use in plastromancy.[50] "Discarded and forgotten, whom can he blame? / He brought upon himself this disaster, did he not?" the speaker asks.

Thus far, then, this is not another lesson about preferring the ostensibly valueless. "Guyi, no. 3" offers us no comparison such as that between the bamboo and the grass. Even as we read that the tortoise is "discarded and forgotten," we are led to see from what turns out to be the diviner-speaker's perspective that this is indeed a tortoise of wondrous value. The language unmistakably is intended to elicit our admiration: the description of its "sumptuous shells" and "delicate flesh," its "lingering spirit" that "remains in the luminous divinations, / To honor us when we pray for blessings with sacrifices," emphasizes only the tortoise's worth. In other words: Wang Ji has turned us full circle. In the previous poem, the legendary bamboo that we would expect to be the object of praise turns out to compare unfavorably, because of its violent death, to the lowly grass that lives out its "blessed life" to the full. In this poem, a precious tortoise similarly suffers a violent death. But counter to our expectations founded on the previous poem's attitude toward the bamboo's fate, here the tortoise is the recipient of the speaker's profound respect and gratitude. What is Wang Ji up to? The real subject of these poems is neither the particular deaths of the bamboo and tortoise nor even the particular responses these deaths elicit from poem to poem. It is instead the problematic nature of the "knowledge" we bring with us to poems about bamboo and tortoises—"knowledge" that, like our "knowledge" of the world generally, is illusory and misleading.

The fourth poem in the "Guyi" series is similar to the second and third in that it takes as its subject an admired natural object, in this case the pine tree. The pine is associated with integrity and the endurance of hardship; in poetry it often symbolizes longevity in contrast to the fleeting human life span. Consider, for example, a poem by Fu Xuan 傅玄 (217–278) that is included in the Tang compendium *Yiwen leiju* as a model for the literary treatment of the pine tree:[51]

Flying tumbleweed is blown about in the wind;	飛蓬隨飄起
Fragrant herbs are crushed in the mountain and marsh.	芳草摧山澤
In the world, there are thousand-year-old pines,	世有千年松
But how can men live to a hundred?	人生詎能百

"Guyi, no. 4" opens by invoking just this conventional association of the pine with strength and longevity. But as we shall see, from this point the perspective toward the pine shifts:

	A pine tree once grew beneath the northern cliff;	松生北巖下
	Here no one had ever set foot.	由來人徑絕
	It spread its branches outward, brushing the clouds;	布葉捎雲煙
4	It planted its roots deep, crowding a grotto.	插根擁巖穴
	It declared its spot ideal for its growth;	自言生得地
	Only clear clouds above it, it was immaculate.[52]	獨負凌雲潔
	When was it ever worried about axes?	何時畏斤斧
8	Time and again it withstood frost and snow.	幾度經霜雪
	Wind shocked its northwestern limb,	風驚西北枝
	Hail damaged its southeastern branching.	雹損東南節
	It wouldn't have known that in the lapse of time,	不知歲月久

12	Its twigs and branches would gradually snap and break off,	稍覺條枝折
	The vines and hanging moss wrapped round it would shatter it into pieces,	藤蘿上下碎
	And its trunk would split, up and down, right and left.	枝幹縱橫裂
	It is about to rot away completely	行當糜爛盡
16	And dissipate into dust altogether.	坐共灰塵滅
	Would it rather that Carpenter Shi took interest in it?	寧關匠石顧
	Is it there for the young prince to pluck?	豈為王孫折
	Thriving and waning have their own due time;	衰盛自有期
20	Sages and worthies have never concerned themselves with it.	聖賢未嘗屑
	I send a word to anxiety-ridden men,	寄言悠悠者
	Don't brood over your advancing age!	無為嗟大耋

In the first eight lines the pine is described as thriving in a place all its own, "ideal for its growth," where "no one had ever set foot." It was a picture of safety, strength, and longevity: "When was it ever worried about axes?" asks the speaker. Though "time and again it withstood frost and snow," it could only do so for so long, however, and ironically the pine's eventual demise is described in language that evokes an image of nature hacking away at it as if with an axe: it is "snapped" and "broken," "shattered into pieces," the trunk is "split up and down, right and left." Suddenly the pine becomes an image of death and waste, on the verge of rotting away to dust. The traditional symbol of the pine tree has been undermined. At this point Wang Ji seems to be inviting us to look back to the previous two poems and ask if, even from the pine's perspective, it would have been better to share the fate of the bamboo and the tortoise.

But as a transition to the poem's conclusion, two questions are posed: "Would it rather that Carpenter Shi took interest in it?" and "Is it there for the young prince to pluck?" The implied answer to these questions, despite the traditionally positive implications of the allusions employed, is clearly no. Carpenter Shi is a character from a story in *Zhuangzi* who passed by a tall and beautiful serrate oak (櫟) without paying any attention to it because he did not consider it a useful timber tree.[53] The "young prince" is an allusion to the recluse in "Summoning the Recluse" from the *Chuci* 楚辭 anthology. In asking if the pine would have preferred to be appreciated for its value, either by a carpenter who would chop it down or by a recluse who would "pluck" it, the speaker not only points out that the inevitable comes in its natural time but suggests that one should not desire otherwise. "Thriving and waning have their own due time, / Sages and worthies have never concerned themselves with it," he says. And he closes by advising "anxiety-ridden men" not to brood over their advancing age because even the "immortal" pine will be struck down one day.

In these final lines, Wang Ji invokes the eleventh and thirteenth of the "Nineteen Ancient Poems." It will be helpful to have them before us to see how "Guyi, no. 3" so completely transforms familiar images and works within this series. The relevant passages follow:

[No. 11]⁵⁴

Thriving and waning, each has its due time;　　　　　盛衰各有時
I lament that I am unable to achieve success early.　　　立身苦不早
Human bodies are not like metal or stone;　　　　　　人生非金石
How can we expect to live forever?　　　　　　　　　豈能長壽考

[No. 13]⁵⁵

Human life is so fleeting, as if passing;　　　　　　　人生忽如寄
Our life span lacks the permanence of metal and stone.　壽無金石固
Thousands of years come and go;　　　　　　　　　　萬歲更相送
Sages and worthies, none was able to live beyond his lot.　聖賢莫能度

We see from these lines that Wang Ji echoes their language while countering their melancholy sentiment. The pine tree, traditionally equivalent to metal and stone as a symbol of longevity, is not contrasted with the lamentably fleeting lives of men, as readers might expect, but serves instead, by its own decay, as evidence of the folly of such a lament.

The fifth poem in the series, on the topic of *gui* trees (*guishu* 桂樹), focuses on the companionship between the recluse and his trees instead of the theme of life and fate. In literary tradition, *gui* referred to osmanthus when associated with the moon or with autumn (its blooming season); but it could also refer to cinnamon, as it does in classical texts (such as *Liji, Shijing, Zhuangzi,* and *Chuci*). While osmanthus was prized for the intense fragance of its blossoms, cinnamon (which blooms in summer and has odorless flowers) was mostly valued for the medicinal value of its bark.

Furthermore, *gui* as cinnamon was commonly associated with reclusion. (The poem "Summoning the Recluse" in *Chuci* is the locus classicus.) As we shall see, it is obvious that the subject of Wang Ji's "Guyi, no. 5" is the osmanthus; yet equally clearly he is invoking the traditional association of *gui* with reclusion and even alluding to "Summoning the Recluse." For this reason, I leave the term *"gui"* untranslated here:

	These *gui* trees, so lush, so green!	桂樹何蒼蒼
	During autumn, their flowers are even more fragrant.	秋來花更芳
	Claiming that by nature they are able to withstand cold,[56]	自然歲寒性
4	They know nothing of dew or frost.	不知露與霜
	The secluded man esteems this quality of theirs,	幽人重其德
	And transplanted them before his hall.	徙植臨前堂
	Snaking and snarling, there are eight or nine trees;	連拳八九樹
8	Twisting and twirling, there are two or three rows.	偃蹇二三行
	Their branches are locked in a tangle,	枝枝自相糾
	Their leaves in symmetry.	葉葉還相當
	A pair of swans fly to and from them;	去來雙鴻鵠
12	Two mandarin ducks stop to rest on them.	棲息兩鴛鴦
	Their foliage is truly not very thick,	榮陰誠不厚
	But then axes would never harm them.	斤斧亦勿傷
	When I gave you my whole heart,	赤心許君時
16	How could I neglect the truth in this?	此意那可忘

In several ways, the previous three poems prepare us for this one: we move from one type of tree (the pine in no. 4) to another *(gui),* and here we are presented with an image of a recluse's apparently proper appreciation of a tree. The first four lines run through the commonplace knowledge of the *gui*'s attributes (osmanthus in this context): it thrives in the cold, and the colder it gets in autumn the more fragrant its blossoms will be. Line 5 introduces the speaker, the "secluded man" who esteems the *gui*'s qualities. But instead of cutting the trees down—the image invoked repeatedly in the previous poems in the series—the recluse transplants them to his home where they continue to grow. Lines 7–10 explicitly echo the opening couplet of *Chuci*'s "Summoning the Recluse." But whereas in that poem the imagery contributes to a representation of nature as a hostile environment for the recluse, in Wang Ji's poem it is transformed into a picture of harmony. The *gui* trees are flourishing in their new location, and the intertwining, "locked" branches and "symmetry" of the leaves suggest an intimate, mutual attraction between the recluse and the trees.

This harmony is further emphasized by the pairs of fowl attracted to the *gui*. Swans are usually associated with loftiness and purity by virtue of their white feathers and their ability to fly high and far. The mandarin ducks symbolize harmony and loyalty because they are always seen in pairs and believed never to separate. At the same time, it is with these fowl that the poem makes a transition to unconventional uses of stock materials. Swans and mandarin ducks, being waterfowl, seem strangely out of place perched in the *gui* trees, even as they symbolize harmony. The following couplet, which returns our attention to the *gui* trees themselves, works similarly. The trees are unattractive, the poet remarks—"their foliage is truly not very thick"—but this is in fact a virtue: for "axes would never harm them." We are invited to recall at this point the comparison between the bamboo and the grass; the lesson of that earlier poem, therefore, seems repeated here. But it also contradicts what readers have always known about *gui* as cinnamon—that it is more akin to bamboo than grass because, as stated in *Zhuangzi*, "The cinnamon bark is edible, and so people chop down its tree."[57]

This ambiguous use of what we would take as familiar images bring us to the poem's ambiguous conclusion. The problem lies in the second to last line, which literally means "When I promise you my red heart." The phrase "red heart" (赤心) generally signifies "loyalty," "devotion," or "wholeheartedness" when it is used with *xu* 許 (make a promise; make a pledge). The word "*jun*" 君 can mean "lord," in an address to a superior, or it can be used as an honorific "you" to express amorous endearment. Nearly all of Wang Ji's recent critics take the line to be Wang Ji's pledge of loyal service to the court and interpret the ending as a reflection of the ambivalence Wang Ji felt about this promise. He wanted to serve the new Tang court, so it is argued, but he was aware of the danger of making himself conspicuous in politics. But just as the fowl and the *gui* are not being used in a conventional manner, *jun* is not functioning as it might in a poem by Ruan Ji. That is: Wang Ji as the "secluded man" is not addressing "his lord" but "you," the *gui*, pledging it his heart just as the *gui* signals its symbolic kinship with him by wrapping itself around his hall.

The last poem in the series has likewise encouraged readers to discover a specific message of political protest or declaration of the poet's worth to the Tang court. But again I think we are seeing rather an expression of Wang Ji's philosophical objection to an intellectual trend then encouraged by the court:

	The striated phoenix is returning,	采鳳欲將歸
	Grabbing their nets, men go to the outskirts seeking it.	提羅出郊訪
	Just as nets are spread over the great marsh,	羅張大澤已
4	The phoenix is already soaring into the deep sky.	鳳入重雲颺
	Morning, it rests on the trees in Kunlun and Langfeng;	朝棲崑閬木
	Night, it drinks from the rising tide at Penglai and Fanghu.	夕飲蓬壺漲
	They ask the phoenix, "Why are you flying far away?	問鳳那遠飛
8	The worthy lord is expecting you."	賢君坐相望
	The phoenix says, "Much obliged to the kindness of His Grace.	鳳言何深德
	How is an insignificant bird like me worthy of such esteem?	微禽安足尚
	For the sake of protecting my chicks and eggs,	但使雛卵全
12	Pray do not have your men release their arrows.	無令繒繳放
	When the Yellow Lord promoted Limu,	皇臣力牧舉
	The lord's music, the 'Xiaoshao,' flowed fluently.	帝樂簫韶暢
	There will be a time when I return to roost—	自有來巢時
16	In the coming year—on your lofty tower."[58]	明年阿閣上

The word "return" (gui 歸) in the first line is quite vague: without a directional suffix, we have no way of knowing if this return means coming back or going away. This point is significant: readers will recognize the allusion to the literary lore associating a phoenix's appearance with sage governance; conversely, the retreat of the phoenix signifies the decline of morality at court. In Huainanzi 淮南子, for instance, it is said: "Formerly in the time of Fuxi 伏羲 and Shennong 神農, the phoenix stopped in their court. In the time of Yao, Shun, and Yu, the phoenix stopped at their gate. In the time of the Zhou, the phoenix stopped at the marsh [in the suburbs]. The more defiled the ruler's virtue, the further out the phoenix stops. The purer the ruler's virtue, the closer in the phoenix stops."[59]

Interestingly, we have a poem on this same theme written by Tang Taizong, the ruling emperor during the latter half of Wang Ji's life. It is the fourth poem in his "Poems on the Imperial Capital" sequence:[60]

	Singing fifes approach the pleasure pavilion,	鳴笳臨樂館
	In this season of fragrance eye and ears rejoice.	眺聽歡芳節
	Shrill flutes in tune with vermilion strings,	急管韻朱絃
4	And clear song that freezes the white snow.	清歌凝白雪
	In dazzling color the stately phoenix descends,	彩鳳肅來儀
	While black cranes form ranks in multitudes.	玄鶴紛成列
	Here we are rid of the degraded songs of Zheng and Wei	去茲鄭衛聲
8	And now can delight in the proper tunes.	雅音方可悅

As Owen observes, Taizong's poem celebrates the Tang court as "exemplary of Confucian morality,"[61] which is attested to by the phoenix that is attracted by the "proper tunes" played in court. In lines 2–3 of Wang Ji's "Guyi, no. 6," by contrast, people have gone to the "outskirts" to find the phoenix, and we sense the speaker's derision in his observation that they are "grabbing their nets" and "looking for it." In other words, they are trying to trap the phoenix—to *force* its coming to the court.

The phoenix, however, "is already soaring into the deep sky" (line 4). This would seem to invite the interpretation that Wang Ji is condemning the Tang court and asserting that the ruler's moral standing is not adequate to the phoenix's legitimizing blessing. But other details of the poem complicate such a reading. For one thing, Wang Ji does not make it clear at the start whether the phoenix was moving closer or farther away from the court when the people went looking for it. And when we do learn that it is soaring away from its pursuers, the phoenix does not answer their question ("Why are you flying far away? / The worthy lord is expecting you") by denying the ruler's worthiness. In fact, it even promises that "there will be a time when I return to roost— / In the coming year—on your lofty tower." At this point it seems to decline the "honor" of attending the lord because it objects to the method of invitation: the men are trying too hard to bring the phoenix to court, hunting it rather than waiting for it to appear in due time, and thus endangering its life and the life of its progeny.

Although I read these lines allegorically, I do not think Wang Ji is protesting against the moral corruption of the court or against its not honoring *him* (represented by the phoenix) with an official title.[62] Rather, I take the people's effort to capture the phoenix to represent the court's confidence that it deserves the phoenix's coming. And what is the basis of such confidence? Precisely the efforts of Wang Ji's contemporaries to codify ritual practice and systems of knowledge or, in such poems as Tang Taizong's, to banish the "degraded" and establish and rejoice in the "proper."

As this process of codification and formalization advanced, its proponents might well assume real progress was being made toward what is "proper" and toward the legitimization of the ruling house—and might even have been feeling impatient for signs of heavenly blessing. But as the phoenix in Wang Ji's poem reminds his pursuers, it will only return at such a time as "When the Yellow Lord promoted Limu," and "The lord's music, the 'Xiaoshao,' flowed fluently." Limu was supposed to have served the Yellow Lord, along with several other ministers the Yellow Lord promoted, during a period when the world was free of crime and enjoyed ever-increasing prosperity.[63] The "Xiaoshao" is said to be a special type of music played only in the court of a moral lord. It signifies harmony and peace in the world—and according to *Shangshu* 尚書, when Shun played nine stanzas of it male and female phoenixes appeared at the court to accompany the music.[64] The implication may seem clear: the phoenix is telling the "worthy lord" that when things are done properly—when "proper tunes" are played at court, as Tang Taizong in his poem boasts is already the case—then the phoenix will appear. But things are not so simple. As the concerted effort to establish what is proper testifies, and as the phoenix's flight symbolizes, knowing what is degraded and what is proper, and thus knowing the appropriate time for the phoenix to appear, is an obscure process. It is too easy to fool oneself into thinking one has got it right— that now the "proper tunes" are being played. As "Guyi, no. 6" playfully argues, one cannot hurry the process: one cannot know for sure that one is playing the genuine "Xiaoshao" tune until the phoenix has actually landed. And since the "Xiaoshao" is legendary, as is the phoenix, we are obliged to concede the slippery nature of this knowledge that is being "established for ten thousand years."

3

The Recluse as Farmer-Scholar

❀

THE PORTION OF Wang Ji's poetry that is most familiar to readers of Chinese literature is that which represents the life of the farmer-scholar. Indeed it is almost solely by appealing to these poems that scholars have written Wang Ji's biography as a recluse. In this chapter's examination of his "country poems," my aim is to show how Wang Ji drew upon nearly the whole range of recluse images from literary tradition to produce an eclectic poetic persona, an unstable literary image, which shifts not only from poem to poem but even within poems. Critics who have remarked on this instability have reacted in various negative ways: some regret that Wang Ji's imitation of his Wei-Jin idols (Ruan Ji and Tao Qian, primarily) falls short;[1] others accuse Wang Ji of creating a self-image as a calculated strategy to win fame or advancement;[2] still others question the sincerity of Wang Ji's identity as a recluse, suggesting that his poetry should be read instead as an expression of his frustrations in political life and his criticisms of the court.[3] We would do better, however, to see in Wang Ji's eclectic portrayals of the life of a farmer-scholar a personification of that philosophy which accepts instability as the one constant. Wang Ji's poetic persona, in other words, should be recognized as a poetic vehicle for staging a range of responses to the ever-changing course of life—a persona that draws upon the materials of traditional recluse literature because the "carefree recluse" most obviously embodies the principle of living in harmony with a world that is always in flux. As we shall see, however, this principle itself precludes consistency—even within such a persona.

Those of Wang Ji's poems that may seem to express criticism of contemporary politics do not, I would stress, betray any personal disappointment, bitterness, frustration, or distrust of either the sovereign or government of Wang Ji's time.[4] Instead they voice the most generalized rejection of striving for political achievement and fame. For example, the poem translated here is representative of Wang Ji's writing on political themes. It is addressed to Fang Xuanling 房玄齡 (578–648), one of the three most eminent ministers serving Taizong.[5] Presumably the poem was composed around 637, when Fang Xuanling was at the height of his official career and had just become Lord of Liang (梁國公), an appointment that gave him hereditary authority over Song prefecture (in modern Henan).[6] The apparent intent of the poem is to persuade Fang Xuanling to withdraw from politics before he is struck down by the dangers around him. Yet the poem's references to the downfall of past ministers are not meant to warn Fang away from service to a bad ruler; they are merely part of a general elucidation of the notion in *Laozi* that success generates calamity:

To the Lord of Liang
(Zeng Lianggong 贈梁公)[7]

	I desire to seek worldly pleasure,	我欲圖世樂
	But this pleasure is hard to make last.	斯樂難可常
	Prominent positions beckon sneers and grudges;	位大招譏嫌
4	Extreme prosperity begets disaster and calamity.	祿極生禍殃
	No one was as sagacious as the Duke of Zhou;	聖莫若周公
	How could anyone be more loyal than Huo Guang?[8]	忠豈踰霍光
	Yet King Cheng still caused censure [against the duke];[9]	成王已興誚
8	Emperor Xuan always felt uneasy [around Huo Guang].	宣帝恆負芒
	How wise was Fan Li!	范蠡何智哉
	He took leave on a raft, carrying little baggage.[10]	單舟戒輕裝
	Did Shu Guang not cherish honor and success?	疏廣豈不懷
12	Yet with staff in hand he returned home.[11]	策杖還故鄉
	Although the vermilion gate delights us enough,	朱門雖足悅
	A reddened clan will also bring us sorrow.[12]	赤族亦可傷
	Frost underfoot leads to the forming of solid ice;[13]	履霜成堅冰
16	Being content with your lot is better than being struck by ill fortune.[14]	知足勝不祥
	I am only a lowly nobody,	我本窮家子
	But I'll say that this is a wise idea:	自言此見長
	Upon achieving success, retreat—	功成皆能退
20	Who in the past was ever brought to demise for this?	在昔誰滅亡

If we read this poem as political allegory—warning Fang Xuanling to be wary of the forces working to bring about his downfall—we should, I believe, interpret the allegory as general rather than topical: Wang Ji is not condemning the Tang court for fostering such forces; he is just repeating what he maintains to be always and everywhere true, invoking the authority of the ninth chapter of *Laozi*:[15]

By holding the vessel upright, one may fill it to the brim,	持而盈之
But it won't be as stable as when you have stopped in time.	不如其已
By pounding out an iron bar, one may give it a piercing tip and a sharp edge,	揣而梲之
But the sharpness will not last long.	不可長保
One may possess enough jade and gold to fill up a hall,	金玉滿堂
But no one is able to keep it all.	莫之能守
One may feel very proud of wealth and rank,	富貴而驕
But this brings on disaster.	自遺其咎
Upon achieving success, retreat—	功遂身退
That is Heaven's Way!	天之道

This passage and Wang Ji's poem share a common underlying metaphor— the cyclical nature of all things: as any given point ascends to the highest extreme, its downward movement necessarily follows. In *Laozi* this cycle is represented in the image of the overfilled vase that cannot long stay upright and in the overly refined blade that cannot long stay sharp; in Wang Ji, examples from history are cited to elucidate the concept. Although Wang Ji's poem sounds warnings of latent danger, he seems to insist this danger lies within one's success itself rather than in one's environment. "Prominent positions" and "extreme prosperity"—these correspond to *Laozi*'s vase that is too full and the blade that is too sharp: they themselves "beget disaster and calamity." Hence the poem's allusions are functioning generally, not allegorically. The misfortunes of the Duke of Zhou and Huo Guang are not invoked to censure the Tang but to serve as contrasts to the cases of Fan Li and Shu Guang, who recognized that their rise to prominence would inevitably lead to a corresponding fall and therefore retired beforehand—supporting Wang Ji's dictum to be "content with your lot" (*zhizu* 知足).

Even so, retreating from the path of success does not bring independence from the ever-changing course of the world. Wang Ji's poems comprise responses to the inherent instability of life in general. And the cause of this instability is not attributed to political turmoil per se but to the cyclical nature of the Way. This, in Wang Ji's view, is what produces, inevitably, political turmoil and ill fortune. The human tendency to react emotionally to life's ups and downs, to rationalize our failures by pinning blame, to hope to defy the changing course of fortune—these represent our misunderstanding of the Way and our vain struggles against the one constant in the world: inconstancy. This is the theme of Wang Ji's "At Night in the Mountains" (Shan ye 山夜):[16]

	When Zhongni first returned to Lu,	仲尼初返魯
	The historian in the archive was about to leave Zhou.[17]	藏史欲辭周
	Untangling himself from the affairs in the world,	脫落四方事
4	He wandered about and roamed 10,000 *li*.	棲遑萬里遊
	With only his shadow trailing along, there was no need for self-censure.	影來徒自責
	His mind was void—what more would he desire?	心盡更何求
	Rites and music sustained the three dynasties,[18]	禮樂存三代
8	But mists and clouds dominate this hillock.	煙霞主一丘
	I sing a long song—the bright moon shines above;	長歌明月在
	I sit in solitude—white clouds drift about.	獨坐白雲浮
	We can toil with the ups and downs in the ways of the world,	物情勞倚伏
12	But the ways of life run their own course.	生涯任去留
	Our hundred-year mortal life is just so;	百年一如此
	The affairs of the world drift back and forth.	世事方悠悠

The poem opens with an allusion to an anecdote that has Confucius seeking instruction on the rites from Laozi (the "historian in the archive"), who advises Confucius: "Get rid of your arrogant attitude and your numerous desires! Let go your ingratiating bearings and your overly ambitious intents."[19] The first couplet thus makes subtle comparisons between the two ideologies these sages represent. The choice the speaker makes between them is clear from his admiring comment in line 6 on Laozi's departure from office and from the mundane world: "His mind was void—what more would he desire?"

This comparison between Laozi and Confucius continues in the contrast between people's attempts to take control of the direction life takes them, on the one hand, and accepting the natural course of the world on the other. We are reminded, in line 7, that the ancient kings established the proper practice of rites and music, observed in Confucian tradition as essential for setting standards of moral conduct and keeping good order among people toward ensuring stability in the state.[20] But at the same time, as the line also makes clear, these accomplishments did not secure permanence. Rites and music only "sustained three dynasties." Compared to this brief span, the way of the world knows only the restraints of "mists and clouds," the "bright moon" and the "white clouds" (lines 8–10), which are all, in turn, conventional metaphors for reclusion, connoting specifically the recluse's carefree and unrestrained lifestyle. In the end, an explicit thesis is stated: people may strive to control the world, to "toil with the ups and downs," but the "ways of life" will just "run their own course" (lines 11–12) in directions that are unpredictable because they are ever-changing, "drift[ing] back and forth" (line 14).

In another poem invoking this image of a drifting world, "To Mr. Cheng, the Scholar in Retirement" (Zeng Chen chushi 贈程處士),[21] Wang Ji similarly ridicules Confucian assumptions of the link between human conduct and the course of the world's affairs:

	Human life is a perpetual jumble of entanglements;	百年長擾擾
	The myriad things in the world drift back and forth.	萬事悉悠悠
	The sun sets whenever it pleases;	日光隨意落
4	The river flows wherever it wishes.	水勢任情流
	The *Rites* and the *Music* imprisoned Ji Dan;	禮樂囚姬旦
	The *Songs* and the *Documents* bound Kong Qiu.[22]	詩書縛孔丘
	It is much better to rest on a high pillow,	不如高枕臥
8	And from time to time dissolve your anxiety in drunkenness.	時取醉消愁

The poem, as we see, contrasts the images of drifting freely with images of constraint. Human life is "a perpetual jumble of entanglements"; the sages are confined by their own doctrine as represented by the four canonical texts. Although the tone of this reference to the classics, which invokes Wei-Jin literati's expressions of scorn for Confucianism, is obviously disparaging, we should not simply take this couplet as evidence that Wang Ji's agenda in the poem is to attack Confucianism. The poem's argument is more general, I think, and takes the position that any submission to any form of social convention is a means to self-confinement. The Duke of Zhou and Confucius are singled out because their doctrines underlie the social conventions in which society was placing its faith; the Duke of Zhou and Confucius are thus portrayed as prisoners of their ideology, victims of their own folly, because that faith is misplaced. And it continues to be misplaced so long as people hope to define, in political and philosophical systems, bases for constancy in this world. The proper alternative, the poem concludes, is to disentangle oneself from the human world. And a proper method is to "rest on a high pillow" and "dissolve" one's "anxiety in drunkenness."[23]

In accordance with this advice, Wang Ji represents himself in many of his poems as a recluse who has detached himself from worldly affairs, politely but firmly turning down offers of fame and wealth in preference of the simple life. An example is in "Declining a Summons, Pleading Illness" (Bei zheng xie bing 被徵謝病):[24]

	In the Han court, they solicited recluses;	漢朝徵隱士
	In the Tang era, they search for disengaged men.	唐年訪逸人
	I reply with "Tune of the Northern Mountains"	還言北山曲
4	While sitting by the eastern bank of the Yellow River.	更坐東河濱
	My home is in the land of Three Jin,[25]	枌榆三晉地
	Amid chimney smoke with neighbors all around.	煙火四家鄰
	I lay a white swine before the village temple,	白豕祠鄉社
8	And sacrifice a black sheep to the household gods.	青羊祭宅神
	To expand my garden, I cut into a corner of my yard;	拓畦侵院角
	To fetch water, I climb up the bank of the canal.	甃水上渠滑
	Liu Gonggan claimed illness;[26]	臥病劉公幹
12	Zheng Zizhen held onto his plow.[27]	躬耕鄭子真
	I cut a gnarled mulberry branch to make a staff,	橫裁桑節杖
	And peel bamboo skin to weave a kerchief.	豎剪竹皮巾
	Cranes call in alarm from the Zither Pavilion at night;[28]	鶴警琴亭夜
16	Orioles sing above my wine jars in spring.	鶯啼酒甕春
	Yan Hui delighted only in the Way;	顏回惟樂道
	Would Yuan Xian lament his poverty?[29]	原憲豈傷貧
	Piling grass to make cushions, I invite in new friends;	藉草邀新友

20	Spreading vitex branches for mats, I greet my old friends.	班荊接故人
	At the market gate, I come upon an herb seller;	市門逢賣藥
	In the mountain garden, I meet a firewood carrier.	山園值肩薪
	Living peacefully in their company,	相將共無事
24	Why should I step into the bustling dust of the world?	何處犯囂塵

In the first lines Wang Ji pairs the court of his own time, the Tang, with that of the Han, the last unified dynasty in history, which the Tang had taken for its model. Thus he acknowledges the Tang's virtuous motives in attempting to recognize and invite into service those "hidden talents" living in exile, many of whom were indeed waiting for this moment to come. Readers are meant to understand, therefore, that the speaker declines an invitation to office, not because of any moral objection to the court, but because he is contented with his simple, peaceful life. This life does not offer much material comfort: the recluse must provide for himself with his own labor (lines 7–8), and he only has grass and branches to serve for seats when friends visit (lines 19–20). But famous recluses of the past are cited as evidence that such a life is enjoyable (lines 11–12 and 17–18), far from the "bustling dust of the world" (line 24). The same sentiment is expressed in Wang Ji's "On Reclusion" (Yongyin 詠隱):[30]

	Only reclusion is pleasurable;	獨有幽棲趣
	It keeps the profane world's entanglements remote.	能令俗網賒
	A tiller, my calling is farming;	耕夫田作業
4	A nester, my dwelling is in a tree.	巢叟樹為家
	At dusk, I gently brush remnants of millet in the valley;	晚谷柔殘黍
	In spring, I sweep up fallen blossoms in the garden.	春園掃落花
	Free of worries, I roam about at my own pleasure;	恝然乘興往
8	Why do I need to drive the cloud chariot?	何必御雲車

Both the "entanglements" of the profane world, as well as the "dust of the world" in the previous poem, are familiar expressions to readers of Tao Qian's poetry. But to begin to distinguish between Wang Ji and his precursors in the tradition of recluse poetry, we may examine the first poem in Tao Qian's "Returning to Dwell in the Country" sequence (Gui tianyuan ju 歸田園居):[31]

In youth I was not suited to sing the common tune;　　少無適俗韻
I was born to love the mountains and hills.　　性本愛丘山
By mistake I fell into the dusty net;　　誤落塵網中
Once trapped, thirteen years went by.[32]　　一去十三年
The detained bird longs for its native woods;　　羈鳥戀舊林
The fish kept in the pond misses its old depths.　　池魚思故淵
....　　...........

Having been confined to a cage for so long,　　久在樊籠里
I now can return to nature once again.[33]　　復得返自然

It is characteristic of Tao Qian to represent his official career as bondage in a "dusty net" or a "trap," and his poems often refer to that part of his life in a regretful or apologetic tone. Here his official career is termed a "mistake," or, as he puts it by way of another of his favorite metaphors, a detour foolishly taken from what should have been a natural migration, while his retirement is represented as a bird's return to the wilds and to freedom. Wang Ji's two poems, in contrast, represent a recluse who has rejected office without being the least tempted. But this is not the most important distinction. After all, Wang Ji's recluse persona does not always appear to be so completely disinterested in entering government service. In some cases, he seems even to be waiting in seclusion for an opportunity to make a name for himself— as in the poem discussed next, "Summoning the Recluse." The topic of summoning a recluse out of retirement had by Wang Ji's time already a long tradition stretching back to the *Chuci* anthology, which contains the original "Summoning the Recluse" poem traditionally attributed to Liu An 劉安 (179–122 B.C.), the Prince of Huainan, of the Later Han. Many variations were made on the model, however. By the Six Dynasties period, poems on the summoning theme argued for leaving the official world for reclusion rather than the other way around. Wang Ji's poem is a response to this later form of "summoning." In particular, his poem seems to have been inspired by one of Zuo Si's 左思 (ca. 250–ca. 305) "Summoning the Recluse" (Zhao yin shi 招隱詩), which starts off with the image of a court official trudging through mountains and woods searching for a recluse, presumably with an intent to summon him out of hiding. The official-speaker recounts:

Leaning on a staff, I beckon the recluse;　　杖策招隱士
His overgrown path cuts off past from present.　　荒塗橫古今
The caves on cliffs contain no structures;　　巖穴無結構
But among the hills flows the sound of a zither.　　丘中有鳴琴

If Zuo Si's speaker begins his journey with a sense of uneasiness about the uninhabited environment, which the opening couplet seems to suggest, it is soon soothed away by the peacefulness of nature. Here he finds:

White snow pauses on the shady ridge;[34]	白雪停陰岡
Red blossoms gleam in the sunny woods.	丹葩曜陽林
Stony brooks burnish agates and jade;	石泉漱瓊瑤
Fine-scaled fish also float up and dive down.	纖鱗亦浮沉

As his senses awaken to the natural beauty, the speaker is led to the discovery of truth embodied in the hills and streams all around him. He comes to a realization:

I do not need strings and reeds,	非必絲與竹
For mountains and streams have their own clear sound.	山水有清音
Why do I need to whistle or sing,	何事待嘯歌
When the crooning of the dense woods is already so moving?	灌木自悲吟
Autumn chrysanthemums can serve as my dried provisions,	秋菊兼餱糧
And the thoroughwort can dress up my double lapel.	幽蘭間重襟
My feet are weary from pacing about;	躊躇足力煩
I wish to throw away my hatpins.[35]	聊欲投吾簪

We shall see that Wang Ji's poem concludes with a sudden twist on this desire (*yu* 欲) to abandon official life:

**On an Ancient Theme, "Leaning on a Staff,
I Go in Search of a Recluse," Composed
at Lu Xinping's Residence
(Lu Xinping zhai fu guti de "Ce zhang [xun]
yinshi"** 盧新平宅賦古題得策杖〔尋〕隱士)[36]

	Leaning on a staff, I go in search of a recluse;	策杖尋隱士
	Walking on, my path gradually extends deeper.	行行路漸賒
	A stone bridge spans the sheer gorge;	石梁橫澗斷
4	An earthen chamber sits opposite the sloping hill.[37]	土室映山斜
	Although Xiaoran had a lodge,	孝然縱有舍
	Weinian had no home.[38]	威輦遂無家
	Setting out wine, I make a fire with dried leaves;	置酒燒枯葉

8   Opening a book, I sit amid the falling blossoms.   披書坐落花
       By the Zi River, I cast with a new fishing pole.[39]   新垂滋水釣
       At Maoling, I darn an old net.[40]   舊結茂陵罝
       Year after year living like this,   歲歲長如此
12   I then know to make light of the world's glory.   方知輕世華

Wang Ji's opening couplet closely resembles Zuo Si's , which has the effect of acknowledging a model and establishing the topic, and the body of the poem stays focused on the theme of searching for the recluse. Yet attention to the details signals Wang Ji's concurrent departure from the model. Zuo Si confronts an "overgrown path" that "cuts off past from present," and Wang Ji's speaker similarly comes to a "sheer gorge" that stands between the hidden world and the outside world. But whereas Zuo Si's path seems impassable, in Wang Ji's poem a bridge spans the gap. Once past this line, Wang Ji's speaker, in contrast to Zuo Si's close observation of natural surroundings, makes few references to the landscape. Instead the recluse's habit of life is described. The speaker situates himself comfortably in this hidden world as if it is already his home. By the fourth line, in fact, any impression that he is an outsider dissolves completely. Suddenly the speaker has long been a man of this hidden realm—one who claims, by the end, to "make light of the world's glory."

It is in the implications of Wang Ji's allusions that the poem contradicts such carefree detachment. The earthen chamber mentioned in line 4 is generally associated with Yuan Hong, a Han official who supposedly sealed himself inside a doorless chamber as a form of withdrawal during the Han court's moral decline. Jiao Xian, alluded to in line 5, reputedly became a recluse when the Wei overthrew the Han; Dong Jing, referred to in the next line, feigned madness when the Sima clan forced the Wei from power. By associating himself with these names, the speaker invites readers to interpret his character as a kind of Confucian moral hero who withdraws from a hostile and perilous environment to preserve his integrity and bide his time until the return of a virtuous ruler.[41] Working in the same way is the reference to fishing by the Zi River (line 9), which alludes to Jiang Taigong's meeting with King Wen of Zhou, who accepted Jiang as his councillor. The reference in the next line to darning a net at Maoling is obscure, but the parallelism of the couplet suggests that it too invokes the image of a recluse waiting in retirement for his discovery by a virtuous king.[42] Thus, by means of these allusions, the poem seems to steer away from Zuo Si's renunciation of the world of honor and fame. Nevertheless, in the last line we have the declaration that the speaker has learned to "make light of the world's glory."

We see, then, that this business of going "in search of a recluse," as Wang Ji claims he is doing in the opening line, is an exploration of the range of the recluse's responses to the world—from biding one's time in retirement during periods of moral decline to utter detachment from worldly affairs. This range of apparently incompatible responses, as we have seen, prompts most readers to view Wang Ji as an insincere recluse or even a sloppy poet. Stephen Owen, one of the more sympathetic readers, argues that "Wang Ji is not an 'imitator' even in the sense of some eighth- and ninth-century poets who tried to rewrite some of Tao Qian's poems. Rather, the model of Tao Qian was a means for renewal; it was an open model."[43] That is: Wang Ji aimed not at imitating wholesale specific personal, ethical, or poetic models but at "capturing the mood or manner of a historical period and making it live in the present."[44] Because the poetry of that historical period reveals, unsurprisingly, a range of moods and manners, Wang Ji in drawing upon it likewise exhibits this range. The result, I am arguing, is a poetic persona whose instability from poem to poem—and even within poems such as "Summoning the Recluse"—personifies the philosophy that denies the possibility of constancy in the human world.

We may witness another dimension of this character in a poem by Wang Ji that represents him in isolation or alienation—typical moods of the recluse in Chinese literary tradition:

Gazing on the Wilds
(Ye wang 野望)[45]

	Gazing from the eastern marsh at dusk,	薄暮東皋望
	Wandering, drifting, where do I rest?	徙倚將何依
	The trees are all imbued in autumn colors;	樹樹皆秋色
4	The hills are all immersed in receding sunglow.	山山唯落暉
	A herdsman drives his calves heading back;	牧人驅犢返
	A hunter's horse carries fowl returning home.	獵馬帶禽歸
	Looking at them, none do I know;	相顧無相識
8	I start a long song, remembering "Plucking the Bracken."	長歌懷採薇

The poem presents a world of tranquility and harmony: the setting sun over the hills and the colors of the leaves tell us that the day and year are approaching their end, and in accordance with these images the herdsman and the hunter are returning home. Everything in both the natural world and human world is settling into correspondence, peacefully and perfectly. We detect something amiss only in the person of the speaker, who is "wandering, drifting," and asking himself, "where do I rest?" This wanderer looks at the scene with a stranger's eyes—"none do I know," he claims—and his singing disrupts its silence.

The speaker's reminiscence of "Plucking the Bracken" is possibly, and ambiguously, a double allusion. It recalls first the story of Bo Yi 伯夷 and Shu Qi 叔齊, who were models of ethical martyrdom in Confucian moral lore. They refused to eat the grain grown on the land of Zhou out of protest against what they considered the immoral conduct of King Wu.[46] Hiding in the mountains, they lived on bracken and eventually starved to death. It would seem, then, that by this reference Wang Ji is protesting the moral state of his times.[47] But in fact he is countering this interpretation by representing a world in which nature and humans are in harmony. The times are not out of joint. Second, "plucking bracken" brings to mind a poem from the *Book of Songs* by that title.[48] Its subject is the homesickness of war-weary soldiers who have been drafted into service on the frontier. The phrase "plucking bracken" that opens each stanza of the song functions as the stimulus (a device termed the *xing* 興) to introduce the main theme, the soldiers' yearning for home. By invoking this song, therefore, the speaker seems to be implying feelings of displacement, suggesting that he is yearning to return home or to a better time.[49] It is crucial to note, though, that this poem departs from the traditional treatment of the displaced scholar in its lack of any explicit expression of lament or moral protest. Only in the last line's allusion do we find any indication of the speaker's emotions—and it is the most longing, or woeful, that we ever find in Wang Ji. As often as we come upon expressions of bitterness, anger, and despair in Wang Ji's Wei-Jin models, and as often as Wang Ji's readers have claimed to find these throughout his corpus, they comprise the one set of emotions Wang Ji does not include in his range of recluse's responses to the world. Yet this is only logical. Bitterness, anger, and despair are reactions to a world that is not what it should be. But if one embraces the view that the world is ever in flux, one can hardly feel bitterness, anger, or despair at whatever state the world is in at present.

This does not mean, of course, that the recluse never feels lonely. But more often Wang Ji's poetry bespeaks contentment in the recluse's alienation and aloofness. "Tuning My Zither at Night on the Mountain" (Shanye tiao qin 山夜調琴)[50] is representative:

Having tightened the pegs under the moonlight,	促軫乘明月
I pluck the strings before the white clouds.	抽弦對白雲
Never has the "Melody of Mountains and Waters"[51]	從來山水韻
Been for mundane men to hear.	不使俗人聽

It was a long-standing literary convention for scholars to invoke the zither and the playing of music to signify a worthy man's high moral quality and lofty mind. When a scholar finds himself at odds with the world, he typically expresses his thoughts and mood through music. The depiction of the morally concerned scholar playing a zither in solitude is usually accompanied with an expression of frustrated desire for some sympathetic listener who is capable of grasping his profound mind.[52] Wang Ji's poem contains several of the conventional tropes: physical and spiritual isolation in the middle of the night somewhere on a mountain, with only the moon and clouds for company. But other expected elements are missing. The poem expresses no feelings of loneliness or regret. In fact, the last two lines seem to indicate that the speaker's isolation is voluntary. The tune he chooses to play is never "for mundane men to hear"—which is to say that he knows very well that he is different from the rest of the world and that it is not even his concern that his lofty tune, or lofty mind, will be appreciated.

In other places, the speaker does not so consciously distance himself from the common world but embraces solitude purely for personal enjoyment, as in "Summer Days in My Mountain Home, no. 5" (Shanjia xiari 山家夏日之五):[53]

	Catching the cool breeze, I am less inclined to return;	追涼剩不歸
	Resting in ease, I am sheltered behind the pine gate.	高臥隱松闌
	Wild bamboos are planted by my front steps;	野竹欄階種
4	Flowers from the cliffs fly into my windows.	巖華入戶飛
	The brook is hidden, scarcely trod by men;	磵幽人路斷
	The mountain is deserted, hardly a bird chirps.	山曠鳥啼稀
	Not that I particularly detest Zhou's grain,	不特嫌周粟
8	But from time to time I have to pluck bracken.	時時須採薇

This poem romanticizes the recluse's solitude and inaction. Again we see in the last couplet's reference to plucking bracken, and its allusion to the story of Bo Yi and Shu Qi, what seems a refutation of the import of their symbolism. That is: the speaker denies the ethical interpretation of his reclusion by insisting that he can be found "from time to time" plucking bracken—not for any moral principle but to supplement an insufficient food supply. His seclusion has nothing to do with making an ethical protest against the court. It is purely a matter of indulging in pleasures—namely, escaping the summer heat (line 1) and the disturbance of social obligations (lines 5–6).

A similar attitude is evident in this next song of a farmer-scholar, "In the Garden on a Spring Night" (Chunwan yuanlin 春晚園林):[54]

	Don't say that I object to reclusion within the court,	不道嫌朝隱
	Or that I obdurately refuse to submerge on dry land.	無情受陸沉
	Just that I chance upon the pleasure of today,	忽逢今旦樂
4	So I return to pursue the love of my heart since youth.	還逐少年心
	I rolled up my books and stored them away in bamboo baskets,	捲書藏篋笥
	Moved my couch into the wooded garden.	移榻就園林
	My old wife is good in urging me to drink;	老妻能勸酒
8	My young son plays the zither to entertain.	少子解彈琴
	Fallen flowers lay wherever they land;	落花隨處下
	Spring birds naturally have to sing.	春鳥自須吟
	Dormant, in a drunken stupor,	兀然成一醉
12	Who knows what is deep in my heart?	誰知懷抱深

The phrase in the first line, "reclusion within the court" (chaoyin 朝隱), had been used to object to the conventional recluse practice of completely withdrawing from the world to preserve one's purity. During the first half of the Six Dynasties period, advocates of chaoyin argued that it is much more difficult and worthy to continue to live amid the "dusty world of men" while still maintaining one's integrity and furthering principles of virtue and that the most lofty-minded of recluses should do so.[55] Similarly, the phrase "submerge on dry land" (luchen 陸沉) in the second line alludes to a conversation between Confucius and Zilu 子路 reported in Zhuangzi, where the master defines for his disciple worthy "servants of a sage" as "submergers on dry land," apparently referring to their ability to maintain their integrity while living among common men.[56] Thus by saying that he does not object to "reclusion within the court" or refuse to "submerge on dry land," the speaker insists that his reclusion is independent of the ethical state of his times. It has only to do with the delight of his heart. And since this heart is completely void of anxiety and desire—in fact, the speaker is "dormant, in a drunken stupor"—the question "Who knows what is deep in my heart?" does not carry its conventional implication of a distressed call for understanding a displaced and lonely man of virtue who is in exile from a world in decline. The sense of the line, rather, is that once one is happily "dormant" and in a "drunken stupor," whatever moral concerns might lie deep in one's heart are unknowable and untroubling.

This depiction of a life of simplicity, free of all desire and anxiety, goes beyond the rejection of Confucian values and a court career. Often, as the following poem illustrates, it extends as well to a rejection of the pursuit of obtaining eternal joy in immortality, an idea that attracted many recluses during the Six Dynasties period:

Portrait of a Farmer, no. 1
(Tian jia 田家之一)[57]

	Ruan Ji was nonchalant about his career;	阮藉生涯嬾
	Xi Kang was wayward in his bearing.	嵇康意氣疎
	When they met, they drank their fill;	相逢一飽醉
4	When sitting alone, they jotted a few lines.	獨坐數行書
	In my small pond, I simply keep a few cranes;	小池聊養鶴
	On my neglected farm, I just raise some pigs.	閑田且牧豬
	Grass sprawls over Yuanliang's walkway,[58]	草生元亮逕
8	Flowers overshadow Ziyun's hut.[59]	花暗子雲居
	Leaning on a staff, I watch my wife weaving;[60]	倚杖看婦織
	Climbing a knoll, I teach my son tilling.	登壟課兒鋤
	I turn my head to look for transcendents,	迴頭尋仙事
12	But it is only an empty void.	併是一空虛

Here is an eccentric character drawn to Ruan Ji's "nonchalant" attitude and Xi Kang's "wayward" bearing—reflected not only in his direct allusion to his two models but also in the image of his neglected farmstead. Pigs graze in his fields, his walkway is overgrown, his house is obscured by untrimmed flowers. The speaker occupies his time with trivial things such as watching his wife weaving or teaching his son farming tasks that he himself is not concerned to practice. The picturesque tranquility of the scene deludes the speaker into thinking just for a moment that he might be in the land of transcendents, so he turns his head to look for them, only to be reminded of his reality by the "empty void" behind him. This last couplet has a dual function: on the one hand, it likens the speaker's carefree life in solitude to the supposedly carefree life of the yonder world; on the other hand, in the speaker's discovery of his momentary delusion there is no betrayal of disappointment, which confirms that his simple life on his "neglected farm" suits the speaker just fine.

As we shall see later in Chapter 5, Wang Ji recognizes the pursuit of transcendence as a seductive motive for reclusion even as he shows its futility. But elsewhere, as in the poem addressed "To Pupils of the Transcendental Art" (Zeng xuexian zhe 贈學仙者),[61] he explicitly criticizes the hope that so many Six Dynasties recluse-writers had expressed in their writings and at times acted upon in their lives:

	The Tiered City is too distant for collecting magic herbs;[62]	採藥層城遠
	The sea journey is too far for seeking the transcendent master.[63]	尋師海路賒
	The jade vase blocks off the sun and moon;[64]	玉壺橫日月
4	Golden portals are obstructed behind the aurora clouds.[65]	金闕斷煙霞
	Where are the music players?[66]	伶人何處在
	The Taoist masters still have not returned.[67]	道士未還家
	Who could understand the thoughts in the Magistrate of Pengze's mind?[68]	誰知彭澤意
8	Let alone speaking about the Infantry Commandant's?[69]	更道步兵耶
	In spring, pine needles ferment in the wine jugs;	春釀煎松葉
	In autumn, chrysanthemums float in the wine cups.	秋蘇泛菊花
	When we chance upon one another, we would rather get drunk,	相逢寧可醉
12	And definitely will not take up mixing the elixirs!	定不學丹砂

As we see, Wang Ji does not so much deny the world of immortals or the desirability of transcendence as he takes the pragmatic position that such a world and such a goal are too remote to be attainable by mortals. It is better simply to enjoy what is readily available, such as the company of friends and wine. Wang Ji makes particular reference to two specific kinds of wine that were known for their medicinal as well as their inebriating benefits—

as if to suggest they are proper substitutes for "magical elixirs" because they truly are effective, good for body and mind. Such practicality, we should note, is characteristic of a philosophy of detachment. The pursuit of immortality is driven by desire, a desire to prolong mortal life indefinitely, to achieve permanence. It is, for Wang Ji, just this desire that burdens people, causes them stress and anxiety, and prevents them from enjoying their lives. Detachment, in contrast, means ridding oneself of desire, focusing on the present, living moment by moment. Put into poetic practice, responding to the moment translates into a style of easygoing spontaneity. Wang Ji's corpus includes many poems that seem to present such spontaneously taken "snapshots of life" that focus strictly on brief and simple moments. It seems that anything can be the topic for a poem, whose casual, almost offhand style reinforces an impression of its free, unstudied thought. These are the poems that are most noted for their disregard of traditional conventions, their free-spirited manner, and their refreshing treatment of even the most time-worn topics. An example is "Early Spring" (Chu chun 初春):[70]

	The morning before, when I went out for a stroll in the garden,	前旦出園遊
	There was not yet a single blossom in the entire grove.	林花都未有
	This morning, when I came down the hall and looked,	今朝下堂望
4	The ice-capped pond had been open for quite some time.	池冰開已久
	Snow fled from the apricot trees by the south balcony;	雪避南軒梅
	Wind urges on the willows in the north court.	風催北庭柳
	Calling from afar, I summon the maid in the kitchen	遙呼竈前妾
8	To go and tell my wife weaving at the loom:	卻報機中婦
	The season has arrived just in time,	年光恰恰來
	Let's fill the jugs and get the spring wine brewing!	滿甕營春酒

To appreciate how differently Wang Ji treats the arrival of spring in this case as opposed to contemporary Sui and Tang writers of court poetry, compare this poem with one on the same topic by Li Boyao:

Matching "An Early Spring Excursion" to His Highness' Command (Feng he "Chu chun chuyou" ying ling 奉和初春出遊應令)[71]

	Singing fifes emerge from Gazing Garden;	鳴笳出望苑
	Flying canopies descend to mushroom fields.	飛蓋下芝田
	The glitter of water drifts in the setting sunlight;	水光浮落照
4	The glow of rosy clouds is hazed by thin mist.	霞彩淡青煙
	The color of willows greets the third month;	柳色迎三月
	Apricot blossoms set apart the two years.	梅花隔二年
	As the sun tilts, the returning carriages move,	日斜歸騎動
8	Our lingering joy fills the mountains and streams.[72]	餘興滿山川

Li Boyao's treatment of his topic is typical of court poetry in its impersonal descriptiveness and rigid structure: the first couplet states the occasion, an outing, with singing fifes and flying canopies that double as a courtesy salute to the host of the party (His Highness, whose poem Li Boyao is commanded to match); the third couplet states the theme—early spring—in a line of tightly structured parallelism. ("The color of willows" corresponds to "apricot blossoms," "greets" contrasts with "set apart," and "third month" is linked with "two years.") At the same time, each couplet is completely independent from those before and after: there is a total lack of sequential unity to the poem. Moreover, there is not one human subject directly presented in the picture: the singing fifes and flying canopies suggest the merrymakers' departure, and the moving carriages tell of their return; but we have no way of perceiving the emotions of the speaker or his group except for the rather flat statement in the last line that their "lingering joy fills the mountains and streams."

Wang Ji's "The First Sign of Spring" certainly contains elements of court poetry,[73] but overall it employs simple diction and direct syntax and is sparing with metaphors. It is a vivid account of the speaker's surprise at discovering the sudden appearance of spring. The poem unfolds naturally, each line leading logically to the next. The third couplet animates nature's response to the change of seasons: snow "fled" at the presence of the apricot blossoms, the willow is "urged" by the wind to sprout. This couplet, positioned right in the middle of the poem, marks an abrupt shift of pace, as if mirroring the abrupt appearance of spring, and transforms the "still scenes" of the first four lines into a scene of "hustle and bustle" in the last four lines as the speaker excitedly stirs up the house. The poem's imperative ending ("Let's fill the jugs and get the spring wine brewing!") concludes the poem in a sudden and purposeful manner that contrasts neatly with the surprise of the opening lines.

Another example of such a snapshot that seems to capture a simple moment in daily life is the poem "On an Autumn Evening, Delighted to Have Run into Yao Yi, the Gentleman in Retirement" (Qiuye xi yu Yao chushi Yi 秋夜喜遇姚處士義):[74]

You just finished weeding the bean field on the north end,	北場耘藿罷
And I am returning from harvesting millet on the eastern bank.	東皋刈黍歸
We run into each other under the full autumn moon,	相逢秋月滿
Just when the fireflies are coming out for the night.	更值夜螢飛

Working with only four lines, each consisting of five characters, a court poet of Wang Ji's time would be expected to write in a dense style—in complete contrast to the casual style of this effort. The poem is concerned merely with the moment when two farmers meet on their way home from a day's farming. A full moon is in the sky, the fireflies are just appearing: the peace and quiet of the scene implies the farmers' mood without help, really, from the poem's title.

A similarly fleeting expression of mood is conveyed in "An Extempore Chant Made Up on My Return to Eastern Creek at Night" (Yehuan dongxi kouhao 夜還東溪口號):[75]

Lichens on rocks should be safe to step on;	石苔應可踐
The shrubs, luckily, are easy to hold onto.	叢枝幸易攀
The road back to Green Creek is straight,	青溪歸路直
By the moonlight, singing, I return at night.	乘月夜歌還

Although this poem is titled as a spontaneous composition, its opening lines are borrowed from a couplet in a poem by Xie Lingyun 謝靈運:[76]

| Lichens are slippery; who can step on them? | 苔滑誰能步 |
| Creepers are weak; how can one hold on? | 葛弱豈可捫 |

While Xie Lingyun's couplet vents frustration and is allegorical—slippery lichen stands for the treacherous path of politics, and weak creepers represent Xie's lack of influential friends at court to assist him along that path—Wang Ji's poem, in contrast, takes the occasion literally and advances a straightforward solution to the problem of walking on a slippery mountain path in the middle of the night: grab the shrubs, not the creepers, and follow the straight road by the light of the moon. The speaker is almost smugly innocent; but it is just this carefree frame of mind, with its ability to respond "extempore" only to what is before him at the moment, that allows him to reject both Xie's allegory and despair, and instead simply sing.

Perhaps the most cursory poem of all among these unconventional short lyrics is "Watching Wine-Making" (Kan niangjiu 看釀酒),[77] which simply comments on the steps in the wine-making process without betraying any of the eager anticipation that one ordinarily sees in Wang Ji's drinking poems:

In the sixth month, the wine starter is mixed;	六月調神麴
The first day of the year, the sweet spring water is drawn.	正朝汲美泉
The procedure of making spring wine	從來作春酒
Is always carried over to the next year.	未省不經年

Though offhand and occasional, this little poem exemplifies Wang Ji's literary manifestation of a philosophical ideal. His understanding of the inconstant nature of the world is cultivated in the detachment of his poetic persona, which in turn motivates a spontaneity of style that results ultimately in the impression of a range of recluse personae in Wang Ji's poems. Wang Ji's self-representation from poem to poem is inconsistent, in other words, not just because one's moment-to-moment responses to life are inevitably varied; rather, this instability of character is a logical necessity in an ever-changing world, where judgments of identity are as illusory as any other form of knowledge.

The poems that force readers to confront this necessity are those like "Summoning the Recluse," analyzed earlier, which contain ambiguities that resist efforts to define the speaker's identity, emotions, and desires because these ultimately are in flux. Another instance of this phenomenon is the poem "To Myself When Sitting Alone on the Mountain" (Shanzhong duzuo zizeng 山中獨坐自贈):[78]

	The secluded man, it seems, is disquieted,	幽人似不平
	Alone, sitting by the portal of Northern Mountain.	獨坐北山楹
	Recluse Liang withdrew hand in hand with his wife;[79]	攜妻梁處士
4	Mr. Xu bid farewell to his.[80]	別婦許先生
	Abandoning the profane world, I am weary of deep sighs;	擯俗勞長歎
	Searching in the mountains—I am tired of long journeys.	尋山倦遠行
	On the empty mountain, the slanting sun falls behind;	空山斜照落
8	From the ancient trees, cold mist rises up.	古樹寒煙生
	Tao Yuanliang untied his official ribbon;[81]	解組陶元亮
	Xiang Ziping left his family.[82]	辭家向子平
	Right and wrong, where do they lie?	是非何處在
12	From pools to lakes, arduously, I wade back and forth.	潭泊苦縱橫

Here we are introduced to a "secluded man," presumably the speaker, feeling disturbed in his heart and pondering reclusion. Looking back on his life, he proclaims himself "weary of deep sighs" and "tired of long journeys." "Deep sighs" are the familiar expression of the melancholy scholar burdened with moral concerns and political distress; "tired of long journeys" implies a speaker who has been searching unsuccessfully for some sort of fulfillment of his ambitions. As the poem ends with his intention to "abandon the profane world" and "search in the mountains," he cites various recluses of the past as a way to spur him toward a life of reclusion.

But this summary glosses over the poem's many ambiguities—both in its images and in the manner of its expression. Although the title indicates that the poet is speaking to himself, he nevertheless begins the poem from an observer's point of view. And instead of stating directly that he is troubled, he reports an observer's tentative impression: he "seems disquieted." Moreover, when we are told that the secluded man is "sitting by the portal of Northern Mountain," it is not clear at that moment whether this recluse is on his way to reclusion or on his way out. And yet the speaker soon supplies a description of his weary heart and his isolated surroundings: lines 5–8 seem unequivocally to situate him as a recluse escaping the troubled world of men. These lines, in turn, are sandwiched between invocations of recluses in history (lines 3–4 and 9–10), which should establish the speaker as their kindred spirit.

We are mistaken, however, if we think the ambiguity of the opening couplet has been resolved. In the final couplet the speaker asks about these model recluses—Liang Hong, Xu Mai, Tao Qian, and Xiang Chang —"Right and wrong, where do they lie?" It appears, for some reason, that he is now questioning their authority as models of reclusion. And next he even seems to challenge the very notion that reclusion can offer an alternative to a life of "deep sighs" and "long journeys": "From pools to lakes," he says, "arduously, I wade back and forth." This closing remark is nothing short of startling. Apparently he did not leave his "disquieted" mood behind on the other side of the mountain portal. His wading back and forth, "from pools to lakes," is an image of uncertain questing, and the word "arduously" implies accompanying frustration—anything but a placid mind. The closer we look at this poem, the harder it is to locate this secluded man.

In short, our attention to the ambiguity of this poem confirms the lesson of Wang Ji's varied corpus of country poems in its insistence that any determination to define and to live the life of a recluse, ultimately, is as unknowable a project as any other in the world.

4

The Recluse as Drunkard

❀

MORE THAN ANY other topic, drinking is the most pervasive theme in Wang Ji's corpus. Over 35 percent of the works in his five-*juan* collection at least make reference to drinking wine, and the proportion is even greater in the abridged three-*juan* collection (50 percent)—which goes a long way toward explaining how various dismissive labels such as "drunken poet" and "tippler hermit" have been applied to Wang Ji. We can concede, of course, that Wang Ji's drinking inspired much of his poetry.[1] But at the same time we must remember how often drinking had been employed, for centuries before Wang Ji, as a literary motif to express particular sets of ideas and emotions. Without attentive reading, one too easily overlooks how deeply Wang Ji drew upon this literary tradition, even as he used its materials for new purposes. As we shall see in this chapter, Wang Ji regularly invokes the famous drinkers and drinking poems of the past. But he seldom attributes to himself the conventional motives for drinking, and his drinking poems do not serve as an opportunity for either the expression or drowning of personal lament. Instead Wang Ji's drunken persona is a vehicle to demonstrate the philosophical precepts of the ever-changing course of the Way and the illusory nature of knowledge. For as we shall see, the state of drunkenness in Wang Ji's imagination is ultimately a metaphor for the enlightened man's realization of these ideas. Wang Ji conveys in his drinking poems an experience of being drunk (when one is aware of one's incapacity to distinguish reality from illusion or to make right judgments) that is analogous to the sobriety of the enlightened man (who recognizes that all perceptions of reality are illusory and that he is no more able to perceive the reality of the Way than the drunken man is able to perceive the reality of the mundane world in his impaired state).

A brief summary of Wang Ji's self-portrait as a drunkard—with an examination of how he incorporates the available motifs from poetic tradition in constructing his unique persona—prepares us to recognize the philosophical significance of drunkenness as he perceives it. Perhaps most frequently in Wang Ji's poems, first of all, drinking is an expression of the poet's carefree spontaneity. His celebrations of natural phenomena, such as the coming of spring, often focus more on joyful descriptions of drinking than on the ostensible topic. In the previous chapter we saw one such response to spring that ended not with a focus on the beauty of the season but with a call for wine.[2] The poem "The Beginning of Spring" (Chu chun 春初)[3] is similar:

At the coming of spring, the days grow longer;	春來日漸長
The drunken visitor loves this time of year.	醉客喜年光
I have barely noticed the lovely pavilion and the pond;	稍覺池亭好
All I can smell is the fragrance from the wine vat.[4]	偏聞酒甕香

After stating his topic in the first line, the speaker introduces himself as a *zuike* 醉客 (drunken visitor). The nature of the *ke* (visitor or guest) in this self-reference identifies him as an excursionist on a spring outing and, at the same time, invokes the conventional metaphor of life on earth as a temporary journey. In fact, this idea of one's brief stay in the world shifts the poem's focus away from spring, because the speaker now admits he is unmindful of his "lovely" surroundings. His mind is only on drinking ("All I can smell is the fragrance from the wine vat").

The intention to represent a spontaneous, unrestrained spirit is evident again in the unconventional treatment of spring we see in another of Wang Ji's poems, "In Spring, in the Garden, After Feeling Exhilarated" (Chunyuan xinghou 春園興後):[5]

	For the last few days I have been drunk, as usual;	比日尋常醉
	When we crossed into a new year, I was not even sober.	經年獨未醒
	Turning around to look at the willow tree in the backyard,	迴瞻後園柳
4	I suddenly notice several green branches.	忽值數行青
	This must mean that spring is here!	定是春來意
	I lower my head and listen: it is even more pleasant!	低頭更好聽

	The singing orioles flutter in a confusion;	歌鶯遼亂動
8	Lotus leaves are growing all around the pond.	蓮葉遶池生
	Running full tilt, I chase after Ruan Ji;	散腰追阮籍
	Waving my hand, I call out to Liu Ling.	招手喚劉伶
	From behind the shelf, I peer at the empty racks—	鬲架窺前空
12	Only a few small bottles left.	未餘幾小瓶
	A beautiful day like this is the time to finish them up;	風光須用卻
	If I leave them here, who is going to empty them?	留此待誰傾

Like "Early Spring," discussed in the previous chapter, this poem's style is relaxed, its narrative flows in a sequential progression, and again Wang Ji positions in the middle (lines 7–8) a neatly parallel and descriptive couplet that is typical of court poetry: "The singing orioles flutter in a confusion; / Lotus leaves are growing all around the pond." This couplet constitutes a turning point—a shifting of the narrative pace from inactive to active, transforming the speaker's sensual experience (singing orioles and burgeoning lotus leaves) into physically responsive action (running, waving and calling, preparing to drink). However neatly symmetrical this poem's structure may be, we are far more likely to be struck by the character of its speaker. He has just regained consciousness after a drunken stupor so extended that spring has arrived without his notice. He responds to the discovery by running about like a madman—an unrestrained spirit, that is (like Ruan Ji and Liu Ling)—but shortly he is eyeing his remaining stock of wine, ready to finish it off and sink back into his stupor. There is no sense that he has any cares or desires other than to let his actions suit the moment—and as he so often asks: when isn't it the proper time to finish off the wine? His poem "Eight Quatrains Scribbled on Tavern Walls, no. 2" (Ti jiudian loubi jueju ba shou 題酒店樓壁絕句八首之二)[6] contains another expression of the same sentiment:

Bamboo-leaf wine, green and unfiltered;	竹葉連糟翠
Grape wine, red and unrefined.	蒲桃帶麴紅
If we don't drink them up when we get together,	相逢不令盡
Who is going to finish them after we part?	別後為誰空

The various cursory accounts that have thus far been written of the differences between Wang Ji's drunken persona and his apparent models from literary tradition have led some scholars to absorb themselves in unprofitable controversies. Literary issues have been neglected in favor of personal questions: Did Wang Ji have a legitimate, moral reason to turn to drink? Was he irresponsibly imitating famous drinker-intellectuals of the past at a time when literati enjoyed great opportunities at court? Was alcoholism just a flaw in Wang Ji's character? Here I hope to offer a more nuanced account of these differences, one that will lead to observations on Wang Ji's poetry rather than on his person.

Since the end of the Later Han, drinking had mainly a hedonistic and escapist significance in early Chinese literature: it was represented as a means of escape to momentary pleasure in a world of pain and sorrow. Certainly the greatly influential "Nineteen Ancient Poems" depicted wine-drinking in this light. This group of pentasyllabic lyrics by anonymous writers of the Han dynasty was praised by Liu Xie 劉勰 (ca. 465–522) as "realistic in describing objective scenes and deeply moving in depicting inner emotions."[7] And in two of them drinking wine is described as providing recourse from melancholy, as the following excerpts show:

from "Nineteen Ancient Poems, no. 3"[8]

Between heaven and earth our lives rush past	人生天地間
Like travelers with a long way to go.	忽如遠行客
Let this pleasure of wine be our merriment;	斗酒相娛樂
Value it highly without disdain.	聊厚不為薄
....	....
Let the feast last forever, delighting the heart—	極宴娛心意
Then what grief or gloom can weigh us down?	戚戚何所迫

from "Nineteen Ancient Poems, no. 13"[9]

Times of heat and cold in unending succession,	浩浩陰陽移
But the years Heaven gives us are like morning dew.	年命如朝露
Man's life is brief as a sojourn;	人生忽如寄
His years lack the firmness of metal or stone.	壽無金石固
Ten thousand ages come and go	萬歲更相送
But sages and wise men discover no cure.	聖賢莫能度
Some seek long life in fasts and potions;	服食求神仙
Many end by poisoning themselves.	多為藥所誤
Far better to drink fine wine,	不如飲美酒
To clothe ourselves in soft white silk.	被服紈與素

Wine is like an elixir in these two pieces—offering escape from the anxiety of this fleeting life and from the painful awareness of our vulnerability to nature's power. It creates the illusion of everlasting pleasure. A similar contemplation of drinking can be found in a poem by Cao Cao, his well-known "Short Song" (Duange xing 短歌行):

Facing wine, I start to sing—	對酒當歌
Human life, how long can it be?	人生幾何
It is like the morning dew;	譬如朝露
So many days are fleeting by, it distresses me.	去日苦多
My feelings stirred, I sigh deeply,	慨當以慷
These grieving thoughts are difficult to forget.	憂思難忘
What is there to dispel my sorrow?	何以解憂
There is only Dukang![10]	唯有杜康

In this poem, interestingly, it is the actual presence of wine that not only triggers the speaker's distress at the impermanence of human life but offers him comfort. The image of wine as a means to dispel melancholy has become so fixed, it seems, it even has the power to elicit that melancholy if it is not already being felt.

In his study of medieval Chinese culture, Wang Yao 王瑤 claims that the popularity of drinking among literati during the Six Dynasties period reflected their fear at a time of bloody political intrigues and epidemics.[11] Putting aside the question of whether or not literati require calamity to exhibit a liking for wine, it is true, as Wang Yao observes, that during this period the representation of drunkenness in poetry was meant to express one's treasuring of life. And it was Tao Qian who introduced the image of a scholar finding not only comfort in drink but personal freedom and happiness during his voluntary reclusion from troubles of the world. But more than this, Tao Qian significantly expanded the image of the drunken poet. In his poetry the drunken poet is not only a man temporarily free of fear and sorrow but one who experiences a spiritual emancipation, whose mind is therefore always free of the burden of worldly worries and the demands of social responsibilities.

In "Drinking Alone in the Rainy Season" (Lianyu duyin 連雨獨飲),[12] for instance, we see Tao Qian contemplating the brevity of life and the potency of wine:

Whatever lives comes to its end at last;	運生會歸盡
From the beginning of time it has been so.	終古謂之然

	If immortals Song and Qiao once lived	世間有松喬
4	Where do you suppose they are today?	於今定何間
	The old fellow who sent this gift of wine	故老贈余酒
	Said to drink it makes man immortal.	乃言飲得仙
	I try a cup, and all my cares are gone,	試酌百情遠
8	More, and all at once I forget Heaven.	重觴忽忘天
	But is Heaven so far from this after all?	天豈去此哉
	Nothing tops the one who trusts the True.	任真無所先
	The cloud-high crane with wonderful wings	雲鶴有奇翼
12	Can reach the ends of the earth in a moment of time.	八表須臾還
	Since I first embraced my solitary state	自我抱茲獨
	I have struggled through forty years.	僶俛四十年
	I have long since surrendered my body to change;	形骸久已化
16	My heart is untouched—what more is there to say?	心在復何言

This philosophical stance of Tao Qian transforms, for the first time in Chinese literature, the image of drunkenness from a temporary escape from sorrow to an enlightened state of mind that allows him to scoff in disregard at his own mortality. In drinking, as Tao Qian strives to show in the following poem, one experiences a sublime feeling of exaltation in one's freedom from care:

Drinking Poems, no. 14
(Yinjiu shi 飲酒詩)[13]

	Sympathetic friends who know my tastes	故人賞我趣
	Bring a wine jug when they come to visit.	挈壺相與至
	Sitting on the ground beneath the pine tree	班荊坐松下
4	A few cups of wine make us drunk,	數斟已復醉
	Venerable elders gabbing all at once	父老雜亂言
	And pouring from the bottle out of turn.	觴酌失行次
	Aware no more that our own "I" exists	不覺知有我
8	How are we to value other things?	安知物為貴
	So rapt we are not sure where we are—	悠悠迷所留
10	In wine there is a taste of profundity.	酒中有深味

In this poem, all measures of consciousness are one after the other abandoned in drinking: first social ritual is discarded (lines 5–6); then awareness of the self and the judgments of others are abandoned (lines 7–8); finally one's own physical presence becomes indeterminate in space (line 9) and even the speaker's verbal articulation dissolves in the wine, leaving him to savor in silence the "taste," rather than the words or thoughts, "of profundity."

Yet, as many critics have noted, despite such representations of his drinking, Tao Qian often betrays a deep ambivalence toward his professed detachment and disregard for personal obligations and moral values. This ambivalence "plagued him half his life," as one scholar puts it,[14] and his writings reflect a constant struggle between his confessed ambition to accomplish great deeds, on the one hand, and his avid desire, on the other, to remain free from the entanglements of political life. As much as he advertises his carefree philosophical disposition as a simple and drunken farmer—and despite his becoming from the Tang onward an icon of contentment and detachment—his drinking poems nonetheless regularly depict this inner conflict. In the thirteenth poem in his series of "Drinking Poems,"[15] Tao Qian personifies this conflict as "two guests who lodge with me":

	I always have two guests who lodge with me	有客常同止
	Whose inclinations keep them far apart;	趣舍邈異境
	One is always getting drunk alone,	一士長獨醉
4	One stays sober all the year round.	一夫終年醒
	They laugh at one another, drunk and sober,	醒醉還相笑
	And neither understands the other's words.	發言各不領
	How very stupid is this hidebound fellow!	規規一何愚
8	The drunkard's detachment seems wiser.	兀傲差若穎
	A word of counsel to the drunken guest:	寄言酣中客
	Light the candles when the sun goes down.	日沒燭當炳

Tao Qian's sober guest clearly represents the side of him that feels obliged to fulfill responsibilities expected from a conscientious man; his drunken guest is the side of him that enjoys the freedom from restraint he feels when drunk. That they scoff at one another attests to their fundamental difference: these are not forces to be balanced or reconciled. When the speaker reminds the drunken guest to "Light the candles when the sun goes down" (line 10), he advises him, through an allusion to "Nineteen Ancient Poems, no. 15," not to interrupt his enjoyment with pointless worries.[16] But the very fact that the self who supposedly embodies detachment needs to be coached to enjoy his carefree life acknowledges the poet's awareness of his own continued reluctance to neglect worldly values and obligations completely.

James Hightower is among those who argue Tao Qian harbored too much concern for the world to lose himself truly and fully in the poetic celebration of unrestrained drunkenness. In his study of Tao Qian's series of poems titled "Twenty Drinking Poems," he observes that Tao Qian hardly writes about drinking at all but instead contemplates his life *after* drinking. Hightower concludes that drunkenness is essentially Tao Qian's excuse for his lack of success in the world—a theme he utilizes for expressing his moral and personal concerns, including criticism of his world. This understanding prompted Hightower to change his English rendition of the title of the series from "Drinking Wine Poems" to "Twenty Poems After Drinking Wine" in his book on Tao Qian's poetry.[17]

Thus Hightower insists that Tao Qian is unable to maintain his carefree and contented image. For Tao Qian, as for his predecessors, wine primarily offered an escape from disappointment and anxiety. Consider, for instance, "Miscellaneous Poems, no. 8,"[18] in which the poet concludes by raising his glass in what seems to be meant as a gesture of philosophical detachment:

	I do not want something in place of plowing,	代耕本非望
	For farming is my proper occupation.	所業在田桑
	Although I never left my work undone,	躬親未曾替
4	In cold and famine, husks are my usual fare.	寒餒常糟糠
	Not hoping for a belly more than full	豈期過滿腹
	I only wish to eat my fill of grain,	但願飽粳糧
	To have coarse cloth enough to cope with winter	御冬足大布
8	And netted hemp to meet the summer sun,	粗絺以應陽
	And even this was more than I could find.	正爾不能得
	Too bad it was, and regrettable too,	哀哉亦可傷
	But what one gets is just what one deserves:	人皆盡獲宜
12	If you are clumsy at life you lose your place;	拙生失其方
	That is the way things are and there is no help,	理也可奈何
	And so you might as well enjoy a drink.	且為陶一觴

Tao Qian begins by self-consciously announcing his chosen occupation—as if to assure us he feels no regret at the simple life he is about to describe—and it seems his aim in this poem is to represent himself as contented. But in fact he admits that this is not just a simple life but one of severe hardship: minimal shelter and sustenance are denied him. He justifies his suffering ("what one gets is just what one deserves: / If you are clumsy at life you lose your place"); he resolves to accept "the way things are" (*li* 理); and he determines to laugh at his fate with a cup of wine. But such philosophical aloofness is compromised by the despair that is conveyed by the image of this hungry, cold man who feels his lot is "too bad" and "regrettable." Drinking is his last resort, since "there is no help" of any other kind.

Overall I would agree that Tao Qian's corpus does not represent him as carefree but indeed as quite self-conscious about the implications of his drunkenness in the eyes of a judgmental world. The conclusion to the last of his "Twenty Drinking Poems,"[19] to take a final instance, has him apologizing for his careless words even as he reasserts his drunken persona:

If I fail to drink to my heart's content	若復不快飲
I will be untrue to the cap I wear.	空負頭上巾
Still I regret the stupid things I've said	但恨多謬誤
And hope you will forgive a man in his cups.	君當恕罪人

The image that we derive of a drunken Wang Ji differs greatly from the apologetic and anxiety-laden example of Tao Qian—both in his poetry and in biographical accounts of his life. To consider a case of the latter, Lü Cai recalls in his preface that in Wang Ji's later years he drank so excessively and without restraint that some of his fellow villagers reproached him. He responded to them with laughter, according to Lü Cai, saying: "You fellows don't understand. It is just the way it should be" (*li zheng dangran* 理正當然).[20] What Wang Ji may have meant (or what his biographer wanted us to understand) by the word "way" (*li* 理)[21] in this response —which in Tao Qian's poem quoted earlier, and in philosophical discourse generally, signifies the natural order or pattern embodied in all living things in the world—is perhaps clarified in Wang Ji's letter to a certain Mr. Cheng explaining his love for wine:

By nature I am fond of drinking; it is what my body depends on. . . . I drink alone behind closed doors, having no need for companions. Whenever I get very drunk, I feel that my mind is clear, calm, and peaceful, that my arteries and veins are open and smooth. [Drinking] not only infringes on nothing in the world but also gives me personal pleasure; therefore, I often indulge myself in self-contentment.[22]

Rather than offering the pleasing befuddlement that distracts the mind from worldly cares, drunkenness in Wang Ji's conception cleanses the body and clears the mind: indeed, as we shall see, drunkenness in Wang Ji's imagination is the "way it should be" or "the state that one should be in" because it represents the "ultimate sobriety" of the mind.

Such an understanding of Wang Ji's conception of drinking as a metaphor for clarity of mind goes far toward explaining the differences between his self-representation and that of his ostensible model, Tao Qian. Wang Ji goes much farther in extolling the benefits of drinking and reveling in his unrestrained drunken behavior. We have already seen examples of this in "Early Spring" and "In Spring, in the Garden, After Feeling Exhilarated." We have also seen, in "Scribbled on a Tavern Wall, no. 3," Wang Ji's willingness to report his public appearances in a drunken stupor. Contrary to Tao Qian's apparent discomfort with the irresponsibility of his drunken persona, Wang Ji never betrays embarrassment, even when he seems to be defending his lifestyle:

In the Village in Spring, After Drinking
(Chunzhuang jiuhou 春莊酒後)[23]

	The farmer's door opens at the crack of dawn;	郊扉乘曉闢
	The mountain brew is unsealed at the coming of the year.	山醅及年開
	Cypress leaves are tossed into a new batch;	柏葉投新釀
4	Pine flowers are splashing in the aged spirit.[24]	松花潑舊醅
	My country wife rests herself against the vats;	野妻臨甕倚
	The village boy brings the bottles to me.	村豎捧瓶來
	I use a bamboo node for a ladle,	竹瘤還作杓
8	And a tree gall for my cup.	樹癭即成杯
	In drunkenness, I make my way to the north pond	北潭因醉往
	And return from the south fields by starlight.	南畝帶星迴
	A farmer has many drinking partners;	田家多酒伴
12	Who can blame the jade mountain for collapsing?	誰怪玉山頹

The collapse of the jade mountain in the last line refers to Xi Kang, who, according to one anecdote, when drunk "leaned crazily like a jade mountain about to collapse."[25] Xi Kang's drinking was traditionally attributed to a desire to avoid political dangers. But in this poem the allusion seems only to serve as a metaphor for the state of drunkenness, for Wang Ji depicts his speaker not only as inebriated from endless drinking with his farmer friends but also intoxicated in his contentment with life. He has nothing to complain of: his family helps him to make wine, and his friends help him to drink it; and once he is drunk he makes his merry way about his farm. All is a picture of perfect contentment underpinned by the subtle allusion—in the image of the poet's crude ladle, made from a bamboo node, and his cup from a tree gall—to the simple fisherman's advice in *Zhuangzi*: "What matters when you drink is that you enjoy yourself ... and to enjoy yourself while you drink, you do not get finicky about your cups."[26]

By comparing two poems probably written at either end of his adult life, we furthermore perceive that Wang Ji consistently represented himself as a self-contented drunken farmer lacking in ambition, desire, anxiety, and worries. In what appears, in the first poem, to be a marriage proposal, Wang Ji presents himself to his future wife with the following self-sketch:

Before Getting Married, in the Mountains, I State My Intent (Weihun shanzhong xuzhi 未婚山中敘志)[27]

	Detached from the world, what do I know of its affairs?	物外知何事
	Living in the mountains, I have nothing to my name.	山中無所有
	Wind carries the sound of my zither through the quiet of the night;	風鳴靜夜琴
4	The moon shines on the fragrant wine in my goblet.	月照芳樽酒
	I only think about this hundred years of mine;	直置百年內
	Who cares what comes after a thousand ages?	誰論千載後
	Zhang Feng took in a worthy wife;	張奉聘賢妻
8	Laolaizi met a fine mate.	老萊藉嘉偶
	If Meng Guang is not married yet,	孟光儻未嫁
	Liang Hong is in need of a spouse.[28]	梁鴻正須婦

Identifying himself with three renowned recluses whose like-minded wives cared little for the comfort of wealth or the luster of fame, Wang Ji depicts himself, and his future wife, completely lacking in ambition and desire for material wealth. Instead they will find contentment in his playing the zither and in drinking wine. In a poem that looks back on life from old age, this contentment in wine and the simple life is still professed:

Sitting in Solitude
(Du zuo 獨坐)[29]

	I ask you, aside from a jug of wine,	問君樽酒外
	Sitting alone, what more do I need?	獨坐更何須
	I have visitors with whom I can discuss Names and Principles,[30]	有客談名理
4	But no one is here to bother me with land taxes.	無人索地租
	My three boys have married into fine families;	三男婚令族
	My five daughters are married to worthy husbands.	五女嫁賢夫
	My life will end when my lot is up;	百年隨分了
8	I have never wished to climb Fanghu Island.[31]	未羨陟方壺

In our study of the differences between Wang Ji's and Tao Qian's self-representations as poor farmers we can compare Tao Qian's poem discussed previously, "Miscellaneous Poems, no. 8," to Wang Ji's "Portrait of a Farmer, no. 3" (Tianjia 田家):[32]

	My only pleasure in life is wine;	平生唯樂酒
	It's my inherent nature, I cannot live without it.	作性不能無
	Every morning I scour the village for it;	朝朝訪鄉里
4	Every night I send my man out to buy more.	夜夜遣人酤
	Though indigent, I urge my guests to stay long,	家貧留客久
	Unconcerned that I may not have decent fare.	不暇道精粗
	I take down the bamboo screen to keep the torch burning bright,	抽簾持益炬
8	And pull off the bamboo mat to rekindle fire in the stove.	拔簀更燃爐
	You always hear people say there isn't enough to drink;	恆聞飲不足
10	Who has ever seen jugs left unfinished?	何見有殘壺

Like Tao Qian, this farmer is strapped for basic necessities: he has no money to entertain his company or even to buy fuel to light his torch or stove. Yet there is only contentment in his tone: the hunger and cold do not bite. He spends his days immersed in the joy of drinking and does not hesitate to exhaust his last few resources to keep the drinking party going to the end of the last jug.

It appears that Wang Ji's drunken-farmer persona differs from Tao Qian's because its function is different: it serves primarily as a personification of an idea rather than to express personal feelings. This is not to deny that Wang Ji's poems convey emotions, but I am insisting here on a crucial distinction between Wang Ji's and Tao Qian's poetic aims. In constructing his poetic self-image, Wang Ji went beyond Tao Qian for his model to include the free-spirited and unrestrained behavior of early Wei-Jin eccentrics such as Ruan Ji, Liu Ling, and others whose stories fill the pages of *Shishuo xinyu* as early exemplars of medieval conduct.[33] In them Wang Ji found precedents for the unapologetically intemperate drinker, sustaining throughout his corpus their joyous disregard for social mores and total lack of embarrassment for reckless behavior. This is true whether he is portraying himself on the farm or in the capital. For in a self-mocking poem supposedly scribbled on a tavern wall in Chang'an, perhaps sometime during the years at the beginning of the Tang dynasty when he was waiting for an official appointment, he jokes about drinking away his meager fortune:

Eight Quatrains Scribbled on Tavern Walls, no. 1[34]

I don't have a grand residence in Luoyang,	洛陽無大宅
And I lack patrons in Chang'an.	長安乏主人
My money is disappearing but not yet all gone,	黃金消未盡
Only because the taverns here are cheap.[35]	祇為酒家貧

And when his money does run out, as he reports in a later poem in the series, Wang Ji unabashedly takes for his subject his dependence on a generous tavern keeper:

Eight Quatrains Scribbled on Tavern Walls, no. 7[36]

I have a guest and I must ask him for a drink,	有客須教飲
But I have no money to buy wine anywhere else.	無錢可別酤
When coming here, I can always say "Put it on credit,"	來時長道貰
Much obliged to the foreign tavern keeper.[37]	慚愧酒家胡

There is no remorse for his drinking or his poverty: he simply "must" entertain his guest. In fact, the only reason Wang Ji "must" ever do anything but drink is to support his bibacity, as he admits in another poem:

Jocularly Inscribed on the Wall of the Oracle-Reading Shop
(Xiti budian bi 戲題卜店壁)[38]

Morning, I run off chasing Liu Ling;	旦逐劉伶去
Evening, I fall asleep along with Bi Zhuo.	宵隨畢卓眠
I really mustn't always read oracles for a living,	不應長賣卜
But I need to get wine money.[39]	須得杖頭錢

Both Liu Ling and Bi Zhuo (d. ca. 329) are notorious drunkards from the Wei-Jin era who came to symbolize the emancipation of the self from worldly concerns in the pure joy of drunkenness.[40] By putting himself in their constant company in his imaginary world, Wang Ji attests to his own emancipation even as he humorously begrudges having to work for the money that keeps him in wine. Thus Wang Ji turns the apologetic mode on its head: for though this poem and the one before are written in the manner of apology, the regret is not for the drinking but for the measures that must be taken to keep oneself in wine.

Scholars often point to two of Wang Ji's poems, however, as evidence that he, like Tao Qian, drank to escape the anxiety of living in a time of turmoil or to drown the disappointment he felt in his failed career. We need to examine these two poems. Whatever Wang Ji's day-to-day reasons for getting drunk, I contend that neither the retreat from troubled times nor self-consolation for life's disappointments is among the motives expressed in his poems:

Drinking Alone
(Du zhuo 獨酌)[41]

This floating life, who knows how long it lasts?[42]	浮生知幾日
It is futile to chase after hollow fame.	無狀逐空名
It is much better to brew lots of wine	不如多釀酒
And frequently tilt your goblet in the Bamboo Grove.	時向竹林傾

Eight Quatrains Scribbled on Tavern Walls, no. 5[43]

Someone asks: "When roaming in the world of men,	或問遊人道
How can you walk alone in sorrow?"	那能獨步憂
"When you drink, you hold in your mouth the remedy;	飲時含救藥
After you are drunk, you can't worry about anything."	醉罷不能愁

The first poem bids the reader to acknowledge the temporality of mortal life and the futility of chasing fame—and urges him to drink by invoking the famous "Seven Worthies of the Bamboo Grove" in the last line. This legendary group includes Ruan Ji, Xi Kang, and Liu Ling, famed for their deliberate self-indulgence in reckless drinking, as we have noted, and it is true their motive was assumed to have been to avoid involvement in political intrigues. This reading has led some to perceive in Wang Ji's poem a tone of resignation, even frustration and despair. I would point out, however, that the reference to the "Bamboo Grove" in this poem rather invites us to imagine the legendary drinking parties of the whole group collectively. Ever since *Shishuo xinyu* immortalized the "seven worthies" in that charismatic role, they have symbolized free and unrestrained spirits. After all, under the heading "The Free and Unrestrained" the compiler of *Shishuo xinyu*, Liu Yiqing 劉義慶 (403–444), describes the worthies "letting their fancy free in merry revelry" and does not draw attention to the political circumstances behind such behavior.[44] I therefore take the reference to the "Bamboo Grove" in Wang Ji's poem as an invitation to recall the legendary drinking parties and "free and unrestrained spirit" of the whole group and would suggest we read the poem as urging us to relinquish our worldly ambitions on general principle, not for specific moral or political reasons. Nor, in sum, is this carefree tone consistent with interpreting the poem as an expression of Wang Ji's desire to find solace in wine for his failures in life.

As for the second poem, it proposes drinking as the solution to life's sorrows or worries, but these seem to be conceived of in the most general sense: they are the cares that arise whenever one is sober and "roaming in the world of men." That the poem does not express Wang Ji's personal desire to find escape from his sorrows is suggested by the poem's question-answer format, which creates the image of a master teaching his listeners the way to rid the mind of melancholy.

Two more short poems further illustrate the point that Wang Ji deliberately disregards his models' motives for drinking while advancing his own reasons. The first is titled "Extempore Chant Written After I Was Drunk" (Zuihou kouhao 醉後口號):[45]

Ruan Ji had few moments sober,	阮籍醒時少
Tao Qian spent many days drunk.	陶潛醉日多
How do we fully enjoy years of our lives?	百年何足度
When the mood rises, sing a long song too.	乘興且長歌

Here Wang Ji invokes the reputations of Ruan Ji and Tao Qian as heavy drinkers but completely ignores the equally commonplace perception that they drank for very different reasons (whatever their actual ones)—Ruan Ji to avoid entangling himself in political intrigue, Tao Qian to satisfy his innate desire to achieve feelings of freedom and contentment. Similarly, when Wang Ji resigned from his first post at Luhe (because, we are told, his drinking caused him to neglect his official duties), his poem explaining his behavior appeals to the examples of Ruan Ji and Tao Qian both (referred to here by their official titles):[46]

The Magistrate of Pengze had land, but he only planted glutinous millet;	彭澤有田惟種黍
The Infantry Commandant took office, but did he care for the salary?[47]	步兵從宦豈論錢
If I can be in a constant drunken stupor morning after morning,[48]	但使百年相繼醉
Why would I refuse to sleep amid wine jugs night after night?	何辭夜夜甕中眠

This eclecticism of Wang Ji's allusions—which would be clumsily contradictory if the expression of personal feelings or motives had been Wang Ji's aim—encourages us to seek another explanation for the prevalence of drinking in his corpus. Another of the poems scribbled on a tavern wall in Chang'an (no. 3)[49] takes us closer to a precise definition of the philosophical significance of Wang Ji's representation as a drunkard and supplies a transition to this chapter's conclusion:

In the presence of wine, I just know I should drink it;	對酒但知飲
If I meet others, I don't force them to oblige.	逢人莫強牽
Leaning against a vat, I quickly drop off;[50]	倚爐便得睡
Crouching over a jar, I am fast asleep.	橫甕足堪眠

It is tempting to interpret this poem as merely the offhand self-portrait of a drunk about to pass out. But I think it is just what Wang Ji's other self-representations as a drunkard prove to be: a poetic materialization of a passage in *Zhuangzi* in which drunkenness serves as a metaphor for "spontaneity of the mind"—a state of being in which a man "remains at the degree where he does not infringe upon others, and stores far back along the skein without beginning where all threads meet, to roam where the myriad things end and begin; he will unify his nature, tend his energies, contain his Power, to circulate through that in which other things find their directions." "A drunken man," the passage continues, "rides without knowing it, falls without knowing it; astonishment and fear never enter his breast, so when he collides with other things he does not flinch." This is a "wholeness from wine" that corresponds to the enlightened man's harmony with the Way, says the *Zhuangzi*.[51] And for Wang Ji, I would argue, drunkenness likewise was imagined figuratively as a state of harmonious integration with the Way. It represents the ultimate sobriety of one who perceives the illusory nature of the physical world, frees himself of all burdens of desire, ambition, and distress, and makes no attempt to control the course of his life in this ever-changing world.

Thus I propose we interpret Wang Ji's drunkard persona as a personification of an idea and an ideal: it is a metaphysical argument, in fact, because his personality and values are premised on a conception of the relationship between the phenomenal world and the Way. This notion is made even plainer in Wang Ji's "Biography of Mr. Five Dippers" (Wudou Xiansheng zhuan 五斗先生傳):[52]

> Mr. Five Dippers roamed in the world of men on account of the virtue of wine. Whenever someone invited him for a drink, nobleman or lowly man, he always went; whenever he went for a drink, he inevitably drank till he was drunk; when he was drunk, he just lay down wherever he found a spot and went to sleep; after he woke up, he went back to drinking. He once drank five dippers of wine at one sitting and thus acquired his sobriquet.
>
> This gentleman's mind was clear of any worries and concerns; he was a person of few words and did not know that there was a concept of goodness, propriety, right, and wrong in the world. He would go off in an instant and come in a flash. When he moved, he modeled the heavens; when he was still, he patterned the earth. To be sure, the myriad things could not have clogged his mind.
>
> Once he said, "I can basically see how the world is.[53] How can anyone nourish life? Yet Xi Kang wrote a treatise on the subject. How can a road run to a dead end? Yet it made Ruan Ji wail. To be sure, obscurity and silence are where a sage resides." Then he carried out his intent and no one knows where he went.

The name "Mr. Five Dippers" is a play on Wang Ji's own nickname, "A-Dipper-of-Wine Scholar" (Doujiu Xueshi 斗酒學士), which he acquired during his years in the capital. By means of this thinly veiled self-reference,

Wang Ji invokes Tao Qian's quasi-autobiographical "Mr. Five Willows" (Wuliu Xiansheng 五柳先生). But the two pieces express very different sentiments. Tao Qian's piece focuses on details of Mr. Five Willows —his life, his moral character, and his conduct—and many of these details are unmistakably autobiographical.[54] Wang Ji is concerned with the idealized personality of his drunkard persona, which is not an individual but a personification of the ideas of naturalness and spontaneity. Mr. Five Dippers drinks without apology, shows no emotion or mental stress, is oblivious to social decorum; his movements are sudden and unpredictable, in accord with the unknowable patterns of heaven and earth. He is, in other words, a manifestation of the Way.

Furthermore, Mr. Five Dippers rejects Xi Kang and Ruan Ji for their inability to comprehend the real meaning of naturalness and spontaneity. Xi Kang is singled out for striving to achieve longevity through the practice of "nurturing life." In his "Disquisition" on the topic (Yangsheng lun 養生論), Xi Kang argues that if a man nurtures life by divesting himself of all emotion and desire, by keeping to a rigid diet devoid of meat, grains, and wine, and by conducting breathing and muscle-toning excercises, he can then achieve the maximum natural life span of one thousand years.[55] Ruan Ji, as Mr. Five Dippers next reminds us, attempted too ardently to realize his naturalness and spontaneity. The reference to Ruan Ji hitting a dead end and wailing alludes to his reputed habit of "driving off alone whenever he was inclined to do so and without following any particular route ... when the trails ran out and he had to turn around, he wailed bitterly."[56] For Mr. Five Dippers, then, Xi Kang and Ruan Ji failed to understand that their methods for pursuing naturalness, though perhaps inactive or unrestrained according to the standards of the "profane world," are misguided. Their methods are founded on self-deception. Xi Kang's devotion to "lifenurturing" practices assumes that humankind has an ultimately certain, uniform, and achievable life span, but his ascetic regimen to achieve this ideal life span ironically requires him to go against humanity's natural lot. And in Ruan Ji's disappointment at the impassable trail in the wilderness, Mr. Five Dippers would have us recognize that a confusion of "natural paths" through the phenomenal world is the truly natural Way that is invisible, noncorporeal, inexhaustible. Concluding with an allusion to *Zhuangzi* that defines the "apex of the utmost Way" as being "obscure and silent,"[57] Mr. Five Dippers holds up his own way of living—lost in drunkenness, obscure and silent, sometimes here and sometimes there—as the embodiment of the ever-changing Way.[58]

In "The Story of Drunkenville" (Zuixiang ji 醉鄉記),[59] Wang Ji supplies an allegory of perfect government to match his description of the perfect man. Here the ideal of inaction (wuwei 無為), represented in the image of drunken stupor, is presented as an alternative to control and regulation:

I don't know how far Drunkenville is from the Middle Kingdom. Its land is vast and boundless; there are no hills or steep slopes. The climate there is always calm and stable; the sky is never too gloomy or too bright, the weather never too cold or too hot. The way of life there is the Grand Harmony; there are no townships or settlements. People there are very free of desire, and they lack the emotions of love, hate, joy, and rage. They inhale wind and drink dew and eat none of the five grains.[60] When lying down, they sleep undisturbed; when up, they move about unconcerned. They mingle with fish, turtles, birds, and beasts; they are ignorant of the use of boats, carriages, instruments, and tools.[61]

Once in the ancient past, the Yellow Lord visited its capital. When he returned, he retired to live quietly; he forsook his reign over the subcelestial realm because he felt that the way of governing by knotting cords had been defiled.[62] When it came to the era of Yao 堯 and Shun 舜, they made sacrificial offerings with a thousand bronze bells and a hundred wine vessels. They attracted the Divine Person from Guye to visit their border region under the pretense of passing through, and throughout their lifetime the subcelestial realm was peaceful.[63]

Then Yu 禹 and Tang 湯 established the law of order; their rites were complicated and their music was perplexing. For ten generations, they were estranged from Drunkenville. Their vassals Xi 羲 and He 和 abandoned their duties as calendar makers and ran away, hoping to get to Drunkenville, but they lost their way and died en route.[64] The subcelestial realm thereupon was in turmoil. By the time it reached to the last generation [of Xia and Shang], Jie 桀 and Zhou 紂[65] in a fury climbed a thousand fathoms of steps to the top of the Hill of Dregs and looked southward, but they never did see Drunkenville.[66]

After King Wu achieved his ambition to rule the world, he ordered the Duke of Zhou to establish an office to oversee the making and the use of wine for ceremonies and to administer five categories of production.[67] He expanded his domain to 7,000 li, just reaching the premises of Drunkenville. After doing so, he did not need to enforce law and punishment for forty years.

Later, from the age of King You 幽 and King Li 厲[68] up to the Qin and the Han, the Middle Kingdom was plagued with chaos and disorder. They had completely broken off from Drunkenville. Those among their vassals who cherished the Way all secretly went there on their own. Ruan Sizong [Ruan Ji], Tao Yuanming [Tao Qian], and ten or so others all roamed in the land of Drunkenville and never returned. When they died, they had themselves buried in the soil there. People in the Middle Kingdom thought that they became wine immortals.

Alas! Isn't the way of Drunkenville just like the state of Huaxu 華胥?[69] How simple and tranquil it is! I have had the fortune to visit this place; therefore I am writing it down for the record.

Drunkenville, obviously, is not a place but a state of mind. Its geography, climate, and inhabitants are all within the "Grand Harmony"; there is nothing to interrupt the constancy of the bland landscape, weather, or the temperament of its citizens, who occupy themselves in the aimless naturalness of the animal kingdom rather than in human social institutions or the arts. As we read Wang Ji's overview of Chinese history, we see that enlightened rulers relinquished control of mundane affairs and governed by paying proper respects to the power of wine. Unsuccessful rulers, even if they loved to drink, failed because they retained their desires and ambitions, or devised complicated rites and perplexing music, or in some such other way became "estranged from Drunkenville." To be in a state or "ville" of drunkenness is, in short, to be in harmony with the Way. As the *Liezi* and *Zhuangzi* describe Huaxu—to which Wang Ji compares his Drunkenville —this is to be "without grudge or regret," or "dread or envy," to be "unaware of what one is doing" or "where one is going."[70] Ruan Ji and Tao Qian, we discover, are among the handful of Drunkenville's residents, not because of their reclusion or virtue, but simply by virtue of their drunkenness.

Thus we are speaking not just of a literal but of a metaphorical drunkenness—which is why to dismiss Wang Ji as a "drunken poet" or to justify his alcoholism by exaggerating the turmoil of his times is to miss the point of his poetic persona. And missing this point has had a long history in commentary on Wang Ji. The Tang moralist and literary reform advocate Han Yu 韓愈 (768–842), for instance, first found Wang Ji's "Story of Drunkenville" unfitting for "the expression of a recluse who detached himself from the world"; instead it was an indication of his "utter devotion to palatal pleasure." Later Han Yu changed his opinion after reading the poetry of Ruan Ji and Tao Qian. He then concluded that Wang Ji wrote about getting drunk to escape his vexation at the world's injustice and to lament his "fellows in Drunkenville" who, like him, had not been born into a proper time (*buyu* 不遇).[71] Similarly, Cao Quan in the seventeenth century found himself initially shocked by the language of the "Story of Drunkenville," which he labeled as "absurd, unconventional, and unorthodox," and he concluded that Wang Ji was "a dispirited and self-indulgent person." Later he retracted this condemnation, arguing that Wang Ji's position in "an era of chaos and turmoil" was "like a bottle on the edge of a well" in constant danger of falling; thus, Cao concludes, Wang Ji "resorted to hiding in the land of stupor to relieve his worries and concerns."[72]

I, however, am arguing that Wang Ji represented himself "in the land of stupor" as a statement of philosophical opposition to the "worries and concerns" of the scholarly activity of his times. The endeavor to codify and canonize rites, music, literature, and other bureaucratic and intellectual institutions was motivated by a desire for a constancy that could not be attained except in a state of mind that, like a drunken stupor, blissfully accepts the ever-changing, illusory nature of knowledge. Hence the "Biography of Mr. Five Dippers" and "The Story of Drunkenville" should be our guides in reading Wang Ji's drinking poems because they so explicitly call attention to the way Wang Ji imagines drunkenness, metaphorically, as a state of "ultimate sobriety."

An additional illustration of this point may be found in the poem "Eight Quatrains Scribbled on Tavern Walls, no. 6":[73]

These days I constantly drink myself to a drunken stupor,	此日長昏飲
But it isn't to nurture my spirit or soul.	非關養性靈
Seeing that all others are drunk,	眼看人盡醉
How can I stand to be sober alone?	何忍獨為醒

At first glance Wang Ji seems merely to be recycling "the venerable theme of true sanity lying behind seeming insanity, in opposition to the true insanity which lies behind the seeming sanity of the world."[74] But in such a case one would expect the poet to distinguish himself from the drunkenness of others, not to be joining them. In fact this poem opposes a classical model that makes just this distinction: "The Fisherman" (Yufu 漁夫) in the *Chuci* anthology,[75] purporting to describe Qu Yuan, has its speaker defend his voluntary exile in terms of the contrast between drunkenness and sobriety. Qu Yuan laments:

The whole world is muddy; I alone remain pure. 　　舉世皆濁我獨清
All men are drunk; I alone stay sober. 　　　　　眾人皆醉我獨醒
For this I am sent into exile. 　　　　　　　　是以見放

The fisherman responds that Qu Yuan should rather "roll in the world's mud and splash in its waves," and "eat the world's lees and drink its wine," because "a sage is not hindered by things in the world and can move with the flow of the world." But Qu Yuan answers that he would rather stand against the crowd—the only sober man in a drunken world.

"The Fisherman" supplies Wang Ji with only the first model for his poem, however. Tao Qian reenacts the discourse of "The Fisherman" in his "Twenty Drinking Poems, no. 9,"[76] where he imagines himself admonished by a "well-intentioned farmer":

Dressed in rags beneath a roof of thatch 　　襤縷茅簷下
Is not the way a gentleman should live. 　　　未足為高栖
All the world agrees on what to do— 　　　　一世皆尚同
I hope that you will join the muddy game. 　　願君汨其泥

To this the poet replies:

My sincere thanks for your advice, old man. 　深感父老言
It is my nature that keeps me out of tune. 　　稟氣寡所諧
Though one can learn of course to pull the reins, 紆轡誠可學
To go against oneself is a real mistake. 　　　違己詎非迷
So let's just have a drink of this together— 　且共歡此飲
There's no turning back my carriage now. 　　吾駕不可回

Tao Qian, we see, redefines the idea of drunkenness that he found in the "The Fisherman." Rather than representing corruption or insanity, it provides solace for the virtuous man who faces a situation that cannot be helped. By offering his companion a drink he changes the subject of the conversation, distracting them both from the regrettable circumstance of his being "out of tune" with the world.

Tao Qian ascribes this circumstance to his nature rather than lofty principles, but his refusal to join the "muddy game" no less aligns him with Qu Yuan in withdrawing from worldly corruption to "nurture [his] spirit or soul," as Wang Ji reminds us in the subtle allusion of his poem's second line. One might reasonably assume that Wang Ji would find these images of reclusion, and at least Tao Qian's conception of drunkenness, satisfactory. But clearly he did not, given his question, "Seeing that all others are drunk, / How can I stand to be sober alone?" Wang Ji rebuffs Qu Yuan and Tao Qian by siding with the fisherman's and farmer's recommendation to "move with the flow" and "join the muddy game" by getting drunk with everyone else. The meaning of drunkenness for Wang Ji thus seems obscure or even to contradict the values of a recluse—until, that is, we abandon Qu Yuan's and Tao Qian's virtue versus corruption distinction, as Wang Ji everywhere does, and understand that this poem instead conceives of drunkenness in the "muddy" and muddled sense of the dream in *Zhuangzi*:

> While we dream, we do not know that we are dreaming, and in the middle of the dream we interpret a dream within it; but until we wake do we know that we are dreaming? Only at the ultimate awakening shall we know that this is the ultimate dream.[77]

There are dreams and there are dreams within dreams, and there is the ultimate dream that we mistake for wakefulness in this life. Correspondingly there is the world's drunkenness and there is Wang Ji's. And any determination on his part or ours to make hard and fast distinctions—to say which represents virtue and which corruption, which is really sobriety and which is just inebriation—is simply and always in vain. This pairing of the *Zhuangzi* dream state and drunkenness is made elsewhere by Wang Ji:

Scribbled on a Tavern Wall (題酒店壁)[78]

Last night, a bottle was just finished,	昨宵瓶始盡
This morning, a jar is opened right away.	今朝甕即開
After interpreting a dream in my dream,	夢中占夢罷
I still come back to the tavern.	還向酒家來

In this poem too, reality for the dreamer and the drunkard is illusory, and it is the enlightened man who comprehends that all human experience is as the dreamer's and drunkard's. In "Eight Quatrains Scribbled on Tavern Walls, no. 6," therefore, when Wang Ji sees "that all others are drunk," he is not leveling a condemnation but stating an insight into the inadequacy of human perception. And when he asks, "How can I stand to be sober alone?" he voices his acceptance of the fact that he, no more than anyone else, is able to skirt the limitations of human perceptions. In accepting this fact, however, and with such equanimity, Wang Ji does distinguish himself from his literary models and from his contemporaries. He is a drunkard in one other sense. For in his perception that an ever-changing world makes all knowledge illusory, he is an enlightened man who understands that his capacity to perceive "ultimate reality" (*Zhuangzi*'s "ultimate awakening") is analogous to the drunken man's condition in relation to what the world judges to be sobriety.

5
"You Beishan fu"
and the Problem of Knowing

❀

THREE YEARS BEFORE Wang Ji died, sometime around 641, he composed "You Beishan fu" 遊北山賦 (*Fu* on roaming the Northern Mountains), the longest *fu* piece in his extant corpus.[1] The title indicates its mode as "travel writing" (*you* 遊: to wander, to roam, to go on an excursion), and the setting—Beishan (the Northern Mountains)—is recognized as the site of Wang Tong's residence and school. The journey prompts Wang Ji to reminisce on his past and his family, so scholars have valued it as a source of biographical information on Wang Ji and his brother. But there has never been a study of "You Beishan fu," in any language, which has attempted a comprehensive critical analysis of the poem. This chapter offers such an analysis and shows how "You Beishan fu" represents Wang Ji's most elaborate and sophisticated example of the poetic strategy we have observed in preceding chapters. That is: "You Beishan fu," like Wang Ji's "On Ancient Themes" series, his "To Myself When Sitting Alone on the Mountain," and his "Eight Quatrains Scribbled on Tavern Walls, no. 6," personifies in the character of its speaker the idea of the permanence-of-impermanence and the illusory nature of the phenomenal world and human knowledge. Like those other poems, this piece forces readers to experience these concepts in the way it exploits ambiguities and unexpected shifts of perspective. As we shall see, "You Beishan fu" is in fact Wang Ji's tour de force in this vein, in the remarkable way that it sustains, over the course of its 434-line length, its manifestation of "constant inconstancy" in a persona who refuses to be grasped.[2]

Wang Ji opens "You Beishan fu" with a preface that serves three functions. First, he asserts his innate nobility by claiming descent from an ancient and hallowed family:

We are the people of Zhou. Our original family home was in Qi. During the Yongjia era [307–312], my ancestor accompanied the Jin emperor to the south. Our land truly nurtures learned men; many of our people are exalted and prominent. Duke Mu was mortified by the Jianyuan affairs and returned to Luoyang. Tongzhou was saddened by the Yongan events and retired to the river bend. It began with Jinyang founding a fief and ended with Ankang receiving a plot of land; our forefathers lived here and they were buried here. In a flash of time, five generations have passed. The mulberry and elm trees are now grown to their maturity; soon they will be a hundred years old.

Here Wang Ji is following the convention established by Qu Yuan in "Li sao" 離騷, which opens similarly with a declaration of the poet's noble pedigree. Wang Ji identifies himself as one in a long line of moral descendants from an illustrious royal family, the Zhou, who are "learned" (*ru* 儒, as in "learned in Confucian learning") and "exalted and prominent." He boasts especially of his two ancestors, Wang Qiu and Wang Yan (by their posthumous titles Duke Mu of Jinyang and Sir Tongzhou), who both withdrew from office when the court they served was plagued by troubles.[3] In this way, Wang Ji implies his own nobility and integrity.

Second, he asserts a parallel spiritual kinship with famous recluses of the past:

I, Wang Ji, have always cherished a passion for the Southern Mountain.[4] It is growing stronger as I advance in age. On the eastern slope, I attend my farm in leisure, carefree and self-content. I have more wine crocks than the Infantry Commandant and a bigger rice field than the Magistrate of Pengze.[5] Like Huangfu Mi, I wish to live out my life on the farm.[6] Like Zhongchang Tong, I too am content with just my garden and grove.[7]

Living alone on the southern islet, I come often to roam about in the Northern Mountains. I take joy in idly passing my days. Without realizing it, years have passed and I have not thought about turning back. I have gone westward all the way to Horse Valley and reached as far north as Ox Creek.

Mountains and ravines remain the same; everywhere I look, wind and mist meet the eye. Sun Deng sat in silence, facing Xi Kang and Ruan Ji without a word;[8] Wang Ba lived in seclusion, taking his wife and children with him and leaving the world behind.[9] Their windows opened to water and rocks; their stone steps wound through pine and bamboo groves. The singing of "Return to the Country," that too was a long time ago.[10] Looking at the familiar path in the mountain groves, how long it extends indeed!

Wang Ji in this passage makes no effort to justify, defend, or apologize for his departure from his ancestors' career track. He has not been forced into reclusion by unfavorable times. He says he is content, lacking all ambition, desire, and anxiety. In the first section of the preface he used the image of full-grown mulberry and elm trees to remind readers of his family's deep roots in Confucian tradition. But here he reroots himself in the recluse tradition by his reference to "the familiar path in the mountain groves." With the title of this *fu* in mind—and having just read of Wang Ji's enjoyment in roaming the Northern Mountains—we are on the one hand invited to take the phrase "the familiar path in the mountain groves" literally, referring to a path he has so often traveled. On the other hand, the phrase "mountain groves" (*shanlin* 山林) is a stock image in Chinese literature signifying both the residence of the recluse and, metonymically, a life of reclusion.

And third, Wang Ji declares his serious intentions in this piece by reiterating two classical statements on the nature of literature:

> One's intent of mind (*zhi* 志) goes into poetry; *fu* is one branch of poetry. I therefore draw together my brief thoughts and present them in this *fu*.

In these sentences, discussed in Chapter 1 in the context of Sui and early Tang literary thought, we see an invocation of two ancient and orthodox statements concerning the nature of poetry and *fu*: the first is from the "Great Preface" of the *Book of Songs*;[11] the second is Ban Gu's famous defense of *fu* in response to the criticism, most notably Yang Xiong's, that *fu* lacks moral and didactic purpose.[12] There is no mistaking the import of these references: Wang Ji is requesting that we take him seriously and take especial note of his intention in this *fu* to communicate his *zhi*. "Intent of mind" is how I have translated this term, but "*zhi*" also captures the notion of "a scholar's heart" or "mind," connoting specifically a *moral mind*, implying the poet's resolve to acquire a moral mind and live a moral life.

This announcement of such a serious and noble aim has had its unfortunate consequences. When Lu Chun compiled his abridged three-*juan* edition of Wang Ji's collected works, "You Beishan fu" was the only piece he selected for the *fu* section—presumably because it appears to declare Wang Ji's "resolve (*zhi*) to hang up his officer's cap and untie his officer's tassel."[13] Moreover, the Song editors of the monumental literary anthology *Wenyuan yinghua* classified Wang Ji's "You Beishan fu" under the category *zhi*. As we have observed, the title suggests it belongs to a genre of writing in which an excursion to a site is recounted poetically, a genre that often contains the expression of personal emotions, private thoughts, and sometimes the poet's comprehension of profound ideas (traditionally a type of writing classified as *youlan* 遊覽 or *yanzhi* 言志). Travel had long been a popular motif among Chinese poets for projecting their thoughts and emotions outward, onto nature, and for linking these thoughts and emotions with their perspectives on the natural world and the cosmos beyond. Qu Yuan's "Li sao" is the great prototype in that it represents a scholar of noble descent and great moral quality who is rejected by a corrupt world. In frustration he leaves, first wandering through the mountains and then flying on a mystical quest for a goddess who will appreciate his virtue.[14]

Han *fu* writers expanded the travel theme to include not only imaginary but apparently genuine journeys that were accompanied by inward reflections of the speaker, usually a dejected or displaced scholar who in the end reaches both his geographic destination and some kind of resolution in his mind.[15] By the Six Dynasties period, the vogue of philosophical discourse on *Laozi* and *Zhuangzi* and on Buddhist religious ideas, as well as the experiment with *xuanyan* (words of the abstruse) poetry, influenced the course of travel writing and landscape literature as it did other literary forms and themes. (See my discussion in Chapter 1.) The theme of the mountain journey was especially popular, and the poetry of Sun Chuo and Xie Lingyun may be taken as representative of its treatment. Their journeys are no longer searches for an inner self or a personal, moral resolution; instead the wandering narrator's experiences in nature lead to a perception of the universe's mysteries; by the end of his journey he is enlightened to an "ultimate wisdom" or reaches "spiritual salvation" in a Buddhist sense.[16]

As we shall see, the narrator of Wang Ji's *fu* is no melancholy wanderer or frustrated scholar tormented by moral dilemmas or self-doubt. Right from the start he declares himself a free-spirited man who is already enlightened because he rejects the conventional values of the mundane world and spurns any attempt to grasp "Heaven's Way." His journey has no purpose but to "give free rein to [his] heart" and to "take pleasure in cultivating a placid mind." He begins his journey resolved on his course and ends with the same resolve. Thus there is no progression from dejection to reflection to self-discovery, as we expect in *sao*-style poetry and travelogue *fu*. Nor do we find the spiritual revelation or philosophical enlightenment that we see in the poetic journeys of Sun Chuo and Xie Lingyun.

Yet in contrast to the consistency and clarity of the narrator's repeatedly announced resolve, we experience persistent ambiguities throughout the narrated journey. I believe that these ambiguities serve a crucial function in Wang Ji's "You Beishan fu." Geographic locations, for instance, are at times specific and at other times remarkably vague. Except in the one section devoted to the site of his brother's school, the speaker never identifies any of the places he passes along the way: we are given only generic nominals, such as mountain peak, cliffs, woods, and creeks, or an indication of directional relations, as in "southern bay" and "northern woods," which seem designed more to satisfy the conventions of the parallel couplet than to convey location. We are confronted, too, with sudden changes in scene that disrupt any sense of a journey. The speaker's efforts to transform his resolution into action prove contradictory. Even at the level of syntax, unexpected shifts in the grammatical subject force us to keep redetermining who is doing what.

The *fu* challenges us, as well, with its eclectic abundance of allusions. Many of these are applied as convention would demand, so that informed readers have no trouble recognizing their logical application to the moment. But Wang Ji regularly uses allusions in three very ambiguous ways. First, he makes well-known allusions that readers can be counted on to recognize as logical in the immediate context of a line, but their sense in the larger context of the passage is puzzling. Second, he combines fragments of recognizable phrases from different sources, making it difficult to pin down the point of the allusion. And third, Wang Ji seems at times to rely on mere fragments of familiar phrases, making it difficult to know at any particular instance even if an allusion is intended. The result: readers of "You Beishan fu" have found Wang Ji's allusions such a confusing hodgepodge that they often conclude he is merely, and clumsily, showing off his learning.

The bewildering progression of "You Beishan fu" similarly unsettles and disappoints readers—it fails to satisfy the expectations raised by the preface and the conventions of its genre. Is Wang Ji just an inferior writer of *fu*? I think not. For one thing, in his other three extant *fu* he is certainly able to employ allusions logically and clearly toward specific points. Moreover, he appears to have had a reputation among his contemporaries as a skilled writer of *fu*. The accomplished poet Xue Daoheng 薛道衡 (540–609), for instance, was reported to have been so impressed by Wang Ji's "*Fu* Remembering Yu upon Ascending Longmen" (Deng Longmen yi Yu fu 登龍門憶禹賦, now lost) that he called Wang Ji "the Yu Xin of our time" (今之庾信也).[17] Is "You Beishan fu," then, Wang Ji's failure? In my view, there is a far more profitable question to ask: what is Wang Ji trying to accomplish in "You Beishan fu"?

I suggest Wang Ji is challenging, by destabilizing, the very notion of resolution. After opening the poem with a declaration of his intent, the speaker sets out to put this *zhi* into action—but this journey has no clear direction, and he finds himself in a "place" inconsistent with his original intentions. The speaker then repeats his resolve, but again we find him in an unexpected location, expressing unexpected sentiments. He repeats his resolve once again, more emphatically, but as the poem concludes we find that the ambiguity of this resolution is again apparent. In other words: embracing the wisdom that he knows propels the speaker on a journey to discover the illusoriness of knowledge; resolution turns to dissolution, again and again, as it must in a world where impermanence is the only permanence and knowledge of the phenomenal world ultimately proves illusory. These constants, "You Beishan fu" would remind us, apply as much to a person's *zhi* as to everything else.

Let us turn now to the text of the poem. It begins with the speaker making a series of pronouncements that, as we shall see, appear to establish once and for all his state of mind and philosophy of life:

	Heaven's Way is vast and extensive;	天道悠悠
	Human life is but a fleeting passage.	人生若浮
	Ancient sages and worthies	古來聖賢
	Have now all become the departed.	皆成去留
5	High lords with eight eyebrows and four nipples[18]	八眉四乳
	And sovereigns with dragon faces and phoenix heads[19]	龍顏鳳頭
	Were burdened with distress for a lifetime,	殷憂一代
	But now lie withered for thousands of years.	零落千秋
	Briefly they faced south,[20]	暫時南山
10	Then one by one they roamed north.[21]	相將北遊
	Their jade halls and gilded chaises marked their grand accomplishments,	玉殿金輿之大業
	Their sacrifices to heaven and earth returned them great blessings.	郊天祭地之洪休
	They held high honors and heavy responsibilities,[22]	榮深責重
	But their joys could not compensate for their worries.	樂不供愁

15	Would it be less true for chancellors and ministers several decades in power?[23]	何況數十年之宰相
	Or dukes and marquis with five-hundred-league fiefs?	五百里之公侯
	They are cautious and vigilant, studious and unrelenting,	兢兢業業
	Always brooding, always concerned.	長思長憂
	In the past, people faulted Yan Zhao and Han Wu,[24]	昔怪燕昭與漢武
20	But now we can see why they quested for immortality.	今識圖仙之有由
	Who wouldn't want to be immortal?	人誰不願
	It is simply difficult to attain.	直是難求
	When hearing the story of Tripod Lake, men wanted to believe it,[25]	聞鼎湖而欲信
	And found it strange that a tomb was built on Qiaoshan.[26]	怪橋山之遽修
25	Jade Terrace and Golden Portal—	玉臺金闕
	They are in the middle of the vast sea!	大海水之中流
	Carnelian Grove and Prase Trees—	瓊林碧樹
	They are on the top of Mount Kunlun![27]	崑崙山之上頭
	But one cannot fly there like a swift stone-swallow,[28]	不得輕飛如石鷰
30	So it would only be a vain effort to ride on an earthen ox.[29]	終是徒勞乘土牛

The *fu* opens with a clichéd but forceful statement contrasting the infinite and constant Way of heaven with the finite and transitory existence of human beings. This contrast is then exemplified by a review of the fates of ancient sages, the legendary lords, the sovereigns, and even noble lords and statesmen—those who are admired, honored, and emulated. Though they may be immortalized in memory for their teaching, virtues, or accomplishments, they are still confined by their mortality and are mere transients in this world. The opposition between what is constant and what is transitory is stressed by the many opposing pairs in the passage's couplets: some are direct and obvious; others are indirect and implied. In lines 3 and 4, for example, we see *gulai* 古來 versus *quliu* 去留 (containing the suffix "come" versus the prefix "go"); in lines 7 and 8, *yidai* 一代 versus *qianqiu* 千秋 ("a lifetime," which is temporary, versus "thousands of years," which implies an everlasting span of time); in lines 9 and 10, *zanshi* 暫時 versus *xiangjiang* 相將 ("briefly" versus "one after another," a recurring pattern); *nanmian* 南面 versus *beiyou* 北遊 ("facing south," an idiomatic expression for occupying the throne, indicating great success in life, versus "roaming north," a euphemism for being dead, when worldy success is irrelevant). The tone in these lines is somewhere between mockery and sympathetic praise. The speaker does not belittle or criticize, for he grants these men their great accomplishments, yet he does focus on their anxieties: they were "burden(ed) with distress," "brooding" and "concerned," their "joys could not compensate for their worries." Such phrases diminish the glory of these honorable heroes. In effect, they are made to look pitiable despite their suprahuman status or illustrious positions.

Having so denied the possibility of human effort to achieve permanent success and power, the speaker turns to the alternative permanence that people desire—immortality—by citing two figures famed for their enthusiastic pursuit of this goal: Prince Zhao of Yan (Warring States period) and Emperor Wu of Han (lines 19–24). They were the targets of criticism and objects of ridicule in many scholars' writings on account of their relentless search for the Islands of Immortals and their desire to discover immortal drugs. Emperor Wu, for instance, was castigated by both Ban Gu and Zhang Heng in their rhapsodies on the western capital for believing in the ludicrous claims of street magicians and alchemists and bestowing on them wealth and power.[30] And Guo Pu, in one of his "Poems on Wandering Immortals" (Youxian shi 遊仙詩, no. 6), sneeringly remarked: "Yanzhao lacked the *qi* for a numen; / Han Wu is no material for an immortal."[31] The speaker of "You Beishan fu," by contrast, is not critical but understanding. He asserts that indeed it is everyone's wish to be immortal, and he does not refute the existence of an immortal world. But he does deny that humans can ever discover the path to immortality, and this leads him to the declaration of his *zhi* in the following lines:

Enough!	已矣哉
From this I can see that this is the way the world is,	世事自此而可見
Why then be distressed about it?	何為而惘惘
I forsake oracle bones and milfoil and divine no more;	棄卜筮而不占
I entrust my heart with a free rein to take me far away.	餘將縱心而長往
35 Following the natural course, I wander alone;	任物孤遊
Leaving behind all my sentiments, I travel straight up.[32]	遺情直上

	I find the words of Laozi and Buddha too prolix;	覺老釋之言煩
	I despise King Wen and Confucius for itching to show off their talents.[33]	恨文宣之技癢
	The course of things changes or shifts,	彼事業之遷斥
40	How can divine gods control it?	豈神明之宰掌
	As for things, there is no medium but they still become plain;[34]	物無往而咸彰
	And for lives, so long as there is sustenance they inevitably will be nurtured.	生有資而必養
	I sigh at the diminishing of the Great Way;	嗟大道之泯沒
	I see how human nature is twisted.	見人情之委枉
45	The *Book of Rites* wastes our time on a thousand ceremonies;	禮費日於千儀
	The *Book of Changes* toils our mind with myriad images.	易勞心於萬象
	Scrutinizing these endless contrivances,[35]	審機事之不息
	I realize that the source has been defiled for too long.	知澆源之浸長
	Why do birds get entangled in snares?	鳥何事而嬰羅
50	How do fish end up trapped in nets?	魚為何而在網
	Living creatures in the world are peculiar and obscure;	生物詭隔
	The divine spirits are mysterious and impalpable.	精靈忽怳
	Zhuangzi pondered for three months without stepping in the court;[36]	莊周三月而不朝
	Siddhartha spent six years absorbed in contemplation.[37]	瞿曇六年而遐想
55	That was the case for men like them,	有是夫
	How much more so for me, unequal to the ancient wise men!	況吾之不如先 達矣
	I will withdraw from the world and disengage myself,	請交息而自逸
	Simply to take pleasure in cultivating a placid mind!	聊習靜而為娛

The opening exclamation of this section—"Enough!"—echoes the first line of the coda in Qu Yuan's "Encountering Sorrow," invoking the *sao*-style closing in which the frustrated and weary moral hero announces his resolve to make his final withdrawal from a hostile world that has repeatedly rejected him. Yet, contrary to the implications of this allusion, it is

Wang Ji's speaker who is voluntarily rejecting the world and dismissing the hallowed teachings and traditions that provide the world with its moral framework. Lines 37 and 38, perhaps Wang Ji's most famous and most frequently cited words in this vein, show his antitraditional, anti-Confucian beliefs. But we see in this passage that he attacks not only sages sacred in the Confucian tradition, King Wen and Confucius himself, but also those sacred to other traditions, Laozi and Buddha. And not only is the *Book of Rites* said to "waste our time on a thousand ceremonies," but the *Book of Changes* too "toils our mind with myriad images." Taking into view this whole passage, we realize the speaker is challenging all the conventional assumptions of what there is to know and how that knowledge is acquired. Those who search the canonical texts for wisdom, turn to oracle bones and milfoil for foreknowledge, or hope that through Zhuangzi or Siddhartha they will acquire insight into the mysteries of the universe, all are doomed to failure. For "the course of things changes or shifts," the Great Way is always, incomprehensibly, shifting—always outside the grasp of human understanding.

Of course, the poem presents this insight as the *real* wisdom to be acquired: the speaker comprehends a fundamental truth about humankind and the Way that others have not. And with this privileged knowledge he confidently announces that he will free himself from the constraints of human ambition and desire, abandon all conventional aspirations, and simply follow the course of nature, taking pleasure only in "cultivating a placid mind." But now the speaker must turn this *zhi* into action, and we see immediately that something goes awry:

	So I push through the shady woods,	乃披林城
60	And scale the steep terrain.	進陟巖區
	A chain of peaks rises and falls;	連峰雜起
	A succession of bluffs coils and winds.	複障環紆
	I comb the cinnabar precipice, searching for a cut-off path;	歷丹危而尋絕徑
	I climb the verdant scarps, looking for a remote trail.	攀翠嶮而覓條塗
65	My soaring spirit is lifted above the auroral road,	聳飛情於霞道
	My wandering mind is sent flying over the misty way.	振逸想於煙衢
	Trees in the thick forest amass and conjoin, neatly arrayed.	重林合沓而齊列
	Fallen boulders from collapsed cliffs support each other.	崩巖磊砢而相扶

I glimpse the deep gloom of the steep gully, 賭森沉於絶磵

70 And gaze at the glaring bright of the towering ridge. 視晃朗於高嶼

I think of beating the whirlwind and flying out of
this dusty world,[38] 自謂搏風飈而
出埃壒

Far away, to attend court in the Dark Palace and
pay a visit to the Purple Capital.[39] 邈若朝玄宮而
謁紫都

But from beneath the emerald crest, 碧巒之下

By the bend of a green creek,[40] 青溪之曲

75 Looking out at the murky dimness, I can barely see
through; 望隱隱而裁通

Hearing their faint voices, I cannot be among them. 聽微微而不屬

Longingly, I crane my neck 眷然引領

And stomp my feet. 茲焉頓足

The opening lines convey a strong impression of haste. The pace of the verse is swift, and we see the speaker "push," "scale," "comb," and "climb," "searching" and "looking" through the mountain terrain. Even when he is not moving physically, as in lines 65–66, his mind is busy and flitting, very far from "placid": his already soaring spirit is "lifted up" even higher; and his already wandering mind is "sent flying." The redundancy of these lines bespeaks restlessness. Even the object-oriented lines in the passage contain activity, as inanimate objects of the natural world come to life in the eyes of our speaker: the mountain peaks "rise and fall," the bluffs "coil and wind," trees "amass and conjoin," boulders "support each other."

More surprising still, the speaker is searching for something beyond the human world, something in another realm, and his failure disappoints him: "Longingly, I crane my neck / And stomp my feet." What exactly is he searching for? Is he seeking guidance? Wisdom? We do not know. But we do know that all of this is inconsistent with the resolution that prompted this journey "through the shady woods" in the first place. We must ask ourselves: does this speaker know his mind?

Curious to learn how he will respond to his experience, we read on:

I wind my way around the rocks crowding the path, 步擁路而邅迴

80 I see the sprawling clouds separating and joining. 視橫煙而斷續

Age-old creepers trail their purple vines, 古藤曳紫

Cold lichens spread out their green hues. 寒苔布綠

Inside a grotto, I steal a glance at sacred writing;[41]　洞裏窺書

On the edge of a cliff, I come across an unfinished　巖邊對局
game of chess.[42]

85　There are vague traces of nymphs' passing;[43]　仿佛靈蹤

Faintly, I can make out the transcendents' footprints.　依稀仙躅

How many ages has gold been fused in　爐何代而銷金
this cauldron?

How many years has jade been swirling in this cup?　杯何年而溜玉

The stone chamber is dark and misty;　石室幽藹

90　The cinnabar pit gleams and glitters.　沙場照燭

Pine trees sough in the swirling wind;　松落落而風迴

Cinnamon trees are luxuriant, moistened with dew.　桂蒼蒼而露溥

Before the moon has tilted west, its brilliance is　月未側而先陰
already dimmed;

Just as the glow of dawn issues forth, there already　霞方昇而已旭
rises the radiant sun.

95　Delighted at the vast span of the yonder realm,　喜方外之浩曠

I sigh at the confinement and restraint of the　歎人間之窘束
human world.

In this passage the dejected speaker, turning from the site of his disap-
pointment, slowly winds his way down the mountain and even pauses now
and again to gaze about at the sights, only to discover himself suddenly
walking right into the environs of the transcendents. He finds himself
peeking at divine writings barred even to Xi Kang's sight, and he sees a
chess game presumably just played by a pair of transcendents. Unlike the
woodcutter in the *Shuyi ji* to whom Wang Ji is alluding, the speaker does
not actually see transcendents playing the game, for once again he seems
to have missed his chance. He finds only "traces" and "footprints" that hint
at their passing. And as his view broadens, turning from individual items—
a scroll, a chessboard, the traces and footprints on the ground, a cauldron,
a cup—to the surrounding stone chamber, the cinnabar pit, and finally the
horizon that divides this realm and the yonder realm, he catches a glimpse
of the other world, a world so vast that it accommodates the moon and the
sun at the same time, a universe where time passes almost without notice.
This glimpse reminds him of "the confinement and restraint of the human
world," and he releases a sigh. Again he seems frustrated at his inability to
enter the other realm; and again we must ask what happened to his resolve.

But abruptly the speaker finds himself next at the open front door of the transcendents. And this, as we observe in the following lines, prompts him to reaffirm his *zhi*:

And then—
In the secluded valley hides the Realized One, 況乃幽谷藏真
No one else lives around him. 傍無四鄰
His purple chamber is left ajar, 紫房半掩
100　And the dark pedestal is still new.[44] 玄壇尚新
I come upon the hermit from Langfeng,[45] 逢閬風之逸客
And encounter the old man from Penglai. 值蓬萊之故人
One casually leans on the sterculia tree, staff in hand; 忽據梧而策杖
He drapes fur over his shoulder and carries 亦披裘而負薪
　　firewood on his back.[46]
105　The other is clothed with a lotus gown and girdled 荷衣薜帶
　　by a fig-leaf belt;
He holds a goosefoot-branch staff and wears a 藜杖葛巾
　　kudzu-vine scarf.
They go out to the mushroom fields to count the 出芝田而計畝
　　acres;[47]
They go to the Peach Blossom Spring to inquire of 入桃園而問津
　　the ford.[48]
Mount Kunlun seems ground into pebbles, 崑山若礪
110　The Great Gulf stirs up dust.[49] 渤澥揚塵
How many days does it take to plant the jade 栽碧奈而何日
　　apples?[50]
How many springs does it take to sow the carnelian 種瓊瓜而幾春
　　melons?
There is a natural peculiarity and mystery about 自然詭異
　　them;
They are not just your ordinary recluses.[51] 非徒隱淪

115　They also have the divine bones of the Highest 乃有上元仙骨
　　Prime[52]
And the magic hands of the Greatest Clarity.[53] 太清神手
They send lightning running and thunder dashing; 走電奔雷
They uproot the hollow and transplant the 耘空蒔朽
　　decayed.[54]
Hejian could not match their power with his skills;[55] 河間之業不齊貫
120　Huainan lacks the acumen to master their arts.[56] 淮南之術無靈受

With one spell, they move the Southern Winnowing Basket; 咒動南箕

Tossing a charm, they turn the Northern Dipper around.[57] 符迴北斗

Woquan brings them herbs as tribute; 偓佺贈藥

Magu presents them wine as offering.[58] 麻姑送酒

125 The Green Dragon waits in attendance at Jiachen; 青龍就養於甲晨

The Black Ox confines itself to Yichou.[59] 玄牛自拘於乙丑

Long have they cared for the world's affairs, 永懷世事

For as long as heaven and earth have lasted. 天地長久

They watch over the people in the profane world, 顧瞻流俗

130 Their cheeks rosy, their hair white. 紅顏白首

Since it is possible to live a thousand years, 儻千歲之可營

Why then do I slight the idea? 亦何為而自輕

I heard that gentlemen of the past 昔時君子

Once made journey to the world above.[60] 曾聞上征

135 Now I suddenly come upon these true visitors;[61] 忽逢真客

I venture to ask them about the scripture of transcendence. 試問仙經

They tell me it is easy to imbibe the Nine Blossoms;[62] 談九華之易就

They say it is possible to perfect the Three Splendors.[63] 敘三英之可成

They rub the cinnabar cauldron and blend the stone marrow, 拭丹鑪而調石髓

140 Coiling steam rises from the green pot, golden elixir appears. 裛翠釜而出金精

It flows like a stream of pearls, congeals like jade pieces, 珠流玉結

Glitters like snow, and glistens like frost. 雪曜霜明

Both say that a pinchful is all it will take 咸謂刀圭暫進

To send the cloud carriages rushing down to greet me. 足使雲車下迎

145 How narrow the vision of my fellow men; 紛吾人之狹見

They are stirred by numerous doubts, but I brush them aside.[64] 攪群疑而自拂

If I am content wherever I set foot,[65] 使投足而咸安

	Why would I need this stuff?	亦何為乎此物
	The Vermilion Wall and the Dark Garden,[66]	彼赤城與玄圃
150	Can it be they are made up out of nothing?	豈憑虛而構窟
	Just as unreal as the moon on the water,	但水月之非真
	Or as shapeless as sound and color?	譬聲色之無佛
	How wrong was Liu Xiang!	過矣劉向
	How pathetic was Ge Hong![67]	吁嗟葛洪
155	They tied their hopes to shadows,	指期繫影
	Relied on their tricks to catch the wind.	依方捕風
	But who can leave this world?	誰能離世
	Where can one go to escape into the void?	何處逃空
	Suppose one is able to roam all the golden chambers in cave heavens in the eight directions	假使遊八洞之 金室
160	Or sit in all the jade palaces in the realms of the Three Clarities,[68]	坐三清之玉宮
	As has always been yearned and anxiously craved.	長懷企羨
	Would that not be like living in a cage all the same?	豈非樊籠
	Why bother to toil on the sea!	徒勞海上
	Why waste energy in the clouds!	何事雲中
165	In the past, Jiang Yuanxu stayed on his three paths;[69]	昔蔣元詡之三逕
	Tao Yuanming lived by his five willow trees;[70]	陶淵明之五柳
	Junping told fortunes by the market gate;[71]	君平坐卜於市門
	Zizhen took up his plow at the mouth of the gully.[72]	子真躬耕於谷口
	They either shielded themselves behind their gates and walls,	或託闤閈
170	Or hid themselves in mountains and marshes.	或潛山藪
	They all complied with their innate natures and shared the same joy.	咸遂性而同樂
	Were they going against the norm by holding fast to their own ways?	豈違方而別守
	I, too, have no other desire;	余亦無求
	So here I am, roaming in solitude.	斯焉獨遊

The first part of this section is startling when we recall the speaker's assertion that immortality, though coveted by everyone, is unattainable:

here it almost seems dropped in his lap, yet he rejects it. What has become of the speaker who asked, "Who wouldn't want to be immortal?" The answer may lie in the frustrating obscurity of this passage (which gets much smoothed over in the process of translation). This obscurity undermines, not only the apparent ease with which the speaker encounters the transcendents and is invited by them to cross over into their world, but also the reliability of our grasp of the speaker's mind and experience. The identity of these transcendents, for instance, is never made clear, even though elements of their description are familiar. The man who "drapes fur over his shoulder and carries firewood on his back" fits the description of the famous legendary recluse Piqiugong 披裘公 (literally "the man who drapes fur over his shoulder"); the adornment of the other man, with fragrant herbs, a conventional symbol of moral purity first seen in Qu Yuan's "Li sao," invites us to recognize a disengaged moral hero. But then the speaker also notes that "there is a natural peculiarity and mystery about them" and "they are not just your ordinary recluses" (lines 113–114). Indeed he recognizes that they are immortals from different temporal and spatial realms: one is a visitor from the "Highest Prime" (上元), the beginning of time, and the other descends from the "Greatest Clarity" (太清), the highest celestial realm (lines 115–116). In the end we must agree with the speaker that the pair are too extraordinary to be earthly recluses, though their identities remain ambiguous.

The more disruptive ambiguities arise in the narrative of the encounter, which forces us to keep revising our understanding of the grammatical subjects and referents. The subject "I" in the couplet "Since it is possible to live a thousand years, / Why then do I slight the idea?" (lines 131–132), for instance, can easily be read as "they" since it is sandwiched between the description of the godlike visitors and the speaker's entrance. The same ambiguity occurs when the speaker refutes the idea of attaining immortality through the elixir (lines 137–146): who is the "they" that the "I" criticizes—ordinary men who do not know better? Or the two visitors who ought to know better?

Such obscurities make us wonder for whom the reconfirmation of resolve at the end of the passage is intended. Is it we who need to be reminded or the speaker? To this point the "journey" has only contradicted his resolve: he has seemed at times obsessed with the immortal world that he condemned others for striving to grasp; now he again rejects immortality and vows again to live the life of past model recluses. Are we to accept the speaker's resolution this time as one strengthened by experience?

Perhaps we would be wiser to read this second declaration of his *zhi* in a way that undermines the very concept of *zhi*—that is, to take his resolution provisionally because we have seen its variability.

As if to guard against such a skeptical reading, Wang Ji moves in the next section into a clear and consistent representation of the speaker putting his idea of detachment into action:

175	It happens to be a time when the world is restless,[73]	屬天下之多事
	And the mountains are enticing me to stay.	遇山中之可留
	Simply whiling away my time,	聊將度日
	Suddenly it is already into autumn.	忽已經秋
	Chrysanthemums bloom everywhere on the banks;	菊花兩岸
180	Pine trees sough all over the hill.	松聲一丘
	I cannot toil my heart to preserve the Way,	不能役心而守道
	So I will entrust myself to fate and drift with its flow.	故將委運而乘流
	In the vast and open woods and ravines,[74]	伊林磵之虛受
	Where woodcutters and hermits take their shelter,	固樵隱之俱託
185	I chance upon a visitor from the past in midstream,	逢故客於中流
	And encounter a rejuvenated man at a sheer precipice.	遇還童於絕壑
	Cloud-covered peaks are piled up like tortoise shells;	雲峰龜甲而重聚
	Auroral-hued cliffs interlink like dragon scales.	霞壁龍鱗而結絡
	Water flows out to the inlet, plashing and splashing.	水出浦而淺淺
190	Fog envelops the stream, thick and dense.	霧合川而漠漠
	How delightful, how enjoyable!	是欣是賞
	I roam and I rove.	爰遊爰豫
	Weaving hanging moss into a curtain, I greet the night;	結羅幌而迎宵
	Opening up my thatched hut, I wait for the dawn.	敞茅軒而待曙
195	Wild tree limbs snarl and tangle in a jumble;	爾其雜枝相糾
	Long branches crisscross and intertwine.	長條交茹
	Leaves rustle and gibbons come;	葉動猿來
	Flowers are startled and birds fly away.	花驚鳥去
	It would excite a young lord's special delight	起公子之殊賞
200	And dispel a prince's remote anxiety.	澹王孫之遠慮

I explore the recess of mountains and streams;	山水幽尋
Amid the wind and clouds, trails run deep.	風雲路深
A magnolia window opens out halfway;	蘭窗左闢
A mushroom chamber overlooks the ravine.	茵蕪邪臨
205 A boulder crouches over the steps like a tiger;	石階當而虎踞
A stream running by the window growls like a dragon.	泉度牖而龍吟
The moon shines over the southern bay;	月照南浦
Mist rises from the northern grove.	煙生北林
Enjoying the new pleasure in the mountains and ravines,	閱丘壑之新趣
210 My mind, always fond of rivers and lakes, drifts free.	縱江湖之舊心
Roads come together at my chamber,	道集吾室
Wind brushes against my lapel.	風吹我襟
I sip the fine wine brewed with pine flowers and cypress leaves,[75]	松花柏葉之淳酎
And play the plain zither with phoenix feet and dragon lips.[76]	鳳翮龍唇之素琴

The speaker seems at last truly to be living out his intention to give his heart "free rein," to follow "the natural course." He is oblivious of his direction and the passage of time. And in contrast to his first journey into the wilderness, where the natural features of the landscape (the steep gulley, towering ridge, emerald crest, and green creek) were barriers preventing his crossing into another realm (lines 67–76), now these features shield him from the restless world. The description in this section, moreover, has a tranquil tone. The speaker's movements are minimal ("Weaving hanging moss into a curtain, I greet the night; / Opening up my thatched hut, I wait for the dawn"), and he explores his surroundings mostly by watching and listening. He seems finally to have attained a "placid mind": he is "enjoying the new pleasure in the mountains and ravines," not searching for something beyond them; he lets his mind "drift freely," as he first resolved.

Yet the passage contains, in lines 193–200, two barely veiled indications that the speaker's resolution may not be as fixed as he insists. First, the language of these lines is reminiscent of Qu Yuan's "Li sao" and, even more so, "Summoning the Recluse," a poem in the *Chuci* anthology that is attributed to Liu An. In Qu Yuan's poem, the speaker grows increasingly frustrated and mournful as he continues his journey in solitude. He yearns to find a companion, only to be cruelly reminded that he is alone in the world. And Liu An's poem attempts to summon a recluse out of, not into, a life of reclusion. Second, the language used to describe the mountain in Liu An's poem, which Wang Ji echoes in his references to the tangled undergrowth and wild animals, is meant to frighten the recluse, impressing on him how hostile the wilderness is, so that he may learn he is in no place for a princely gentleman. In sum, when the speaker of "You Beishan fu" comments with joy, "It would excite a young lord's special delight, / And dispel a prince's remote anxiety," we have in mind too Liu An's summoner who cries out despairingly, "O Prince, return! / In the mountains you cannot stay long!"[77]

Such an invocation reminds us of the provisional nature of this section's contented embracing of the recluse life. But even so the sudden shift in the following passage comes as a shock: the speaker jumps abruptly from sipping wine and playing his zither in his mountain abode, undisturbed by anxiety, to an emotionally painful visit to his late brother's residence:

215	In the valley of White Ox Creek,	白牛溪裏
	Enclosed by the rolling hills,	崗巒四峙
	In the deepest recess of this mountain,	信茲山之奧域
	Is the place where my brother lived in the past.	昔吾兄之所止
	Like Xu You, he withdrew from the world;[78]	許由避地
220	Like Zhang Chao, his valley swarmed like a market.[79]	張超成市
	He observed customs and edited the *Songs*;	察俗刪詩
	In accord with the classics, he rectified the histories.[80]	依經正史
	Kangcheng carried a bookbasket on his back and followed him;[81]	康成負笈而相繼
	Genju held his robe in hand and never put it down.[82]	根矩摳衣而未已
225	His disciples, wearing silk ribbons and blue collars,	組帶青衿
	Flourished and prospered.	鏘鏘儗儗
	Performing rites and music on the steps of the court,	階庭禮樂
	They stood like purple osier and catalpa trees.[83]	生徒杞梓
	This mountain reminded people of Ni Hill,[84]	山似尼丘
230	This creek called to mind the Zhu and the Si.[85]	泉凝洙泗

[Wang Ji's note:] My brother Tong, *zi* Zhongyan, lived during the final years of the Sui. He held steadfast to the proper Way and refused to take office. During the years of the Daye era, he came to this creek and retired into seclusion. He continued Confucius' course by compiling the *Six Classics*, which nearly exceeded a hundred *juan*. His disciples swarmed here in great numbers. For this reason, the creek is called Wang Kongzi Creek today.[86]

	Suddenly these men scattered in all directions;	忽焉四散
	Two decades have since gone by.	于今二紀
	The place looks still the same as it was before,	地猶如昨
	But most of the people have now passed on.	人多已矣
235	Remembering the good time we shared in the past,	念昔日之良遊
	I think of gentlemen from those days.	憶當時之君子
	They girdled themselves with thoroughwort, sat in the bamboo shade,	佩蘭蔭竹
	Cut reeds for the roof, and braided angelica into mats.	誅茅蔪茝
	The trees formed a circular grove,[87]	樹即環林
240	The gate opened into Queli.[88]	門成闕里
	Yao Zhongyou had an austere demeanor;	姚仲由之正色
	Xue Zhuangzhou was eloquent in argumentation.	薛莊周之言理

The disciples who gathered at this creek often numbered over a hundred. Among them, Dong Heng of Henan, Cheng Yuan of Nanyang, Jia Qiong of Zhongshan, Xue Shou of Hedong, Yao Yi of Taishan, Wen Yanbo of Taiyuan, Du Yan of Jingzhao, and others, altogether more than ten of them, were regarded as outstanding talents. Yao Yi was very vehement, so his fellow companions compared him to Zhongyou.[89] Xue Shou was acclaimed for his eloquence, and so was compared to Zhuang Zhou.[90] Xue [Shou] was truly ingenious in discoursing.

	They leaned against rocks, bending their arms for pillows;[91]	觸石橫肱
	When coming upon streams, they washed their ears.[92]	逢流洗耳
245	They took delight in the classics,	取樂經典
	And forgot all about sorrow and joy.	忘懷憂喜
	Sometimes they carried books with them while herding sheep;[93]	時挾冊而驅羊
	Sometimes they tossed fishing lines to catch carp.	或投竿而釣鯉

	Who would have thought that one day	何圖一旦
250	All would become so distant as if it were a thousand years ago?	邈成千紀
	Trees fell down, hillsides eroded,	木壞山頹
	Their boats drifted away and the valley has moved.	舟移谷徙

	On the north ridge,	北崗之上
	In front of the east cliff,	東巖之前
255	The lecture hall is still there;	講堂猶在
	The stele inscriptions are as before.	碑石宛然
	I recall listening to his lectures in the central chamber,	想聞道於中室
	And remember spreading out the classics down in the hall.	憶橫經於下筵
	The ceremonial ground is covered by weeds and trees;	壇場草樹
260	The courtyard is swallowed in wind and mist.	苑宇風煙

	Formerly Master Wenzhong withdrew from the world	昔文中之僻處
	Because it was a time of decline and chaos.	諒遭時之喪亂
	He drew back his haughty steps and bided his time,	守逸步而須時
	Preserved his lofty calling and waited for the dawn.	蓄奇聲而待旦
265	He was a traveler who succeeded through smallness;	旅人小節
	He darkened the light in great adversity.[94]	明夷大難
	He achieved merits, but the phoenix's call fell silent;[95]	建功則鳴鳳不聞
	When compiling history, he stopped at the capturing of the unicorn.[96]	修書則獲麟為斷

	Oh, what a pity for my brother,	惜矣吾兄
270	He met a troubled time!	遭時不平
	After his passing,	沒身之後
	The empire returned to order and enlightenment.	天下文明
	His disciples are now seated in the grand halls;	坐門人於廊廟
	The master is laid in his resting place.	瘞夫子於佳城
275	If it's possible that the dead can rise again,	死而可作
	When will he return to life?	何時復生

As I survey his empty hall, 式瞻虛館

And pace his front corridor, 載步前楹

My thoughts linger; 眷眷長想

280 Unremitting is my sorrow. 悠悠我情

At this familiar sacrificial and ceremonial ground, 俎豆衣冠之舊地

There still echoes the sound of bells and drums, 金石絲竹之餘聲
strings and pipes.

Though he is gone, he does not perish; 歿而不朽

He will be remembered for his deeds.[97] 知何所營

In the thirteenth year of Daye [617], my brother Zhongyan
died at his school in the country. He was thirty-four years of
age at the time.[98] His disciples gave him the posthumous name
Master Wenzhong. By the time the [Tang] imperial house
received heaven's decree, most of his disciples had advanced
to the ranks of ministers and counselors. But for Master
Wenzhong, he was unable to carry out his course while he was
alive. As I am here visiting this creek, I see the remains of his
old residence and I lament that this worthy man did not meet
his proper time.

Here we feel that Wang Ji the author, not a persona who encounters
immortals, is speaking to us. There are three striking features of this sec-
tion: Wang Ji's conscientious concern for factual details, emphasized by
the inclusion of his own annotations; his unmistakable admiration for Wang
Tong's legacy as a Confucian scholar; and his deep regret for Wang Tong's
misfortune at not having been fully appreciated while he was alive. This
admiration and regret is so great, however, that the concern for factual
detail does not prevent Wang Tong from becoming mythologized into a
second Confucius. Wang Tong is first presented to us through comparison
to two recluses—the famous Xu You, who turned down the sage-lord Yao's
offer of the empire, and then the Han recluse Zhang Kai (a.k.a. Zhang
Chao), whose reputation for virtue attracted so much attention that the
entire valley to which he retired filled with his followers. We are then told
of Wang Tong's intellectual emulation of Confucius through his compila-
tion of the classics and recording of history. Next his learned disciples are
introduced, and these include some of the most noted Confucian scholars
in history, making Wang Tong's school appear the reincarnation of Con-
fucius'. As if Wang Ji is afraid this romanticization will be taken as sheer
hyperbole, he inserts his first of several footnotes, justifying his bold com-
parison of Wang Tong to the sage himself.

As he returns to describe the flourishing days of Wang Tong's school, he continues to parallel Wang Tong and his followers with Confucius and his disciples. Moreover, Wang Ji includes himself in this portrait of Confucian worthies, informing the reader of his own training at the foot of his master brother (lines 257–258). The account is accompanied by so much biographical detail that the poem seems to shift away from the mode of *youlan*, with its description of an excursion, to *huaigu* 懷古 (remembrance of the past) in which the poet, upon visiting a historical site, contemplates the past in order to reflect on the present, usually with political intent.[99] The difference is that this is exceptionally personal: Wang Ji is viewing the present remains of his brother's school, remembering him as a talented man worthy of his Confucian values and court recognition.

What is remarkable here is the utter inconsistency of these sentiments in the poem we have been reading up to this point. The *fu* opened by criticizing Confucian study and values. The speaker mocked the sages King Wen and even Confucius himself for "itching to show off their talents" (line 38), accusing them and their believers of "wast[ing] our time" and "toil[ing] our mind" with the *Book of Rites* and the *Book of Changes*. He referred as well to the "endless contrivances" of Confucian teaching, which he says have defiled the source of Heaven's Way (lines 45–48).

Moreover, the detached recluse of the poem's previous section assured us there is no need to brood over the earning of merit and recognition in this world: the course of life and the Way is unpredictable, so it is better simply to relinquish all desire and anxiety and follow instead the course of nature. But now this same speaker is filled with painful emotions as he takes leave of his brother's abandoned residence:

285	Standing over the remains of his former home,	臨故墟而掩抑
	I cover my face and hold back my grief;	
	Turning onto the road home, I sigh with sorrow.	指歸途而歎息
	Over and again, creeks cut across my trail;	往往溪橫
	Now and then, my path is blocked.	時時路塞
	Suddenly I am atop a lofty peak,	忽登崇岫
290	Still the familiar surrounding that I know.	依然舊識
	The place is remote when my mind is detached;	地迴心遙
	The mountain is tall and I look straight ahead.	山高直視
	Watching smoke rise from my home village,	望煙火於桑梓
	I recognize the canals and the dikes of my native land.	辨溝塍於鄉國

295	It inclines on the west side of Guye Mountain,	斜連姑射之西
	And lies due north of the Yellow and the Fen Rivers.[100]	正是河汾之北
	How listless is my heart!	悵矣懷抱
	How still are the rivers and the land!	悠哉川域

The constant obstructions in the speaker's path seem to be further reminders of the difficulty in keeping to one's path of life. Yet soon he reverts to the contented tone of the philosophical recluse as he stands atop the mountain looking into the distance. Lines 291–292 contain an allusion to one of Tao Qian's "Drinking Poem" series:

I built my hut in the realm of men,	結廬在人境
But I hear no noise of carts and horses passing.	而無車馬喧
Do you know how one can do it?	問君何能爾
When the mind is detached, one's place becomes remote.[101]	心遠地自偏

Tao Qian's point is that no matter what situation you find yourself in, so long as you attain a detached mind the disturbances of the mundane world will disappear. Thus he cannot hear the passing carts and horses. By invoking Tao Qian's poem the speaker of "You Beishan fu" reminds his readers —but perhaps more importantly himself—that he too has attained that detachment and all the personal sorrows and troubles in life do not matter to him. It is, in other words, a reassertion of his *zhi*.

And it is a shaky one. Only a few lines later Wang Ji appears to reflect regretfully on his own lost youth and his lost opportunity in service. These feelings are triggered by the sight of his home village in the distance, which he espies while gazing from the mountaintop. Yet just as suddenly there is an abrupt, discordant shift out of this state of mind:

	I recall the past in my days of learning,	憶昔過庭
300	Just a child in my tender age.	童顏稚齡
	What fun did I not fully enjoy?	何賞不極
	What excursion did I not take?	何遊不經
	I played in the spring breeze at the mouth of the brook,	弄春風於磵戶
	And chanted odes to the autumn moon by the mountain gate.	詠秋月於山扃

305	I stole light from glare off the snow through my north window,[102]	北窗照雪
	And gathered fireflies to light my south studio.[103]	南軒聚螢
	Wearing a colorful gown, I fanned my parents' pillows;[104]	彩衣扇枕
	Donning a black cloth cap, I studied classics.[105]	緇布開經
	But how easily happiness is lost;	何斯樂之易失
310	Suddenly I am biting grief, swallowing sorrow.	焂銜哀而茹恤
	Before heaven had dispelled its casts of calamity,	天未悔禍
	My family encountered misfortune and did not prosper.	遭家不秩
	Zijing passed away early;	子敬先亡
	Gongming died young.[106]	公明早卒
315	Since then I have been adrift	餘自此而浩蕩
	And caught in an inimical time.	又逢時之不仁
	Heaven and earth slowly closed in;	天地遂閉
	Thunder and clouds gradually amassed.[107]	雷雲漸屯
	I shared the same intent with Chang Ju and Jie Ni,[108]	與沮溺而同恥
320	And concealed myself in the company of Bo Yi and Shu Qi.[109]	共夷齊而隱身
	Fate blesses me with great fortune;	幸收元吉
	I chance on a favorable time,	生偶昌辰
	Which permits the North Sea man to cheerfully retreat[110]	容北海之嘉遁
	And allows Southern Mountain men to decline to serve.[111]	許南山之不臣
325	Nurturing ineptitude, I resign from office;	養拙辭官
	Embracing harmony, I preserve my trueness.	含和保真
	Would I act like Feng Jingtong and blame the world for my failure?[112]	豈若馮敬生之誹世
	Or like Zhao Yuanshu fault others for my dire straits?[113]	趙元叔之尤人
	They burdened themselves with sorrow and shame for their humble status,	殷憂恥賤
330	And exhausted themselves with distress and lament for their poverty.	憔悴傷貧

They found no joy in drawing water from wells or hulling rice in a mortar,	探井臼而無樂
And roaming mountains and rivers was too arduous.	歷山河而苦辛
How can they live like I do—	豈如我家生事
To abandon all worldly attachments completely?	都盧棄置
335 I do not think about "time-to-return";	不念當歸
I would rather pursue "lofty ambition."[114]	寧圖遠志
Sitting in the green hills, I am not hiding from the world;	坐青山而非隱
Roaming the limpid tarns, joy arises.[115]	遊淥潭而巳喜

Here the speaker credits himself with conventional, orthodox traits, building an image of himself as a reputable young man worthy of recognition by Confucian standards, clearly at odds with his earlier pronouncements. This image is presented to us through a series of allusions to well-known stories of filial piety and tales of studious young men in history who relentlessly pursued knowledge. But the fond manner in which he refers to his experiences as an aspiring youth is puzzling. It now seems we are supposed to forget that our speaker is a recluse who has no ambition for office, who is content with just his wine, his farm, his garden and groves, and who once said that an official's "joy could not compensate for his worries."

But he explains, too, with the vague term *"buzhi"* 不秩 (literally "unranked" or "not salaried"), that his generation was unable to attain official status due to the early deaths of his brothers. Then in lines 315–316 he claims he has been drifting in "an inimical time." Contrary to our previous impression, we are now encouraged to think of the speaker as an exile from adversity. And his allusions to the hexagrams of the *Book of Changes* (lines 317–318 and 323) indeed confirm that his leaving office is in accord with the sage advice to withdraw in "an inimical time." Yet his subsequent references to legendary recluses muddle this picture. Chang Ju and Jie Ni advocated total withdrawal from the world whether danger was imminent or not; Bo Yi and Shu Qi withdrew in protest against their new sovereign, who had conquered the former court. Wang Ji's new sovereign, we might note, was the Tang emperor, of whom he had spoken favorably in lines 271–272.[116] And in fact in lines 321–324 he completely denies his statement of a few lines earlier when he observes that he is living not in an "inimical" but a "favorable time" that allows him—not forces him—to drift as he pleases.

Perhaps it is just these unsettling self-contradictions that, at this point, prompt the speaker again to assert his resolution. He does so through invocations of past recluses:

	My old friends are here in the mountains, cut off from the mundane world;[117]	舊知山裏絕氛埃
340	Ascending high in the sunset, my mind wanders far.	登高日暮心悠哉
	Ziping took his leave, when would he return?[118]	子平一去何時返
	When Zhongshu went on a distant roaming, he never came back.[119]	仲叔長遊遂不來
	Amid the secluded thoroughwort in the solitary night, I play a tune on my zither;	幽蘭獨夜之琴曲
	Under the cinnamon tree into the early morn, I hold a wine cup in hand.	桂樹凌晨之酒盃
345	On the hills and in the gardens I am free and unrestrained;	丘園散誕
	In the caves and grottoes, I linger and loiter.	窟室徘徊
	When I sit, I am dormant like a withered tree;	坐等枯木
	My mind is as calm as dead ashes.[120]	心如死灰

As if to demonstrate how "free and unrestrained" he is, the speaker slips back into a vague mode of narrative, paying no attention to specificity of location. We presume for a time that the "journey" is continuing, for the speaker wanders "on the hills and in the gardens," "in the caves and grottoes." Yet he is also "dormant like a withered tree," and his mind, we are told, "is as calm as dead ashes." The excursion narrative is conceding to the concerted self-presentation of an ideal recluse:

	Moreover, I have delicacies from mountains and savories of the wild,	亦有山羞野饌
350	Thoroughwort juice and birthwort powder,	蘭漿朮麨
	Simmered broth with matrimony-vine leaves,	杞葉煎羹
	Clear brew distilled from pine roots.	松根溜醑
	I collect herbs for medicine and for food;	既採藥而為食
	I follow my innate feeling and never constrain it.	諒隨情而不矯

355 In early spring, I carry a spade on my back;	負鍤春前
At the year's end, I tuck a sickle into my waistband.	腰鐮歲杪
Where the grass grows thick, animals are abundant;	草漸密而饒獸
Where woods grow deeper, birds are ample.	樹彌深而足鳥
The land is serene, lush and luxuriant;	地寂寞而森沉
360 Roads crisscross, secluded and sequestered.	路縱橫而窈窕
A crane whoops from the pavilion in the wild;	野亭鶴唳
A pheasant chick cries from the ridge of the mountain.	山梁雉鷕
At this place for distant wandering,	遠遊之所
And the lodge for seclusion,	幽棲之次
365 Some have just come, still holding calves in their arms;[121]	或抱犢而新來
They have arrived as roosters begin to crow.[122]	乍聞雞而始至
There are a couple of pigweed patches	藋畦一兩
And three or four thatched huts.	茅齋數四
The mountains are rugged, there is no one around.	山為險而無人
370 Where slopes level off, there are parcels of land.	嶺時平而有地
Rock fungi sprout out their leaves,	石菌抽葉
Golden mushrooms shoot out their caps.	金芝吐穗
Mirrors ward off mountain sprites;	鏡厭山精
Broadswords drive away tree dryads.	刀驅木魅
375 A spring winds along the paved step, and in it fish leap.	泉邊砌而魚躍
A tree branch stretches across the window, and on it birds gather.	樹橫窗而鳥萃

The speaker seems to be keeping in mind how difficult it has been for him to "follow the course of nature" without finding himself off track, distracted by desires and memories. He has been enticed by the unconfined yonder realm, tempted by the opportunity to join the world of immortals, and stirred by remembrances of his family's past, so this time he concentrates intently on the trivial routine of ordinary life and the details of his immediate natural surroundings. Yet the stream of stock phrases and allusions invoking reclusion gives the impression that he feels the need to "drive home" his resolution—to strengthen his (and our own) confidence in his resolve through the sheer weight of number. As this effort continues, the pace of the narrative quickens:

	Wide and vast is heaven's web,	天網寬寬
	How difficult can life be?	人生豈難
	I drink from the river and stop when I have enough;	飲河知足
380	Nesting in the woods, I am certainly content.[123]	巢林必安
	What honor can lure me to don a purple robe?	亦何榮而拾紫
	Why would I yearn for the Elixir of Return?[124]	亦何羨而還丹
	Holding my red goosefoot staff, which taps a rapid rhythm,	紅藜促節之杖
	Wearing my green bamboo-leaf hat with mottled pattern,	綠簜班文之冠
385	I load my baskets with savors of the wild	野餐二簋
	And fill my tray with garden greens.	園蔬一盤
	I send off Ruan Ji with a long whistle	送阮籍而長嘯
	And welcome Liu Ling with great delight.	得劉伶而甚歡
	At dawn, I enter the brushwood gate;	曉入柴戶
390	At dusk, I return to the herb garden.	暮歸藥欄
	Lao Lai's place is isolated,	老萊地僻
	Zou Yan's valley is cold.[125]	鄒生谷寒
	Under the drooping willow branches, I forge iron;[126]	楊柳則條垂鍛沼
	Amid the flying apricot blossoms, I sit to meditate.[127]	杏樹則花飛坐壇
395	My rhapsodies resound like drums and pipes;[128]	賦成鼓吹
	My poems chant like pellets and balls.[129]	詩成彈丸
	I take the young Minghe in my arms,[130]	擕始晬之鳴鶴
	And face the newly married Boluan.[131]	對新婚之伯鸞

Again we encounter an explicit statement of the speaker's resolution in detachment. But as we progress through this final section of the *fu*, both the style and the logic of the argument break down. There is not a stream but an avalanche of allusions, similes, and declamatory statements supporting the speaker's assurance that he is, indeed, a model recluse. We confront a cluttered abundance of place and proper names, from many different sources, and the result contrasts unfavorably with the clarity and specificity of the previous section's account of the excursion in the Northern Mountains. This obscurity is even more pronounced in the last lines of the poem:

	I embrace my own ideal,	我有懷抱
400	I am detached to preserve my purity.	蕭然自保

It is difficult for me to return in the company of
    ancient men, 　　　　　　　　　　　　　古人則難與同歸

So I will happily stay here to face my old age. 　　紛吾則此焉將老

I gather duckweed and lotus leaves from streams
    and marshes, 　　　　　　　　　　　　礀溪沼渚之蘋荇

Pick mulberries and jujubes from hills and bluffs. 丘陵阪險之桑棗

405 I plant fruits, graft pears, 　　　　　　　　　接果移棠

Grow young stalks, sow rice. 　　　　　　　　栽苗散稻

I do not collect useless implements, 　　　　　不藏無用之器

Nor am I fond of extraordinary treasure. 　　　不愛非常之寶

I toss jade to startle fowls, 　　　　　　　　抵玉驚禽

410 Swing gold to cut down weeds. 　　　　　　揮金薙草

I greet friends with food and wine; 　　　　　接朋友於杯案

Play with my swaddled youngsters. 　　　　　弄兒孫於襁褓

I delight in roaming mountains and marshes, 　樂山澤之浮遊

Laughing as my body shrivels and withers in rivers
    and lakes. 　　　　　　　　　　　　　笑江潭之枯槁

415 I practice abstinence but not to enchant Buddha; 戒非佞佛

I exercise temperance but not to charm the Way. 齋非媚道

There is no merit in my words and fame; 　　　言譽無功

My body turns into a hollow shell. 　　　　　形骸自空

For leisure, I am an old gardener; 　　　　　坐成老圃

420 For livelihood, I am a lowly farmer. 　　　　居為下農

I abandon the world all on my own; 　　　　　身與世而相棄

Walking the mountain paths, I find endless joy. 　賞隨山而不窮

Draping a gown over my shoulder, I stay behind
    the stove; 　　　　　　　　　　　　　披衣竈北

I search for food by the eastern wall.[132] 　　　逐食牆東

425 There are as well four hoary-headed worthies, 　儻有白頭四皓

Eight thick-browed noblemen,[133] 　　　　　　厖眉八公

Young lads riding the sun, 　　　　　　　　小童乘日

Transcendents yoking the wind, 　　　　　　仙人馭風

Village elders with birds perched on their canes, 　鄉老則杖頭安鳥

430 And rulers of states with bears painted on their
    carriages. 　　　　　　　　　　　　　邦君則車邊畫熊

Their minds understand mine tacitly; 　　　　心期闇合

Their Way, though concealed, coincides with mine. 道術潛同

> Now and again, they come to visit me　解來相訪
> 434　In the Valley of the Foolish Old Man.　愚公谷中

To begin with, we see that the speaker contradicts his assertion of isolation by indicating a rather active social life. He resigns himself to the fact that it is difficult for him to "return in the company of ancient men," by which we assume he means to enjoy retirement (the implication of *gui* 歸) with his recluse idols of the past (although just a few lines ago he was entertaining them) and "will happily stay here to face my old age" (lines 401–402). He abandons all worldly attachments, he says, in order to experience the "endless joy" of living in nature (lines 421–422). Yet we find him joyfully receiving visitors from all corners of the human and other world: the four hoary-headed recluses who denounced fame in officialdom, the eight ministers who were awarded transcendence for their loyal service to their lord, sun-riding lads who never grow old, wind-yoking transcendents who have the power to transport earthlings to the immortal realm, and then village elders who preside over local administrative affairs and even sovereigns of states who honor those of great achievement and reputation (lines 425–430). Here is a grab bag of figures, presumably all with different values and aspirations. Yet the speaker confidently asserts: "Their minds understand mine tacitly; / Their Way, though concealed, coincides with mine" (lines 431–432).

These last lines are particularly slippery and deserve extended analysis—partly because we cannot help but react with skepticism to the speaker's claim that others understand this mind of his whose *zhi*, as we have seen over the course of this *fu*, has proved so unstable. Liu Xiang's anecdote about the "Valley of the Foolish Old Man" is our starting point:

> Duke Huan of Qi went out hunting one day, and while chasing a fleeing deer he entered a valley. There the duke met an old man, and he asked him: "What valley is this?" The old man said: "It is the Valley of the Foolish Old Man." Duke Huan asked: "Why is it called so?" The old man answered: "It is named after me." The duke then said: "But as I look at your appearance and your manner now, you don't look like a fool. Why do people call you that?" The old man said: "I request your permission to explain. In the past I raised a cow and it gave birth to a calf. When the calf grew big, I sold the cow to a young man in exchange for his pony. The young man later said, 'This cow can't give birth to a horse,' and he took his pony and walked away. My neighbors heard about

this and thought I was foolish. Therefore, they call this the Valley of the Foolish Old Man." Duke Huan said: "You are foolish indeed. Why did you let him have it?" Having said that, Duke Huan returned home. The next day at court, he told of his encounter to Guan Zhong. Guan Zhong straightened his robe, bowed twice, and said: "This is my fault. If Yao were the ruler above and Jiugun were his assistant, how could there be anyone who would take another person's pony? If one were to encounter such an unreasonable person as this old man met, one certainly would not have given him the pony. But this old man knew that he would not have a fair hearing if he brought the case to court—which is why he let the young man take his pony. I request to step down and study governing."[134]

The moral of Liu Xiang's story is this: a wise man will act foolish sometimes, but it is only because he is wise and knows that when the world is in disorder, acting foolish is the wisest means to protect himself. Yet in the unknowing eyes of foolish people, who think they are wise, they view a wise man's "foolish act" in isolation as being merely foolish.

Now let us return to the *fu*'s concluding line. It seems, on the one hand, that Wang Ji's allusion to the Foolish Old Man might simply characterize him as a recluse, for by his time that was its stock significance. On the other hand, Wang Ji seems also to be asking, just as the old man challenged Duke Huan, "Do you indeed know who I am?" This question has in fact already been begged by the previous two lines, where we are assured there is no need to spell out what one knows when one is confident in that knowledge: though the Way is concealed, right paths will coincide if minds comprehend one another tacitly. Words are unnecessary: those who know do not speak, those who speak do not know. This notion recalls the speaker's earlier criticism of Laozi, Buddha, King Wen, and Confucius for being too prolix in their words; specifically it invokes Laozi's claim that "a way-able Way is not the constant Way; a namable name is not the permanent name."[135] Zhuangzi puts it plainer in his discussion of *bian* 辨 (distinctions):

In any case, the Great Way has not had a boundary since the beginning. Speech has not had a constant standard since the beginning.... So surely, as for those who debate over the boundaries, it is because they are ignorant about them; as for those who debate over the distinctions, it is because they are ignorant about them.... The Great Way is not stated by name; the Great Distinction is not put in words.[136]

Embracing the Way means to comprehend it intuitively; active effort or explanation may seem to clarify the Way's nature, but in fact they only demonstrate one's misunderstanding.

Tao Qian expresses his grasp of this precept in his "Yinjiu shi, no. 5":[137]

I built my thatched hut amid the realm of man,	結廬在人境
But I hear no noise from the carts and horse.	而無車馬喧
You ask how I manage to do so?	問君何能爾
If you detach your mind, the place naturally becomes remote.	心遠地自偏
While picking chrysanthemums by the eastern hedge,	採菊東籬下
I catch the sight of the Southern Mountain in the distance.	悠然見南山
In the mountain mist, the sun sets and is beautiful;	山氣日夕佳
Flying birds, following one another, are turning back.	飛鳥相與還
This setting bears the profound truth;	此中有深意
I was just about to articulate it, but already forget the words.	欲辨已忘言

His inarticulation attests to Tao Qian's attainment of understanding and confirms the wisdom of *Zhuangzi* that "profound truth" is unspoken and the wise man is silent. The final four lines of "You Beishan fu," read in isolation, echo this idea: the speaker's companions understand him "tacitly"; they know intuitively that "Their Way, though concealed, coincides with" his, the "Foolish Old Man" in appearance who is in reality wise.

But what is his wisdom, after all? The experience of reading this *fu* has taught us, if anything, that knowing "the scholar's mind" or *zhi* is illusory because the speaker's repeated efforts to communicate his resolve seemed to prove ultimately uncertain and disappointing. But this is precisely the reason the poem ends where it does: the excursion has been transformed into an image of settling, of inaction, and an assurance that no longer will the speaker strive to state his resolve. He has determined to rely now on the "tacit" understanding that accommodates unproblematically the seeming disparateness of his companions, and his own variable character, because he understands this impression is based on transitory worldly distinctions rather than the "concealed" Way.

It is this "tacit understanding" that Wang Ji upholds as the wiser alternative to the efforts of so many of his contemporaries to codify intellectual systems and cultural and political practices. Their activity was premised on

a faith in the articulation of timeless standards and an attainable perma-
nency in human affairs. Wang Ji, with other devotees of Laozi-Zhuangzi
ideas, simply denied that these could ever be achieved. What makes Wang
Ji unique in his time, and in some measure a pivotal figure in Chinese liter-
ary history, is the means by which he communicated his philosophical con-
victions through the imaginative performance of his recluse persona.

Conclusion
The Idealization of the Recluse

❀

LET US RETURN now to the traditional assumption that Wang Ji's poetry communicates the essence of his personal identity as a recluse. Here I want to consider some of the consequences of this assumption, because ultimately it has affected not only our interpretations of Wang Ji's poetry but those of other Chinese poets as well. And in this we have important lessons to learn as scholars of Chinese literary history.

To begin we discover that the judgment of scholars who choose to consider (or ignore) questions of attribution, dating, and variants in Wang Ji's corpus has been affected by their desire to shore up preferred notions of the poet's "true character." In the editions of Wang Ji's collected works, most of the authorship problems are raised by the issue of dual attribution—that is, a number of poems are found both in Wang Ji's and in other Tang poets' collections. For the most part, the evidence clearly suggests that these pieces were mistakenly ascribed to Wang Ji through editorial carelessness in the Ming and Qing dynasties. Take, for example, the poem "On Passing an Ancient Han City" (Guo Han gucheng 過漢故城), which is attributed in *Quan Tang shi* to Wang Ji in one place and to Wu Shaowei 吳少微 (fl. early eighth century) in another. There are several reasons to believe that the poem is not by Wang Ji: it is not included in any of the five-*juan* editions; nor was it included in the Song three-*juan* edition of Wang Ji's works later reproduced by Sun Xingyan 孫星衍 (1753–1818). Sun added it to his edition only after discovering it in the other three-*juan* editions available to him, all of more recent issue than his own source text. How, then, did the poem find its way into Wang Ji's collection? This, I think, is no great mystery. The poem is in *Wenyuan yinghua*, ascribed to Wu Shaowei. Right before it, incidentally, is a poem by one Wang Wujing 王無兢. I suspect a Ming editor, while collecting poems for a supplemented three-*juan* edition of Wang Ji's works, mistook Wang Wujing for the author of "On Passing an Ancient Han City" and misread Wang Wujing as Wang Wugong 王無功, Wang Ji's courtesy name.[1]

In any case, literary scholars have ignored this attribution problem, treating the poem as if it were unproblematically by Wang Ji. And the reason for this is not a mystery either. Its speaker contemplates the rise and fall of an unspecified Han city lying in ruins, a traditional poetic means for reflecting on the fallen moral state of one's own times. Most of Wang Ji's critics matter-of-factly cite "On Passing an Ancient Han City" as an illustration of Wang Ji's disdain for the Sui court. Simply put: their determination to portray Wang Ji as a morally upright recluse who shunned the immorality of his times outweighs the dangers of relying on fallacious evidence.

The same motive has led other scholars to speculate on the dating of Wang Ji's works and events in his life.[2] As we have seen, the little information that we have about Wang Ji's life permits us to speculate only occasionally along these lines. But in their resolve to tell the story either of a moral recluse or a conflicted misfit of his time, scholars have taken great liberties with the limited record to argue the dates of Wang Ji's works— and then have done the same with his works to attempt a chronicle of his life. Consider, for example, the argument of Kang Jinsheng and Xia Lianbao concerning Wang Ji's "Six Poems on Ancient Themes." There is nothing in this series to indicate when it may have been composed. Kang and Xia nonetheless propose that it was written in or around 614 (the tenth year of Daye under the reign of Yangdi of Sui) on the basis of a report that Wang Ji compared the Sui court to a "heaven's net" (天網) before leaving his post in Luhe,[3] as well as the fact that in the last poem of the series Wang Ji describes men attempting to use a net to catch the phoenix.[4] Thus Kang and Xia confidently assert that "Six Poems on Ancient Themes" must have been written around the time of Wang Ji's first retirement.[5]

Similarly, decisions about textual variants and discrepancies often indicate scholars' interpretive preconceptions rather than sound editing practices. While most editors simply note variants and discrepancies without offering recommended readings—despite the fact that most have resulted from simple graphic confusions—on occasion the alternatives cannot easily be resolved and present significant differences in the tone of the poem in question. For instance, among the major editions of Wang Ji's collection there are three possible readings for the closing couplet of "To Zhai

Zhengshi, the Scholar at Home: Expressing My Resolve in Old Age"
(Wannian xuzhi zeng Zhai chushi Zhengshi 晚年敘志贈翟處士正師):[6]

1. 自有常居樂　誰知我世憂[7]
   There is naturally joy in the simple life;
   Who can tell that there is worry in this world of mine?
2. 自有常居樂　誰知身後憂[8]
   There is naturally joy in the simple life;
   Who can tell that there will be worry after life?
3. 自有常居樂　誰知身世憂[9]
   There is naturally joy in the simple life;
   Who can tell that my life is filled with worries?

The difference in the final three characters of the last line alters the words
subtly but the meaning and tone substantially. The first version asserts a
moral scholar's concern for his world, as he wonders aloud if his worldly
cares will be understood. The second version sounds detached and philo-
sophical: the speaker rejects concern for the unknowable afterlife in favor
of the simple pleasures of the present. The third version complains that no
one knows the concerns in the speaker's mind. Which of the readings is
authentic cannot be known; no version has more claim to authority than
the others. The version that particular editors have selected—and that lit-
erary scholars have quoted—thus supplies a good clue to their conception
of who Wang Ji was: a moral man who despairs over his fallen times, or
laments his lack of recognition (both implied by options 1 and 3) or a
detached and carefree hermit (implied by option 2)?

Precisely the same motivation lies behind scholars' decisions to adopt
or to ignore the substantial new evidence on Wang Ji's life and writings
that is represented by the discovery of the five-*juan* edition of his works.
Not only does the three-*juan* edition contain fewer poems than the five-
juan text, it should be emphasized, but there are also portions of a number
of poems that have been omitted in the three-*juan* edition as well as lexical
variants that significantly alter the sense of a line (perhaps the result of
cosmetic surgery performed by Lu Chun). Take, for example, the poem
"On Chinese Pink" (Shizhu yong 石竹詠), a *yongwu* 詠物 poem whose
speaker is a "Chinese pink" (a kind of fern).[10] The three-*juan* version
opens with the plant describing its physical appearance; it then turns to
contemplate its life at the mercy of the fickle elements, finally coming to a

reluctant acceptance of the variability of fate. The same poem in the five-*juan* collection is titled "The Chinese Pink by My Steps" (Jieqian shizhu 階前石竹)[11] and is longer by two couplets at the beginning (printed here in italics), which express gratitude to *shangtian* 上天 (august heaven) for treating all things in the world equally and for endowing even a humble fern with its benevolent nourishment:

	August heaven spreads sweet rain	上天布甘雨
	Onto ten thousand miles of land, even and fair;	萬里咸均平
	Insignificant and worthless as I thought I was,	自顧微且賤
4	*Yet I too was nurtured to flourish and bloom.*	亦得蒙滋榮
	My verdant branches interlock in their lushness;	萋萋結綠枝
	My vermilion blossoms droop in their splendor.	曄曄垂朱英
	But constantly I fear that the dew will fall	常恐零露降
8	And I will not survive intact.	不得全其生
	Heaving and sighing, I think to myself:	歎息聊自思
	How can I fathom the Way of life?	此生豈我情
	Formerly, before I was yet born,	昔我未生時
12	Who was it that made me sprout?	誰者令我萌
	Forget it, never mention it again!	棄置勿重陳
	What can one do about nature's transformations?	委化何所營

As we see, the first two couplets supply a note of humility and gratitude that tempers the melancholy in the six lines that open the abridged, three-*juan* version. These omitted lines also contrast with the apparent pose of philosophical resignation that concludes the poem. In other words: the three-*juan* edition in this instance conveys a different reading experience, a different tone, a different impression of the "I" behind the voice than does the full version. Thus it would seem to be imperative that any scholar writing on Wang Ji since 1987 (the publication date of Han Lizhou's critical edition of the five-*juan* text) would have to take into account the textual differences between the two versions—and, moreover, would have to rely primarily on the latter. Yet I have not seen one study that does so.

Despite the commonplace that Wang Ji is a "transitional figure" in literary history, another consequence of accepting him simply as an imitator of Wei-Jin recluse-poets in his life and in his writings is the neglect of his influence on later poets, especially Bo Juyi 白居易 and Su Shi 蘇軾. Bo Juyi explicitly emulates Wang Ji's drunken persona in several respects. He took for himself the sobriquet Zuiyin Xiansheng 醉吟先生 (Mr. Chanting-in-Drunkenness); he composed a pseudo-autobiography after the fashion of Wang Ji's "Biography of Mr. Five Dippers" and a tomb inscription for himself modeled on both Tao Qian's and Wang Ji's. Moreover, in his poetry he more than once invokes Wang Ji's name when emphasizing his own persona as a drunken poet.[12] As for Su Shi, we discover that he copied Wang Ji's "Zui xiang ji" 醉鄉記 (The story of Drunkenville),[13] and he wrote a postscript to Wang Ji's biography in which he boasts of his own drinking capacity.[14] His sobriquet "Dongpo" 東坡 (Eastern Slope) recalls Wang Ji's "Donggao" 東皋 (Eastern Slope by the River). And Su Shi's much-celebrated drunken farmer persona, in details and in spirit, bears a much closer resemblance to Wang Ji's than to Tao Qian's. These are the most obvious signs of Wang Ji's influence on Bo Juyi and Su Shi, yet modern scholars fail to mention them. This is an especial weakness in studies of Su Shi, whom scholars regard as a "second Tao Qian" in the history of Chinese poetry while overlooking Su Shi's own testimony that he follows Wang Ji's lead in his imitation of Tao Qian. Neither of the otherwise fine studies of Su Shi recently published in the West mentions Wang Ji once, let alone explores the significance of Wang Ji's poetic persona and practices to Su Shi's own, even though one of these studies is specifically devoted to tracing "the development of Su Shi's poetic voice."[15]

I call attention to this oversight not to argue that the "minor poet" who is the subject of my study deserves greater respect and a higher canonical status. In fact there are greater rewards—namely, our own enriched understanding of Wang Ji's, Bo Juyi's, and Su Shi's poetry, to begin with just these names. So long as scholars of late classical and early medieval Chinese poetry continue to assume that we read primarily to discover the poet's thoughts and feelings and morals, the study of this poetry and the poetry that it influenced will offer few interpretive insights. My goal in this book has been to illustrate such a literary explication that begins with an effort to understand the historical and intellectual circumstances behind a poet's selection and arrangement of words. Thus I have argued that Wang Ji's self-idealization as a recluse was meant to communicate a philosophical objection to the scholarly activity of his times. His self-image personifies the Lao-Zhuang notion of an ever-changing world that disallows sure knowledge; it is a multifaceted, unstable image, which by its example objects to scholars' efforts during the Sui and early Tang to establish, "permanently," proper codes of conduct, ritual practice, government institutions, and cultural knowledge. This opposition to the dominant intellectual trend in his time was not based on political or moral grounds; nor was it polemical. (Wang Ji's poems, as we have seen, suggest bemusement at the wasted labors of his fellow men, not indignation.) It was an opposition based instead on metaphysical principle. And for us this means that the reward of reading Wang Ji is not to perceive his politics or his moral character but to discover the diverse, surprising, and often humorous ways that a metaphysics has been imagined in the figure of a literary persona and to experience this metaphysics through the process of reading.

Notes

❁

Abbreviations

CSJC	*Congshu jicheng* 叢書集成
MS	*Maoshi* 毛詩
QSG	*Quan Shanggu Sandai Qin Han Sanguo Liuchao wen* 全上古三代秦漢三國六朝文
QTS	*Quan Tang Shi* 全唐詩
QTW	*Quan Tang Wen* 全唐文
SBBY	*Sibu beiyao* 四部備要
SBCK	*Sibu congkan* 四部叢刊
SBCKXB	*Sibu congkan xubian* 四部叢刊續編
SKQS	*Siku quanshu* 四庫全書
TWC	*Tang wen cui* 唐文粹
WX	*Wen xuan* 文選
WYYH	*Wenyuan yinghua* 文苑英華
XQHW	*Xian Qin Han Wei Jin Nanbeichao shi* 先秦漢魏晉南北朝詩
YWLJ	*Yiwen leiju* 藝文類聚

Introduction

1. For example, Wang Wei 王維 (701–761) and Su Shi 蘇軾 (1037–1101). The recognition of symbolic method in these poets' writings informs the analyses in Yu, *Poetry of Wang Wei*; Fuller, *Road to the East Slope*; and Egan, *Word, Image, and Deed*.

2. The original five-*juan* collection compiled by Lü Cai was so rarely seen after Lu Chun's edition (see next note) that eventually most scholars assumed it was lost. Not until 1984, when Han Lizhou and Zhang Xihou reported their discovery of three Qing manuscripts of the five-*juan* collection, were modern scholars alerted to its continual existence. See Han Lizhou, "Lun Wang Ji de shi," 78–83; Zhang Xihou, "Lun Wang Ji de shiwen ji qi wenxue chengjiu," 116–126, and "Guanyu 'Wang Ji ji' de liuchuan yu wujuanben de faxian," 70–95. Unless otherwise indicated, all references in this study to Wang Ji's writings are to the five-*juan* edition prepared by Han Lizhou, *Wang Wugong wenji* (hereafter *Wenji*).

3. Lu Chun's identity is uncertain. Both of the Tang histories contain entries for a man named Lu Zhi 陸質 and mention that Lu Zhi's original name was Lu Chun, which he changed to avoid the taboo name of Emperor Xian 憲宗 (Li Chun 李純, r. 805–820). This Lu Chun, later Lu Zhi, lived in the second half of the eighth century and studied under Zhao Kuang 趙匡, a disciple of Dan Zhu 啖助. Both were renowned unorthodox Confucian scholars. Lu Zhi died sometime around 805. Many scholars believe Lu Zhi is the Lu Chun who edited Wang Ji's three-*juan* collection, but some doubt this identification because the Tang histories record that Lu Zhi was a native of Wu commandery and his courtesy name was Bochong 伯沖, while the postface in the standard three-*juan* edition is signed "Lu Chun, courtesy name Huaqing 化卿, of Pingyuan 平原." See *Jiu Tang shu*, 189b. 4977–4978; *Xin Tang shu*, 168.5127–5128; and Lu Chun, "*Donggaozi ji xu*," in *Donggaozi ji* (*SKQS*), 1b. The full title of this last piece is "Shan *Donggaozi ji* houxu" 刪東皋子集後序, and though it is listed as a postface in the five-*juan* collection and in *QTW*, it is treated as a preface in most of the three-*juan* texts, including the *SKQS* edition to which I refer in this study.

4. *Donggaozi ji*, 1b.

5. Lü Cai's preface included in *QTW* (160.7b–10a) is Lu Chun's abridged version.

6. In the *Zhongshuo* 中說, a collection of Wang Tong's teachings and his dialogues with his disciples and associates, Dong Heng is referred to by the name Dong Chang 董常.

7. Compare *Zhuangzi*, 26: "That which lies in words is the intention. When the intention is achieved then words can be forgotten" (Wang Shumin, *Zhuangzi jiaoquan*, 26.1082; all references to *Zhuangzi* in this study are to this edition).

8. *Donggaozi ji*, 1a.

9. Ibid., 1a–b.

10. Xin Wenfang, *Tang caizi zhuan*, 3–4.

11. Compare *Lun yu* 論語, 8.13: "Enter not a state that is in peril; stay not in a state that is in danger. Show yourself when the Way prevails in the Empire, but hide yourself when it does not. It is a shameful matter to be poor and humble when the Way prevails in the state. Equally, it is a shameful matter to be rich and noble when the Way falls into disuse in the state" (Lau, *Confucius*, 94).

12. Cao Quan produced the Ming woodblock edition of Wang Ji's collection, which later became the base text for the *SBCKXB* edition and the authoritative edition for most reproductions and all previous studies of Wang Ji's literature.

13. *Wenji*, app. A, 223.

14. Referring to Tao Qian, who lived in Li Village 栗里 (in modern Jiangxi) in his retirement.

15. The group of famous recluses conventionally listed together as "Seven Worthies of the Bamboo Grove" 竹林七賢. This group included Wang Ji's idols Ruan Ji, Xi Kang, and Liu Ling.

16. *Wenji*, app. A, 224.

17. Modern scholars who, like Xin Wenfang and Cao Quan, cite Wang Ji's writings in praise of his character include Han Lizhou in "Lun Wang Ji de shi" and Zhang Xihou in "Lun Wang Ji de shiwen ji qi wenxue chengjiu," "Wang Ji sheng-

ping bianxi," 71–75, and "Yingdang quanmian pingjia Wang Ji de tijiu yongyin shi," 22–27.

18. See Ji Yun et al., *Siku quanshu zongmu tiyao*, 29.3114.

19. Zhang Daxin and Zhang Bai'ang, "Wang Ji sanyin sanshi bubian," 66–67.

20. Another scholar who criticizes Wang Ji's weakness of character is Ye Qingbin in "Wang Ji yanjiu," 167–189.

21. This story is related in a letter purportedly penned by Wang Ji; however, it is not found in Wang Ji's collection nor is it included in the *Tangwen cui*, a Song anthology of Tang prose. Instead it is found among the collected prose of Wang Fuzhi 王福畤, Wang Ji's nephew; see "Lu Donggaozi da Chen Shangshu shuliie" 錄東皋子答陳尚書書略 in the Qing anthology *QTW*, 161.2a–3a. Many scholars question the letter's authenticity, suspecting it is a forgery. For a good summary of this issue see Wechsler, "The Confucian Teacher Wang T'ung," 232 and 243–244.

22. See Jia Jinhua, "Wang Ji yu Wei Jin fengdu," 1–7. For a comparably sympathetic view of Wang Ji's reclusion see Zhang Mingfei, "Shilun chu Tang shiren Wang Ji de yinyi," in *Tangyin lunsou*, 268–278.

23. For other examples see Takagi Masakazu, "Ō Seki no denki to bungaku," 40–70; Ōno Jitsunosuke, "Ō Seki to sono shifū," 64–92; You Xinli, "Wang Ji ji qi zuopin," 151–177; Ogasawara Hiroe, "Ō Seki ron," 65–105.

24. See Owen, *Poetry of the Early T'ang*, 62–63.

25. Ibid., 67. For Owen's discussion of an "opposition poetics" in the Sui and early Tang see "An Opposition Poetics and the Sui" and "The Sui Legacy: Wei Cheng and Li Pai-yao," chaps. 2 and 3 in *Poetry of the Early T'ang*, 14–26 and 27–41. A similar emphasis on Wang Ji's "opposition poetics" is found in a more recent study of the history of Tang poetry; see Xu Zong, *Tangshi shi*, 1:112–129.

26. See Weng Fanggang, *Shizhou shihua*, 2.1364. The simurgh is a phoenix-like bird in Eastern mythology. See also Stephen Owen: "Wang Ji's poetry is a unique phenomenon in his age.... He possesses a simplicity of diction, a directness of syntax, and a lack of ornament which are like a fresh breeze in the rarefied atmosphere of contemporary court poetry" (*Poetry of the Early T'ang*, 62).

Chapter 1: Wang Ji and Sui-Tang Literati Culture

1. In this study I refer to Lü Cai's preface in the five-*juan* editions only. As explained in the introduction, the five-*juan* collection of Wang Ji's works (*Wenji*) was unknown to most readers until the mid-1980s, and this holds true of the longer version of the preface as well. The obscure history of the transmission of the longer collection seems fortunately to have prevented it from serious contamination, and I therefore take it as the more reliable.

2. See *Jiu Tang shu*, 192.5116, and *Xin Tang shu*, 196.5594–5596. For a comprehensive survey of the representation of recluse culture and personalities in early China through the sixth century see Berkowitz, *Patterns of Disengagement*. See also Jiang Xingyu, *Zhongguo yinshi yu wenhua*, and Liu Xiangfei, "Tangren yinyi fengqi ji qi yingxiang."

3. There are other sources in which we find occasional accounts of Wang Ji's life. One of them is a short story titled "Tale of an Ancient Mirror" (Gujing ji 古鏡

記), which tells of Wang Ji's journey round the country after his first retirement. This story of fantastic adventures and strange encounters is narrated by an otherwise unknown Wang Du 王度 (n.d.) of the Sui dynasty, to whom the authorship has also been attributed. In it the narrator refers to Wang Ji as his younger brother. Although scholars agree that one of Wang Ji's brothers wrote "Tale of an Ancient Mirror," there has always been disagreement over which brother it was. Most have assumed that it was actually Wang Ji's third brother, Wang Ning 王凝, because Wang Ji mentions Wang Ning in his writings but never a Wang Du. Two recent studies have argued convincingly against such an assumption: Sun Wang, "Wang Du kao," in *Wosou zagao*, 1–26; and Han Lizhou, "'Gujing ji' shi Sui Tang zhi ji de Wang Du suozuo xinzheng," 43–49. The text of the short story can be found in *Taiping guangji*, 230.1761–1767. For a modern critical edition see Wang Bijiang, *Tangren xiaoshuo*, 3–17. Two additional sources provide information on Wang Ji and his family: an unofficial biography of Wang Tong, the most famous of Wang Ji's brothers, titled "Wenzhongzi shijia" 文中子世家; and the *Zhongshuo* (also referred to by the title *Wenzhongzi* 文中子), a collection of dialogues ostensibly between Wang Tong and his disciples patterned after *The Analects* of Confucius. "Wenzhongzi shijia" was written by one of Wang Tong's disciples, Du Yan. The text is appended to *Zhongshuo* and included among Du Yan's prose works in *QTW*, 135.18b–23a. The existence of Wang Tong and the authenticity of the *Zhongshuo*, however, have been issues of heated debate since the Song dynasty. Scholars in the twentieth century have generally accepted Wang Tong's historical existence and hold that *Zhongshuo* accurately represents Wang Tong's ideas and philosophy while maintaining that at least portions of the *Zhongshuo* are either corrupt or outright forgery. For a discussion of these issues see Wechsler, "The Confucian Teacher Wang T'ung," and Warner, "Wang Tong," 370–390.

4. While there is no question about the date of Wang Ji's death, none of the historical sources indicate his date of birth or exact age at the time of death. Zheng Zhenduo 鄭振鐸 (1897–1958) was the first to suggest 590 as the estimated year of Wang Ji's birth (see *Chatuben Zhongguo wenxueshi*, 364), but he does not explain how he arrived at this date. A different year, 585, has been suggested by others, making Wang Ji only a year younger than Wang Tong and leaving little time between them for the birth of Wang Ning (see note 3). Scholars who accept the second date base their conclusion on a comment Wang Ji makes in his "You Beishan fu," but textual discrepancies among different editions cause many to question the reliability of this evidence. For recent studies on the matter see You Xinli, "Wang Ji yinianlu," 149–185; Fu Xuancong, "Tangdai shiren kaolüe," 159–163; Han Lizhou, "Wang Ji shengping qiushi," 177–188. Here I follow the general consensus and accept the date 590 as a reasonable estimate.

5. According to popular belief, the Wang clan of Taiyuan descends from Prince Jin 太子晉, the deposed heir-apparent of King Ling of Zhou 周靈王 (r. 571–545 B.C.). After having offended his father with his outspokenness, the prince was demoted to the status of a commoner. He is better remembered in popular legend as the immortal Wang Ziqiao 王子喬, who travels about on the back of a crane. For an official account of the genealogy of the Wang clan of Taiyuan see

"Genealogy of the Grand Councillors" (Zaixiang shixi biao 宰相世系表) in *Xin Tang shu*, 72.2601. See also Moriya Mitsuo, *Rikuchō monbatsu no ichi kenkyū*. Du Yan, author of Wang Tong's unofficial biography, "Wenzhongzi shijia," begins his account of the Wang family history with Wang Ba, the famous farmer-hermit of the Later Han, without mentioning a lineage from the House of Zhou; he does, however, provide an impressive list of the forebears of the Wang family who were accomplished and served with distinction at court during the centuries before the Sui; see "Wenzhongzi shijia," 5a–8a.

6. *Wenji*, 1.

7. See *Nan Qi shu*, 1.9–13, and *Song shu*, 89.2232–2234. Yuan Can's biography can be found in *Song shu*, 89.2229–2234.

8. *Zhongshuo* records the following conversation between Wang Tong, his brother Wang Ning, and his student Pei Xi 裴晞: "Pei Xi asked about the deeds of Duke Mu, and the Master [Wang Tong] replied, 'Haven't you heard about the phoenix? It lands wherever it sees the radiance of moral power. Why should it fixate on one particular place?' Shutian 叔恬 [Wang Ning] said, 'Duke Mu's action made clear the difference between the Qi and the Wei'" (*SBBY*, 7.4a).

9. For details of these events see *Wei shu*, 10.255–269 and 75.1661–1665.

10. According to the *Zhongshuo*, when Wang Ning asked Wang Tong about Wen Zisheng's character, Wang Tong replied: "He was a treacherous man. He had petty wit but big schemes. Tongzhou [Wang Yan] had reason to gnash his teeth about the Yongan events" (4.3a). An account of the career and life of both Wang Qiu and Wang Yan can also be found in "Lu Guan Ziming shi" 錄關子明事, a document ascribed to Wang Tong's son Wang Fuzhi 王福畤 and included among the appendixes to the *Zhongshuo* (10.11a–15a). But serious factual discrepancies in this document invite questions about its authenticity and credibility. See Warner, "Wang Tong."

11. The claim is even made that at the height of their careers Wang Long and Wang Tong each attracted followings of over a thousand students, a number exaggerated by convention, of course, but underscoring their reputations. See Du Yan, "Wenzhongzi shijia," 5b.

12. *Wenji*, preface, 1.

13. In several of Wang Ji's writings, particularly in his "*Fu* on Roaming the Northern Mountains" (*Wenji*, 5–6), he speaks with great familiarity of activities at his brother's school.

14. In several of Wang Ji's poems we read that in retirement he supplemented his farming income by selling divinations. Lü Cai, too, praises his expertise in these arts.

15. "To Zhai Zhengshi, the Scholar at Home: Expressing My Resolve in Old Age," *Wenji*, 110.

16. *Han shu*, 64.2819–2820.

17. *Hou Han shu*, 80b.2653.

18. Lü Cai affirms this image of a proud and highly moral young Wang Ji in a story of his visit as a fifteen-year-old to Yang Su 楊素 (d. 606), a powerful minister at Chang'an:

When Wang Ji was in Chang'an, he sought an audience with the Lord of Yue [越公], Yang Su. On the day of his calling, Lord Yang's residence was crowded with visitors. Having seen Wang Ji's calling card, Lord Yang had Wang Ji brought in but received him insolently. Wang Ji thereupon said to him, "I have heard that when worthy men called on the Duke of Zhou, he would immediately put down his half-eaten food or leave his hair half-done to receive them. If you, my perspicacious lord, want to guarantee your noble prosperity, it would not be wise of you to receive the world's talented men in an insolent manner." [*Wenji*, preface, 1]

19. See *Sui shu*, 4.87. "Filial and Brotherly" and "Incorrupt and Pure" are two nomination categories; see Hucker, *Dictionary of Official Titles*, no. 2418. Different sources give different dates, none specific, for Wang Ji's nomination for official appointment. On this issue see note 24 in this chapter.

20. The official title of his first position is *mishu zhengzi* 秘書正字, which Hucker translates as "proofreader in the palace library" (*Dictionary of Official Titles*, no. 450).

21. *Wenji*, preface, 2.

22. Wang Ji may have suffered mildly from rheumatism, variously referred to as *zuji* 足疾, *fengji* 風疾, and *fengbi* 風痹.

23. *Wenji*, preface, 2.

24. Precisely when Wang Ji first took office and how long he remained in service is uncertain. According to Lü Cai, Wang Ji was recommended to the throne sometime in "Daye *mo*" 大業末 (the final year[s] of Daye, that is, the end of Emperor Yang's reign), but he mentions no specific year. Wang Ji's biographies in the two Tang histories record simply "Daye *zhong*" 大業中, leaving two possible interpretations: "in the middle of Daye," which sets the date of Wang Ji's first appointment around 610 so that his service lasts four years, or simply "during the Daye years," which could be any year including the final years of the period, as Lü Cai states. In *Sui shu* there is only one record of Emperor Yang issuing an edict to request local magistrates to recommend candidates from among the Filial and Brotherly (*xiaodi*) and the Incorrupt and Pure (*lianjie*) jointly, leading many scholars to believe that Wang Ji took office in 614; see *Sui shu*, 3.87; Feng Chengji, "Guanyu Wang Wugong de jixiang kaozheng"; You Xinli, "Wang Ji yinianlu"; and Fu Xuancong, "Tangdai shiren kaolüe." Others are skeptical of this date, arguing that one year is not enough for a man to receive an appointment, request and receive a transfer to another office in the south, establish a pattern of reckless negligence while on duty, and then retire. They suggest that Wang Ji probably took office sometime around 610; see, for example, Han Lizhou, "Wang Ji shengping qiushi." Whichever the case may be, it is generally accepted that Wang Ji's first tenure in office was remarkably short.

25. *Wenji*, preface, 2. Wang Ji's biography in *Xin Tang shu* reports a slightly different version of his departing words. There the quote reads: "The snares and nets are hanging in the sky. Where am I going to go?" 網羅在天, 吾且安之 (196.5594).

26. *Wenji*, preface, 2.

27. *Wenji*, 61–62.

28. This is a reference to Tao Qian. Glutinous millet is the main ingredient for making fermented beverages. In the "Biography of Tao Qian" in *Jin shu* we read:

In the public fields [Tao] ordered his subordinates to plant only glutinous millet, saying, "That should give me enough to make wine so that I can always be drunk." Only after his wife and sons persistently begged him to plant some nonglutinous millet [for food], then he agreed to use one *qing*, fifty *mu* for planting glutinous millet and fifty *mu* for nonglutinous millet. [94.2461]

29. Infantry commandant is the official position for which Ruan Ji allegedly requested an appointment. According to his *Jin shu* biography, "Ruan Ji heard that the attendant in the infantry's kitchen was very good at brewing wine and there was 300 *hu* of wine stocked there. Thereupon he pleaded to be appointed infantry commandant" (49.1360).

30. Han Lizhou's edition reads: 但使百年相續醉, 何辭夜夜甕間眠. Han notes that in the Li text, which he used as his base text, 使百年相續醉 is crossed out. A marginal note suggests an alternative reading: 願朝朝長得醉. I choose to follow the latter for two reasons. First, the closing couplet in Wang Ji's "Composed After Stopping by Mr. Cheng's Place for a Drink" (Guo Cheng chushi yin shuai'er cheng yong 過程處士飲率爾成詠), just four poems earlier in the collection, contains one line that is identical to the first line of Han's version. The couplet reads: 但使百年相續醉, 何愁萬里客衣單 (*Wenji*, 58). It is unlikely that Wang Ji would have used the exact same line in these two different poems. And a close examination of the parallel structures of these two couplets suggests that the line in Han's version properly belongs to the poem addressed to Mr. Cheng and was copied into this poem by mistake.

31. *Wenji*, 33.

32. It is believed that the custom of observing the Lustration Festival originated in the state of Zheng 鄭, where people would gather along the Zhen and Wei Rivers at a certain time in spring, wading and bathing in the streams among floating peach blossoms. Later the date became fixed on the third day of the third month. See, for example, *YWLJ*, 4.62. For a discussion of the history and customs of the Lustration Festival in ancient China see Bodde, *Festivals in Classical China*, 273–288.

33. Ye refers to the capital of Wei 魏 (220–264) during the Three Kingdoms period. Luo is Luoyang 洛陽, the ancient capital of imperial China.

34. Nandu Bridge is a place outside Luoyang famous for celebration gatherings for the Lustration Festival.

35. This is an allusion to a story about the Jin-period recluse Xia Tong 夏統 (third century), who in the midst of the festival celebration was completely unaffected by the merrymaking around him, paying attention only to sun-drying herbs on his boat. See his biography in *Jin shu*, 94.2429.

36. King Zhao of Qin 秦昭王 (r. 306–251 B.C.) was said to be holding a feast on the river bend on the first *si* 巳 day of the third month when a bronze figure emerged out of the river with a sword in his hand, which he presented to the king

saying: "This will make you rule Western China." Thus began the custom of floating wine cups by the river bend on the Lustration Festival. See Wu Jun, *Xu Qi Xie ji*, 6b.

37. See note 32 in this chapter.

38. Refers to a place in Guiji 會稽 of present-day Zhejiang 浙江 province, famous for a reputed gathering of literati on the Lustration Festival during the Jin dynasty. Hosted by Wang Xizhi 王羲之 (321–379; alt. 303–361), a renowned calligrapher, author, and owner of the Magnolia Leaf Pavilion, these writers were said to have spent the day drinking wine and writing poetry commemorating the festival. An account of their gathering can be found in Wang Xizhi's biography in *Jin shu*, 80.2099.

39. "On an Ancient Theme: Composed in Haste and Presented to Xue Shou, the Secretarial Aide to the Prince, When He Stopped by My Village for a Visit" (Xue Jishi Shou guo zhuang jian xun ti guyi yi zeng 薛記室收過莊見尋率題古意以贈), *Wenji*, 55.

40. The source of this allusion is actually not Tao Yuanming (that is, Tao Qian) but a letter written by the Later Han scholar Cai Yong 蔡邕 (133–192) in which he describes his life in retirement with the sentence, "I pour out some wine and roast some dry fish; it is such a pleasure, I am completely delighted." See *Cai Zhonglang ji waiji* 蔡中郎集外集 (*SBBY*), 2.11b.

41. Gongsun Hong 公孫弘 (199–120 B.C.) was a prominent minister in the court of Emperor Wu of the Han 漢武帝. He was said to have come from a very poor family, and he had to herd pigs when he was young. See *Han shu*, 58.2613–2624.

42. "Being Recommended to Court, I Answer the Summons and Bid Farewell to Old Friends in My Home Village" (Bei ju ying zheng bie xiangzhong guren 被舉應徵別鄉中故人), *Wenji*, 113.

43. Traditionally these items were presented as token gifts to those invited to attend the ruler at court. The items represented the ruler's recognition of a person's honorable character and praiseworthy talents. For an example see Ge Hong, "Yi min" 逸民 in the "Outer Chapters" of *Baopuzi*, 2.172b–173a.

44. Early accounts of this story differ in what happened to Jie Zitui. While *Zuo zhuan* 左傳 (Xigong 24 僖公二十四年) simply states that Jie went into hiding together with his mother and later died (see Du Yu, *Chunqiu jing zhuan jijie*, 6.340–341), Sima Qian 司馬遷 (145–86? B.C.) follows the version provided here in his *Shi ji* account of Jie's fate (39.1662). According to the Qing scholar Gu Yanwu 顧炎武 (1613–1682), the legend of Jie Zitui being burned to death is first recorded in *Zhuangzi* (see Gu Yanwu, *Ri zhi lu jishi*, 25.880–883). For *Zhuangzi*'s version of this story see 29.1186–1187.

45. Xu Ling 徐陵 (507–583), for example, wrote in his "Yuanyang fu" 鴛鴦賦: "Seeing its reflection in water, the pheasant is content; / Looking at its own image in the mirror, the lone simurgh will remain unpaired." See "Quan Chen wen" 全陳文 in *QSG*, 3431a. Liu Jingshu 劉敬叔 (ca. 468), in the *Yi yuan* 異苑, records:

Pheasants are fond of their own feathers. Whenever [they see their images] reflected in the water, they [begin to] dance. During the reign of Emperor

Wu of Wei [Cao Cao 曹操], someone brought a pheasant from the south and presented it to the throne. The emperor wanted to hear it sing and see it dance, but he could not make it do so. Prince Cangshu 蒼舒 [Cao Chong 曹沖] had someone put a mirror in front of it. Upon seeing its own reflection, the pheasant began to dance and would not stop until it died of exhaustion. Wei Zhongjiang 韋仲將 composed a *fu* to record this. [*Xuejin taoyuan* 學津討源, 3.2a]

46. In the category "Auspicious Omens" 祥瑞 in *YWLJ*, under the heading "Auspicious Clouds," there are several passages from historical works such as the *Book of Documents, Han shu*, and *Hanwu gushi* 漢武故事 that report the appearance of white clouds when the legendary ruler Yao 堯 and Emperor Wu of Han 漢 武帝 performed the proper rituals and sacrificial ceremonies (98.1696–1697). In *YWLJ*, these passages exemplify auspicious omens that confirm the virtuous deeds of the rulers. For this reason I take "white clouds" in Wang Ji's poem, especially given its coupling with "the vermilion color of the sun," to represent a virtuous court rather than its other conventional association with hermits.

47. There is evidence that Wang Ji traveled to Chang'an to join the Tang court sometime toward the end of 621. A poem by Wang Ji titled "After the Defeat of Dou Jiande, I Entered Chang'an and Wrote a Poem on Autumn Tumbleweed to Academician Xin" (Jiande po hou ru Chang'an yong qiupeng shi Xin xueshi 建德破 後入長安詠秋蓬示辛學士; *Wenji*, 126) alludes to Tang's victorious campaign against one of its powerful rivals, Dou Jiande, who was captured and executed in the seventh month of 621. (See *Jiu Tang shu*, 54.2242, and *Xin Tang shu*, 85.3696.) The time indicated in the title of Wang Ji's poem then eliminates the possibility of Wang Ji arriving in Chang'an earlier than the time of Dou's death. Likewise there is an anecdote recorded in Lü Cai's preface about Wang Ji receiving special favor from Chen Shuda 陳叔達 (d. 635) when he lived in the capital during the Wude era. Here Chen is referred to as Jiangguo Gong 江國公, a noble title he received in 622 (*Wenji*, preface, 4), which places Wang Ji in the capital at least by then.

48. "In the Capital, Homesick for My Old Garden, I See My Fellow Villager and Inquire" (Zai jing si guyuan jian xiangren wen 在京思故園見鄉人問), *Wenji*, 127–128. In all three-*juan* editions, attached to the end of this poem is a matching one in response attributed to a certain Zhu Zhonghui 朱仲晦. *QTS* also credits this poem to Zhu Zhonghui, his only entry. Its title is "Response to Wang Wugong's 'Homesick for My Old Garden, I See My Fellow Villager and Inquire'" (Da Wang Wugong si guyuan jian xiangren wen 答王無功思故園見鄉人問), and the *QTS* compilers further note that Zhu Zhonghui was the fellow villager whom Wang Ji addressed in his poem (38.494). But Wang Guo'an 王國安 points out that the same poem is found in the collected works of Zhu Xi 朱熹 (1130–1200); see *Zhu Wengong wenji*, 4.393. Zhu Xi's courtesy name *(zi)* is Zhonghui 仲晦. It is quite likely that Zhu Xi wrote the poem to match Wang Ji's as a literary exercise, but later the Ming or Qing editors were misled by the title into believing that it was written by Wang Ji's fellow villager; see Wang Guo'an, *Wang Ji shi zhu*, 25.

49. Han's text reads: 忘去不知回 (Oblivious to the time passing, I had no sense of return). Here I follow the reading found in all other editions.

50. *Mei* 梅, commonly translated "plum," is identified as *Prunus mume* by Stuart and Read, who identify it as the black plum or white plum (depending on style of preparation; Stuart, *Chinese Materia Medica*, 355) or dark plum (Read, *Chinese Medicinal Plants*, no. 447). But "the ornamental *Prunus mume*, called 'plum' (梅) in its native Japan, is actually an apricot," according to Bailey and Bailey, *Hortus Third*, 887.

51. *Zhou li* 周禮 (*Shisanjing*, 934a) stipulates that for traveling through marshland, it is more appropriate to use carriages with wheels that have short hubs and wide rims. This kind of carriage is called *xiaze che* 下澤車 (or *xingze che* 行澤 車). In literary tradition, the phrase "*xiaze che*" or "*xingze che*" was conventionally invoked, as Wang Ji does in this line, to indicate a rustic lifestyle in the country as opposed to the life of an official at court. The earliest known record of this association is in Ma Yuan's 馬援 (ca. 13 B.C.–ca. 48 A.D.) biography in *Hou Han shu* (24.838), where Ma Yuan recounts the advice of his cousin: "If a man for his whole life can have sufficient food and clothing, ride in a marsh-traveling carriage and drive a slow-footed horse, if he can become a commandary administrative clerk, whose duty is to guard graves, if he can earn the praise of locals for being a good man, then that is enough. If you desire anything more beyond that, you will only be making yourself suffer."

52. Stuart and Read identify *lai* 萊 (alternative name *li* 藜; common name pigweed, goosefoot, or lamb's quarters) as *Chenopodium album* (Stuart, *Chinese Materia Medica*, 104; Read, *Chinese Medicinal Plants*, no. 561a).

53. Again Lü Cai indicates only the general time frame *zhenguan zhong* 貞觀 中 (during or in the middle of the Zhenguan years; *Wenji*, preface, 4). You Xinli and Han Lizhou suggest that it was about the eleventh or twelfth year of Zhenguan (637–638), taking Lü Cai's statement literally as "in the middle of Zhenguan." See You Xinli, "Wang Ji yinianlu," 155; and Han Lizhou, "Wang Ji shengping qiushi," 186.

54. *Wenji*, preface, 4.

55. For general histories of the Sui and Tang see Lü Simian, *Sui Tang Wudai shi*; Bingham, *Founding of the T'ang Dynasty*; Wright, *Sui Dynasty*; Twitchett, *Cambridge History of China*, vol. 3, pt. 1; Cen Zhongmian, *Sui Tang shi*.

56. Wright and Twitchett, *Perspectives on the T'ang*, 1.

57. Twitchett, *Cambridge History of China*, vol. 3, pt. 1, 12.

58. A good account of these contrasting traditions may be found in Mou Runsun, "Tangchu nanbei xueren lunxue zhi yiqu ji qi yinxiang," 50–88.

59. Lu Deming's biography can be found in *Jiu Tang shu*, 189a.4944–4945, and *Xin Tang shu*, 198.5639–5640.

60. *Lun yu*, 13.3.

61. See Lu Deming's preface to *Jingdian shiwen*, 1.

62. The text of Lu Fayan's preface is preserved in *Guangyun* 廣韻; see *Jiaozheng Songben Guangyun*, 12–14.

63. Ibid., 13.

64. Bol, *"This Culture of Ours,"* 10.

65. Yan Zhitui, *Yanshi jiaxun*, 8.34a.

66. In addition to Wright and Twitchett, *Perspectives on the T'ang* (especially

14–25), see Wechsler, *Offerings of Jade and Silk*; Somers, "Time, Space, and Structure," 971–994; McMullen, *State and Scholars*.

67. Twitchett and Wright, *Perspectives on the T'ang*, 4.

68. On this feature of Tang rule see Cen Zhongmian, *Sui Tang shi*, 1:113–126. Cen's view represents a revision of an opposite account first advanced by Chen Yinke 陳寅恪. In his several studies on the political structure of the Sui and the early Tang, Chen argues that the Sui ruling class formed a trusted inner circle in the high court with those who had a blood relationship with the elite class, mostly with military power, of northwestern China, consisting of families of inter-racial marriages between non-Chinese and Chinese. Chen terms this circle "Guan-long Hu-Han jituan" 關隴胡漢集團 and refers to their policy on government bureaucracy as "*guanzhong benwei zhengce*" 關中本位政策. See Chen Yinke, *Sui Tang zhidu yuanyuan lüelun gao* and *Tangdai zhengzhishi shulun gao*.

69. McMullen, *State and Scholars*, 6.

70. Ibid., 258.

71. *Tang hui yao*, 64.1316. Another entry in the *Tang hui yao* reads:

In the tenth month of the fourth year of Wude [621], having just brought stability to the empire, the Prince of Qin [Li Shimin, the future Emperor Taizong] focused his attention on the study of classics. He established the College of Refined Learning west of the Imperial Palace to host learned men from all over the empire.... The congregation of scholars [in the college] were feasted with delicacies reserved for fifth-rank officials, and they were divided into three shifts, waiting on call in the agency even at night. Every day the Prince of Qin brought them in for audience, discussing literature and canonical texts with them. People at the time referred to those who gained admission to the college as "ascending Ying Isle." [64.1319; Ying Isle 瀛洲 is a legendary island of immortals in the Eastern Sea]

72. McMullen, *State and Scholars*, 257.

73. Ibid., 259.

74. Ibid., 8.

75. *Jiu Tang shu*, 89.4945.

76. The drive to reform literature may be dated even earlier than this—to the reign of Yuwen Tai 宇文泰 (r. 534–551), the Toba ruler who established the Western Wei dynasty; see the biography of Su Chuo 蘇綽 (498–546) in *Bei shi* 北史, 63.2239. When Yang Jian called for a similar reform of literature, he received an enthusiastic response from Li E 李諤 (fl. 600), who denounced Six Dynasties literature (especially of the later period) for being utterly decadent and depraved, and he urged the emperor to ban such immoral literary practice in both official and private compositions; see the biography of Li E in *Sui shu*, 66.1544–1545.

77. *YWLJ*, preface, 27.

78. Originally designating the *Ya* (Elegantia) section of the *Book of Songs*, "*ya*" later evolved into a term for the proper poetic principle conforming to ortho-dox Confucian ethics.

79. A.k.a. Jizha of Wu 吳季札 of the Spring and Autumn period, famous for

his ability to forecast the rise and fall of a state by evaluating the music of the *Songs* played at court. See Yang Bojun, *Chunqiu Zuozhuan zhu, Xiang* 29, 1161–1165.

80. *Sui shu*, 76.1730.

81. For further discussion of the idea of *ya* in the early Tang see Wilhelm and Knechtges, "T'ang T'ai-tsung's Poetry," 16.

82. See, for example, Li Boyao's preface to "Wenyuan zhuan" 文苑傳 in *Bei Qi shu*, 45.602, and Linghu Defen's discussion at the end of the biographies of Wang Bao 王襃 (sixth century B.C.) and Yu Xin 庾信 (513–581) in *Zhou shu* 41.742–745.

83. Preface to "Poems on the Imperial Capital" (Dijing pian 帝京篇), *QTS*, 1.1.

84. Refers to the application of phonetic and tonal regulations among literary circles of the Six Dynasties period.

85. *Sui shu*, 76.1730. This passage is also integrated into the introduction to "Wenyuan zhuan" in *Bei shi* (83.2781–2782).

86. *Zhou shu*, 41.742–745.

87. On Taizong's poetry see Wilhelm and Knechtges, "T'ang T'ai-tsung's Poetry"; see also Owen, *Poetry of the Early T'ang*, 52–59.

88. *Wenji*, 2.

89. For a translation and discussion of the "Great Preface" see Owen, *Readings in Chinese Literary Thought*, 37–49.

90. Ban Gu, preface to "Rhapsody on Two Capitals" (Liang du fu 兩都賦) in *WX*, 1.1.

91. *Wenji*, 148.

92. K. C. Hsiao, *Zhongguo zhengzhi sixiang shi*, 365; translated by F. Mote as *A History of Chinese Political Thought*, 1:605.

93. Holcombe, *In the Shadow of the Han*, 86–87.

94. Ibid., 88–89.

95. Mather, "Controversy over Conformity and Naturalness," 163. I rely primarily on Mather's concise account of *xuanxue*'s development in the summary to follow; but see also (in addition to Holcolmbe, *In the Shadow of the Han*, especially 85–134) Feng Youlan, *Zhongguo zhexue shi*, 2:94–135; translated by Derk Bodde as *History of Chinese Philosophy*, 2:168–236.

96. Quoted and translated by Mather in "Controversy over Conformity and Naturalness," 164. The complete text of He Yan's *Wuming lun* is no longer extant, but a fragment of it, which includes the passage cited here, is preserved in *Quan Sanguo wen* 全三國文, 39 (*QSG*, 1274b–1275a). For Wang Bi's discussion on *ziran* see his commentary to *Laozi Daode jing* (*SBBY*), 5.3b.

97. Mather, "Controversy over Conformity and Naturalness," 164–165.

98. See Dai Mingyang, *Xi Kang ji*, 234; quoted and translated by Mather, "Controversy over Conformity and Naturalness," 166.

99. Mather, "Controversy over Conformity and Naturalness," 168–169; emphasis in the original.

100. Ibid., 176.

101. Chan, *Source Book*, 315.

102. *Shishuo xinyu jiaojian*, 4.6; Mather, *Shih-shuo hsin-yü*, 95. For an

extensive study on the discursive practice of the Wei-Jin period see Kong Fan, *Wei Jin xuantan*.

103. See, for example, Kong Fan, *Wei Jin xuanxue he wenxue*. For an essay in English on the topic, with conclusions that are likewise sweeping and obscure, see Tu Wei-ming, "Profound Learning," 3–31.

104. Holzman, *Poetry and Politics*, 102.

105. Mather, "Controversy over Conformity and Naturalness," 175.

106. "Sitting in Solitude" (Du zuo 獨坐), lines 1–4, *Wenji*, 114.

107. "A Reply to Mr. Cheng, the Taoist Adept" (Da Cheng Daoshi shu 答程道士書), *Wenji*, 158.

108. Ibid.

109. Having commented on various historical personalities who withdrew from society, Confucius is recorded saying: "I, however, am different. I have no preconceptions about the permissible and the impermissible." See *Lun yu*, 18.8; Lau, *Analects*, 151.

110. Ibid., 9.14.

111. *Laozi*, 1.

112. According to his biography in *Shi ji* (63.2141), Laozi departed from the land of Zhou when he perceived its moral decline.

113. Wang Ji seems to be quoting a line from *The Sūtra of the Heart of Prajñā*. Se 色 (form) in Sanskrit is *rūpa*, designating all things in reality.

114. Here the phrase "all things" translates 諸法 (elsewhere 萬法 and 一切法), in Sanskrit *sarvadharma*, designating the most basic elements of existence.

115. *Lun yu*, 11.20.

116. See *Laozi*, 48: "One does less and less until one does nothing at all / and when one does nothing at all there is nothing undone" (Lau, *Lao Tzu*, 109).

117. The twelfth chapter of the *Abhidharma-kośa-śāstra* defines the "three calamities" (三災) (*saṃvartani*) as one of two types: the three smaller calamities are war, pestilence, and famine, which occur at the end of the *kalpa* of continuance (住劫); the three greater calamities are fire, flood, and storm, which occur at the end of the *kalpa* of destruction (壞劫). "Karmic accumulation" (行業), in Sanskrit *karma-abhisaṃskāra*, is the store of one's good and bad words, deeds, and thoughts (that is, karma) accumulated in previous lives. I cannot trace the original source of Wang Ji's quote in the scriptures of the Buddhist canon. Most likely he is not quoting directly from Buddhist scripture but repeating a dictum that was commonly attributed to scriptural sources in his time.

118. See *Zhuangzi*, 2.42–43.

119. See *Yijing*, hexagram 32: "Thunder and wind: the image of Duration. Thus the superior man stands firm and does not change his direction." For a translation and discussion see Wilhelm, *I Ching*, 127 and 547.

120. *Zhuangzi*, 8.313.

121. Ibid., 6.258.

122. Donald Holzman makes this observation in *Poetry and Politics*, 235.

123. Ibid., 234–235.

124. See Lu Kanru and Feng Yuanjun, *Zhongguo shishi*, 2:320–326 (on Ruan Ji's poetry) and 2:258–268 (on Tao Qian's poetry).

125. Owen, *Poetry of the Early T'ang*, especially 14–26.

Chapter 2: The Recluse as Philosopher

1. *QTS*, 31.441. In *Tangshi jishi* (4.86), Ji Yougong (*jinshi*, 1121) recorded this poem under the title "Chu guan" 出關 (Leaving the pass). It is generally believed that Wei Zheng wrote "Shu huai" between 618 and 619, when he traveled to the northeastern territory as the Tang emperor's personal emissary to persuade the remaining rival groups to surrender to the newly established Tang court; see, for example, Wechsler, *Mirror to the Son of Heaven*, 60. For an account of Wei Zheng's mission see *Jiu Tang shu*, 71.2546, and *Xin Tang shu*, 97.3867–3868.

2. That is, "contending for control of the empire." The locus classicus of this expression is a remark that Kuai Tong 蒯通 made to Emperor Gaozu of Han: "When Qin lost its deer [that is, its seat on the throne], everyone in the empire chased after it. The one with great talent and speed captured it first" (*Shi ji*, 92.2692).

3. The "pass" refers to Tongguan 潼關, a vitally strategic pass near the confluence of the Wei River and the Yellow River (some 400 *li* west of Chang'an) and the gateway to the northeastern plain. See Li Jifu, *Yuanhe junxian tu zhi*, 2.35–36.

4. This couplet contains allusions to two Han personalities: Zhong Jun 終軍 and Li Yiji 酈食其. Zhong Jun was sent by Emperor Wu of Han to persuade the king of Nanyue (that is, Vietnam) that his kingdom should recognize Han as its suzerain and he should present himself in court before the Han emperor accordingly. At his departure, Zhong Jun asked the emperor to give him a long rein and pledged, "I will bring the king of Nanyue to Your Majesty's gate, even if I have to tie him up [and drag him here]." See *Han shu*, 64.2821. Li Yiji was famous for his skills of persuasion. When Liu Bang was contending for the throne against the king of Chu, Xiang Yu 項羽, Li Yiji persuaded the king of Qi, Tian Guang 田廣—without using any military force—to subjugate himself to Liu Bang 劉邦 (later Emperor Gaozu of Han 漢高祖) and proclaim Qi the "eastern vassal state" (*dong fan* 東藩) of Han. See *Shi ji*, 97.2693–2696; *Han shu*, 43.2107–2110.

5. See "Chou si" 抽思 (Outpouring of sad thoughts) of the "Jiu zhang" 九章 (Nine pieces): "The road to Ying is so long, / Yet my soul flies there many a time each night" 惟郢路之遙遠兮魂一夕而九逝 (Hong Xingzu, *Chuci buzhu*, 4.232).

6. Ji Bu of the early Han was well known for being true to his word. In his home region, there was purportedly a proverb: "Obtaining a hundred catties of gold is not as good as obtaining one promise from Ji Bu" (*Shi ji*, 100.2731; *Han shu*, 37.1978). Hou Ying of the Warring States period was a recluse from whom Lord Xinling 信陵君, the youngest son of the king of Wei, sought counsel. When Lord Xinling took part in a military campaign against the state of Qin, Hou Ying thought he was too old to join his patron. Instead he promised to show his support by committing suicide on the day of the attack, a promise he purportedly kept (*Shi ji*, 77.2380–2381).

7. Owen, *Poetry of the Early T'ang*, 28. For Owen's analysis of Wei Zheng's poem see pp. 27–30. It is also discussed by Wechsler, *Mirror to the Son of Heaven*, 60–62.

8. *Wenji*, 55. Although Wang Ji's poem is undated, most likely he wrote it sometime in late 621. Xue Shou was appointed *Tiance fu jishi canjun* 天策府記室 參軍 (secretarial aide to the office of heavenly strategies) in the tenth month of 621

(*Jiu Tang shu*, 73.2588; *Xin Tang shu*, 98.3891). Wang Ji obviously was aware of Xue's new position as shown in the way he dedicated his poem to Xue. Yet it is unlikely that Xue's visit occurred after 621, because Wang left his home in retirement later that year to go to Chang'an for an official appointment and ended up staying in the capital for several years before returning home again (see Chapter 1). See Kang Jinsheng and Xia Lianbo, *Wang Ji ji biannian jiaozhu*, 84 n. 1.

9. Here I am translating the phrase "*sangzi*" 桑梓 (mulberry and catalpa) figuratively. Because mulberry and catalpa were typically planted next to one's residence in ancient times, by metonymy the binomial term "*sangzi*" later was understood to mean "native land," "hometown," or "former residence." See, for example, the final lines of "*Fu* on the Southern Capital" (Nandu fu 南都賦) by Zhang Heng 張衡 (78–139): "The ruler shall forever be filial, / And always remember the mulberry and catalpa of home. / The Perfect Man tours the south / To visit his old village" 永世克孝, 懷桑梓焉. 真人南巡, 覿舊里焉 (*WX*, 4.162; Knechtges, *Wen xuan*, 1:335).

10. The "great bird riding on the wind" alludes to the great Peng in *Zhuangzi*. As legend has it, "When the Peng travels to the South Ocean, the wake it thrashes on the water is three thousand miles long, it mounts spiralling on the whirlwind ninety thousand miles high, and is gone six months before it is out of its breath" (1.6; Graham, *Chuang-tzu*, 43). The "fish stranded in the carriage rut" alludes to a passage in chap. 26 of *Zhuangzi* (26.1049).

11. "Mr. Yao" refers to Yao Yi 姚義, a follower of Wang Tong. In Wang Ji's collected works there is a poem titled "On an Autumn Night, I Was Pleasantly Surprised to Run into Yao Yi, a Scholar in Retirement" (Qiuye xiyu Yao chushi Yi 秋夜喜遇姚處士義). In addition, Wang Ji mentions Yao Yi in several personal letters and also in his "*Fu* on Roaming the Northern Mountains," suggesting a close relationship between the two. The identity of Mr. Xu, however, is unclear.

12. See Chapter 1, note 40.

13. See Chapter 1, note 41.

14. *Zhuangzi*, 26: "The bait [荃; or rather "trap"] is the means to get a fish where you want it; catch the fish and you forget the bait. The snare is the means to get the rabbit where you want it; catch the rabbit and you forget the snare. Words are means to get the idea where you want it; catch onto the idea and you forget about the words" (26.1082; Graham, *Chuang-tzu*, 190).

15. Feng Youlan, *History of Chinese Philosophy*, 1:258.

16. *Wenji*, 48.

17. Holzman, *Poetry and Politics*, 1.

18. Cao Zhi 曹植 (192–232), for example, is one of the early poets who frequently invokes the image of the tumbleweed buffeted by the wind to represent his own "buffeting" from place to place—first by his brother, Cao Pi 曹丕 (187–226), the self-declared emperor of the Wei dynasty, then by his nephew, Cao Rui 曹叡 (r. 226–239), who succeeded Cao Pi as emperor. An example of Cao Zhi's self-representation as a tumbleweed may be found in his "Xujue pian" 吁嗟篇. See Zhao Youwen, *Cao Zhi ji jiaozhu*, 382–383. For a translation and discussion of this poem see Frankel, "Fifteen Poems," 10.

19. *Zhuangzi*, 4.134; Graham, *Chuang-tzu*, 66–69.

20. *Wenji*, 54.

21. *Wenji*, 47.

22. *Wenji*, 118–124.

23. It has been argued, but not at all persuasively, that the "Guyi" poems were originally independent and only later grouped by Wang Ji's editors. Ōno Jitsunosuke, for example, puzzlingly argues that these poems could not have been composed as a group because they are not all the same length; see "Ō Seki to sono shifū," 81. In contrast, Imaba Masami 今場正美 argues that a clear sequential structure is evident in the "Guyi" series; see "Ō Seki no 'Koyi' roku shu ni tsuite," 27–39.

24. See, for example, Ōno Jitsunosuke, "Ō Seki to sono shifū," 64–92 (especially 81–85); Kang Jinsheng and Xia Lianbao's commentary notes to these six poems in *Biannian jiaozhu*, 71–79; Gao Guangfu, "Lüelun Wang Ji de zongdan ji qi shi de pingdan," 35–40.

25. See Imaba Masami, "Ō Seki no 'Koyi' roku shu ni tsuite," 27–39.

26. In the "Yu gong" 禹貢 chapter of *Shang shu* it is recorded: "Between the sea, Mount Dai [Mount Tai 泰], and the Huai 淮 River is Xuzhou 徐州.... Its tribute is ... the solitary paulownia (桐) tree from the south slope of Mount Yi 嶧." Kong Anguo's 孔安國 commentary to this line reads: "On the sunny side of Mount Yi, there grows a special paulownia tree, fitting material for making zithers and lutes" (*Shisanjing*, 184b).

27. Mount Kun 崑丘 refers to Mount Kunlun, which produces very fine jade. According to the "Shidi" 釋地 chapter of the *Erya* 爾雅: "A fine place in the northwest is the range of Mount Kunlun, in which there is *qiulin* 璆琳 (fine jade of dark color) and *langgan* 琅玕 (pearl-shaped jade)" (*Shisanjing*, 2615b). The "Quan yan" 詮言 chapter of *Huainanzi* 淮南子, attributed to Liu An 劉安 (179–122 B.C.), contains the line: "Plug one's ears with jade from Mount Kun[lun], and dust and filth cannot dirty them" (*SBBY*, 14.7b).

28. In a letter to Feng Zihua, Wang Ji reports that one Pei Kongming 裴孔明 made him a zither as a gift, and he describes it as unadorned with "the stand shaped like phoenix feet and the ends shaped like dragon lips; it is truly different from commonly seen zithers" (*Wenji*, 149).

29. The origin of "Guangling san" 廣陵散 is unknown. According to Xi Kang's *Jin shu* biography, once in the middle of the night a man who claimed to have come from antiquity called on Xi Kang. This ancient visitor taught Xi Kang to play a tune that turned out to be "Guangling san," and he made Xi Kang promise that he would never teach it to anyone else (*Jin shu*, 49.1374). In *Shishuo xinyu*, a passage recounting the night before Xi Kang's execution reads:

On the eve of Xi Kang's execution in the Eastern Marketplace of Loyang, his spirit and manner showed no change. Taking out his seven-stringed zither, he plucked the strings and played the "Melody of Guangling" (Guangling san). When the song was ended, he said: "Yuan Chun once asked to learn this melody, but I remained firm in my stubbornness, and never gave it to him. From now on the 'Melody of Guangling' is no more!" [*Shishuo xinyu jiaojian*, 6.265; Mather, *New Account*, 180]

30. The composer of "Mingguang qu" 明光曲 is believed to be Zhao Mingguang 趙明光, a grandee of the ancient state of Chu. He purportedly wrote the song upon learning that a petty-minded minister slandered him in front of King Zhao of Chu 楚昭王. See Cai Yong, *Qin cao*, 2.6a–6b (in *Shaowu Xushi congshu*). Kang Jinsheng and Xia Lianbao cite the following story from *Xu Qi Xie ji* (*Biannian jiaozhu*, 71 n. 9): A certain Wang Yanbo 王彥伯 encountered a young lady one night and heard her play a remarkable tune he had never heard before. The young lady told him that it was a song called "Chu Mingguang" 楚明光 and that, other than Xi Kang, few people could play it. When Wang Yanbo asked to learn the tune, she said: "This song is not for the entertainment of a voluptuous layman. It is only for those men who live in caves and hide in valleys to delight themselves with." I cannot, however, locate this story in the edition of *Xu Qi Xie ji* included in the *Han Wei congshu* collection available to me.

31. Zhong Ziqi 鍾子期 is famous for his ability to understand another man's mind simply by listening to the music he played. In the "Tangwen" 湯問 chapter of *Liezi* 列子, we learn that "Boya 伯牙 was an excellent zither player; Zhong Ziqi was an excellent listener. Boya once played the zither and his mind was focused on Mount Tai; Zhong Ziqi said, 'Splendid! Grand and lofty, it is like Mount Tai!' When Boya's mind shifted to the flowing water, Zhong Ziqi said, 'Vast and mighty, it is like the flowing water!' Whatever that was on Boya's mind, Zhong Ziqi would surely comprehend it" (*SBBY*, 16a–b).

32. *XQHW*, 1.496; see also Holzman's translation in *Poetry and Politics*, 229.

33. Holzman, *Poetry and Politics*, 229.

34. A variation on this view is Imaba Masami's, which takes Wang Ji as the subject of the first couplet as well as the rest of the poem, so that one might paraphrase the opening lines thus: "'Where is the secluded man?' you ask. 'You will find the sign of me beneath the purple cliff,' I reply. Here I lay out my precious zither, and have nothing more I desire." Of course, the absence of pronouns in the original makes it difficult to argue which reading is more likely. But in any case, Imaba argues for an unsupportable topical interpretation: that the poem laments Wang Ji's loss of his friend Xue Shou, whom the poet regarded as his Zhong Ziqi (line 13); see Imaba, "Ō Seki no 'Koyi' rokushu ni tsuite," 28–29.

35. *Wenji*, 71.

36. See the case of the "primitivist" objection to people's dependence on "artifice" in *Zhuangzi*, 12.444–445; Graham, *Chuang-tzu*, 185–187.

37. The state of Bactria was known to ancient China by the name Daxia 大夏. *Shi ji* records that "Daxia is over 2,000 *li* southwest of Dayuan. It is situated south of the Gui River" (*Shi ji*, 123.3164), or in the northern part of modern Afghanistan.

38. The legend of the creation of the pitch pipes varies slightly from version to version, one of which is the following in *Han shu*:

Formerly, the Yellow Lord sent Ling Lun to the western part of Bactria and the north side of Mount Kunlun to find the bamboo grown in the Xie Valley. He took those that were hollow and had even thickness, cut them at the joints of two sections, and blew. Thus he made the yellow-bell pitch. He made twelve pipes and listened to the calls of phoenixes. The male phoenix made six calls, and so did the female. He tried out their calls with the yellow-bell pitch; he could make all the sounds. This became the base tune for pitch pipes. [21A.959]

39. Han's edition reads: 翠莖犯雪密 (Its green stalks, standing against the snow, are dense). Han chooses to follow the reading in his base text, the Li edition, which is the only version that reads 雪 (snow) for 霄 (sky). It has been conventional practice to associate bamboos as well as evergreens with integrity and endurance of hardship. This association derives from the fact that bamboo and evergreens stay green through the harshest conditions of winter and, moreover, the word for their joints (*jie* 節) is the same as the word for "integrity." It is perhaps this assumed association that led editors of the Li edition and Han Lizhou to believe that a graphic confusion had occurred mistaking 霄 for 雪, both of which share classifier no. 173 (雨). But the element of snow is introduced in the following line. If line 4 indeed includes the element of snow, then this would be a very uncharacteristic instance of repetitiveness. Although one hesitates to make a textual argument on aesthetic grounds, it does strengthen the case against Han's acceptance of the unique reading in the Li edition.

40. A.k.a. the Yellow Lord. According to Sima Qian's 司馬遷 "Wudi benji" 五帝本記, "the Yellow Lord is the son of Shaodian 少典. His surname is Gongsun 公孫 and his personal name is Xuanyuan" (*Shi ji*, 1.1).

41. See note 38.

42. Owen, *Poetry of the Early T'ang*, 284.

43. See *Zhuangzi*, 17.633.

44. *Zhuangzi*, 4.167.

45. For a discussion of the controversy over the identification of the "Five Lakes" and "Three Rivers" see Knechtges, *Wen xuan*, 2:322 nn. 23 and 24.

46. The Zhen River 溱水 originates from Shenshui Yu 聖水峪 (Sacred Water Valley) in Mi Xian 密縣 (in modern Henan province). Running southeast, it joins the Wei River 洧水 and the two turn into the Ziji River 淄洎河.

47. Han's edition reads 枯骨 for 豐骨, the reading in all other editions.

48. The *Shiji* passage reads: "Only when a tortoise is a thousand years old does it reach one foot and two inches in length. Right before a ruler mobilizes his army and sends out his general, he will drill holes in the tortoise shell in the temple to decide whether [the deployment] is auspicious or not" (128.3227). Wang Guo'an cites a passage from *Yi Li* 逸禮 which stipulates that for sacrificial ceremonies and divination purposes, "the Son of Heaven uses tortoises that are one foot two inches long; feudal lords use those that are eight inches long; grandees use those that are six inches long; scholars and commoners use those that are four inches long" (*Wang Ji shi zhu*, 3, n. 2). This same reference is cited in Kang Jinsheng and Xia Lianbao's annotation to Wang Ji's collected works (*Biannian jiaozhu*, 73 n. 1).

49. It is also quite likely that Wang Ji is making an allusion here to the poem "Zhen Wei" 溱洧 in the "Zheng feng" 鄭風 section of the *Book of Songs* (*MS*, no. 95; Waley, *Book of Songs*, 28). Constructed in the form of a dialogue between male and female speakers, the poem reenacts courtship and mating rituals between

young men and women by the Zhen and Wei Rivers during a festival in spring. Traditionally, Confucian commentators had condemned this poem for being one of the examples of the licentiousness underlying the music of the state of Zheng, which ultimately led to the state's downfall. Their interpretation of the poem goes like this: aroused by the surging tide of the Zhen and Wei Rivers in early spring, young men and women gave way to licentious pleasure; but they failed to see that what attracted them to the rivers in springtime would be exactly what led them to their eventual moral fall. If indeed Wang Ji is alluding to this poem, then I should note that his emphasis is simply on the aspect that the tortoise, too, fails to see that danger—in this case, physical rather than moral—is waiting for him up ahead in the Zhen and Wei.

50. See *Zhuangzi*, chap. 26, for the story of the tortoise who cannot prevent its capture (to which this poem alludes). According to that story, a man named Yuanjun 元君 in the state of Song one day had a dream in which a young man appeared in front of him and claimed that he was a white tortoise. A few days later, Yuanjun was given a white tortoise as a tributary gift. He killed the tortoise to cast divinations. He drilled the shell seventy-two times, and each time the shell provided a prognostic reading. In *Zhuangzi* the moral is stated by Confucius, who upon hearing this story says:

> The divine tortoise is able to appear in Yuanjun's dream, yet it is unable to avoid the fisherman's net. Its knowledge enables it to provide seventy-two prognostic readings in succession without fail, yet it is unable to avoid the disaster of having its innards pulled out. If this is so, then knowledge has its limit and the divine spirit has its unreachable points. Although the tortoise might have ultimate knowledge, myriad people will be hunting it. A fish does not know to fear nets, but it is afraid of cormorants. When one gets rid of petty knowledge, then the great knowledge will be clear. When one gets rid of refinement, then he naturally becomes refined. [26.1067]

See also another adaptation of this story in Wang Ji's "The Divine Tortoise" (*Wenji*, 43).

51. *YWLJ*, 88.1513.

52. Han Lizhou's edition reads: 獨負凌寒潔 (Alone to withstand the chilling cold, it was immaculate). I follow all other editions in reading 凌雲 (clear clouds) for 凌寒 (chilling cold).

53. *Zhuangzi*, 4.150–151; Watson, *Chuang Tzu*, 59–61.

54. *WX*, 29.1347.

55. *WX*, 29.1348.

56. Han Lizhou's edition reads: 自然歲寒性 (By nature, it can withstand cold weather); I follow the more common reading, 自言 for 自然.

57. *Zhuangzi*, 4.167.

58. *YWLJ* cites *Shangshu Zhonghou* 尚書中候 "Yao governed his empire for seven decades, the male and female phoenix stopped at his court, building their nest on his lofty tower" (99.1707).

59. *Huainanzi* (*SBBY*), 10.12b.

60. *QTS*, 1.2; Owen, *Poetry of the Early T'ang*, 56, with my modification to line 7.

61. Owen, *Poetry of the Early T'ang*, 56.

62. See, for example, Han Lizhou, "Wang Ji shiwen xinian kao," 64–65; Imaba Masami, "Ō Seki no 'Koyi' rokushu ni tsuite."

63. See *Shiji*, 1.6; *Huainanzi*, 6.6b.

64. See *Shisanjing*, 1.144a.

Chapter 3: The Recluse as Farmer-Scholar

1. See Ye Qingbing, "Wang Ji yanjiu," 183–189; Gao Guangfu, "Lüelun Wang Ji de zongdan ji qi shi de pingdan," 37.

2. Jia Jinhua, "Wang Ji yu Wei Jin fengdu," 7.

3. Han Lizhou, "Lun Wang Ji de shi," 78–83. An exception to these three general tendencies is Zhang Mingfei's "Lun Wang Ji de tianyuan shi," in *Tangyin lunsou*, 184–194, which argues that Wang Ji's merging of pastoral and landscape themes was a significant contribution to the development of nature poetry in the Tang.

4. Although there are a few poems in Wang Ji's corpus that make explicit and disparaging references to the Sui, these poems were almost all written during the Tang period.

5. The other two are Wei Zheng and Li 李 (originally Xu 徐) Shiji 世勣 (549–669); see Twitchett, *Cambridge History of China*, vol. 3, pt. 1, 213. Both *Zhongshuo* and "Wenzhongzi shijia" claim that Fang Xuanling was a disciple of Wang Tong. Whether this is true or not, there is no reason for us to doubt that Fang was an acquaintance of the Wang brothers. See Warner, "Wang Tong," 384.

6. For Fang Xuanling's biography see *Jiu Tang shu*, 66.2459–2467; *Xin Tang shu*, 96.3853–3857.

7. *Wenji*, 72.

8. Huo Guang (d. 68 B.C.), younger brother of the Han general Huo Qubing 霍去病 (d. 116 B.C.), served in the court of Emperor Wu (r. 141–87 B.C.) and was entrusted to assist the emperor's young successor, Emperor Zhao 昭帝 (r. 87–74 B.C.), to the throne. After Emperor Zhao died, Huo first supported Liu He's 劉賀 (d. 59 B.C.) succession; but when Liu He demonstrated himself morally unfit as an emperor, Huo Guang was responsible for removing him and establishing Liu Xun 劉詢 on the throne, who became Emperor Xuan 宣帝 (r. 74–49 B.C.). Huo Guang's official biography describes him as loyal to the emperor, but the emperor is said to have felt "prickles down his back" whenever in his company. After Huo died, his entire family was accused of treason and executed. See *Han shu*, 68.2931–2959.

9. When King Wu 武王 of Zhou died, King Cheng 成王 (who was still a young child) succeeded to the throne and his uncle, the Duke of Zhou, was appointed regent. But soon a rumor started in the court that the Duke of Zhou harbored ill intentions toward the new king, because he was seen placing some bamboo prayer tallies in a metal-bound casket when King Wu was on his deathbed. This inspired suspicion in King Cheng toward the Duke of Zhou, who decided it best to withdraw from court and live quietly for two years to prove his innocence. Later, when King Cheng found out that the tallies were in fact the Duke of Zhou's prayer to

die in the place of King Wu, he invited the Duke of Zhou back to court. See *Shang shu (Shisanjing)*, 197a.

10. Fan Li 范蠡 was a grandee in the state of Yue 越 of the Warring States period (453–221 B.C.). After the state of Wu 吳 annexed Yue, Fan Li masterminded the King of Yue Gou Jian's 句踐 plot to reclaim his kingdom. But after Gou Jian's successful defeat of the state of Wu, Fan Li quietly went into hiding, leaving behind a word of advice to his fellow grandee, Wen Zhong 文種, who also helped Gou Jian in his campaign against Wu. Fan Li urged Wen Zhong to follow his example and run away, saying: "When the flying birds are extinct, fine bows will be stored away. When the cunning rabbits are finally killed, the hunting dogs will be boiled. The King of Yue is such a person ... with whom you can share his misery but not his joy." Wen Zhong took Fan's advice and declined to attend court, but he did not go into hiding. Soon Gou Jian ordered him to commit suicide. See *Shi ji*, 41.1746–1747.

11. Shu Guang 疏廣 (fl. 107–102 B.C.) was grand tutor to the crown prince in the court of Emperor Xuan of the Former Han. Five years after Shu Guang was promoted to the post of grand tutor, at the prime of his career, he retired pleading illness. He remained in retirement for the rest of his life. See *Han shu*, 71.3039–3040.

12. Vermilion (*zhu* 朱) is the color of the residential gate of high officials and nobility, here symbolizing riches and honor. Red (*chi* 赤) here refers to the color of blood, and the term "reddened clan" (*chizu* 赤族) is a euphemism for a blood purge. This couplet alludes to Yang Xiong's "Dissolving Ridicule" (Jie chao, 解嘲), in which Yang Xiong's persona ("Master Yang") puns on the word "*zhudan*" 朱丹 ("vermeil cinnabar," the color of the wheel hubs of high officials and nobility) and "*chi*" 赤, saying: "You only want to vermilion my wheel hubs. / You do not seem to know that just one slip will redden my entire clan." See *Han shu*, 87B.3566–3573; *WX*, 45.2005–2012; Knechtges, *Han Rhapsody*, 98.

13. A reference to hexagram 2 in the *Book of Changes*. The lines read: "Six at the beginning means, when there is hoarfrost underfoot, solid ice is not far" (Wilhelm, *I Ching*, 13, 389). That is, the autumn frost forewarns the coming cold winter, which symbolizes difficulty and treachery.

14. This couplet is a borrowing from the "desk inscription" (*zuoyouming* 座右銘) of the Later Han writer Cui Yuan 崔瑗 (78–143 B.C.): "Be cautious when you speak. Be restrained when you eat and drink. Knowing to be content is better than being struck by ill fortune. If you can always keep it in practice, then you will naturally thrive forever and ever" (*WX*, 56.2410).

15. *SBBY*, 5a; see also Lau, *Lao Tzu*, 65, and Henricks, *Lao-tzu*, 61.

16. *Wenji*, 49.

17. This refers to Confucius' supposed trip to seek advice from Laozi, at that time the historian in the archive of Zhou. The biography of Confucius in *Shi ji* records:

Nangong Jingshu of Lu said to the lord of Lu, "May your vassal be granted permission to go to Zhou with Confucius." The lord of Lu gave them a carriage, two horses, together with one young servant. They went to Zhou to ask about the rites. It was probably then that Confucius met Laozi. It is said that when Confucius took his leave, Laozi saw him off and said to him, "I have heard that a man with wealth and rank gives gifts of money while a man who has compassion for his fellow men gives gifts of words. I am unable to obtain either wealth or rank, but I have undeservedly acquired the reputation of a compassionate man. So I offer you these words as my parting gift: 'The reason that people who are clever and perceptive are always close to death is because they are fond of criticizing others. The reason that people who are learned and eloquent are always endangering themselves is because they expose the bad nature in others. Being the son of others, one should not regard his person as his own; being the vassal of others, one should not regard his person as his own.'" [47.1909]

Laozi's biography in *Shi ji* contains a different version of Laozi's parting words to Confucius. There Laozi is reported saying:

I have heard that a good merchant hides well his goods and makes it look as if his store is empty. Although a gentleman is endowed with great inner capacity, he wears a foolish countenance. Get rid of your arrogant attitude and your numerous desires! Let go your ingratiating bearings and your overly ambitious intents. These have no beneficial consequences to your person. That's all that I have to say to you. [63.2140; adapted from Lau, *Lao Tzu*, 8]

Laozi's *Shi ji* biography also reports that "Laozi cultivated the way and virtue, and his teachings aimed at self-effacement. He lived in Zhou for a long time, but seeing its decline he departed.... No one knew where he went in the end" (63.2141; Lau, *Lao Tzu*, 9).

18. *Sandai* 三代 refers to the dynasties Xia, Shang, and Zhou of antiquity.

19. The full passage is cited in note 17.

20. For a concise summary of early thinking about the rites see Wechsler, *Offerings of Jade and Silk*, 23–27.

21. *Wenji*, 60.

22. These two lines refer to four texts of the Confucian classics, the *Book of Rites*, *Book of Music*, *Book of Songs*, and *Book of Documents*. Ji Dan was the Duke of Zhou's personal name; and Kong Qiu was Confucius'.

23. In Wang Ji's collected works is a letter responding to one from this very Mr. Cheng, who seems to be urging Wang Ji to consider the pursuit of fame by taking up service or to rectify his wild behavior by conforming to social conventions. In any event, Wang Ji's letter centers on one theme—the virtue of being *zishi* 自適 (literally, according as nature suits)—and he jabs at Mr. Cheng for his inability to comprehend this idea. An excerpt from this letter is quoted in Chapter 1. For the full text of the letter see *Wenji*, 157–159.

24. *Wenji*, 45.

25. During the Warring States period, around 453 B.C. the Lord of Jin, Zhibo 知伯, was killed by his three powerful grandees who then divided his territory among themselves and established their own states (see *Shi ji*, 34.1553). Since

then the term "Three Jin" (*sanjin* 三晉) has been an alternative name for the area formerly comprising the state of Jin. Most of this area is now within modern Shanxi province.

26. Liu Gonggan is the courtesy name of Liu Zhen 劉楨 (d. 217), a literary master of the Jian'an period. When Cao Cao offered him an official appointment, he declined on the ground of illness. See *Sanguo zhi*, 21.599.

27. Zheng Zizhen is the courtesy name of the Han recluse Zheng Pu 鄭樸, who turned down an invitation to serve on Grand General Wang Feng's 王鳳 staff, living all his life as a farmer in a place called Gukou 谷口 (literally, mouth of a valley). See *Han shu*, 72.3056–3057.

28. *YWLJ* preserves the following excerpt on cranes from Zhou Chu's 周處 (d. 299) *Feng tu ji* 風土記:

Crying cranes (*ming he* 鳴鶴) are sensitive to dew. This kind of bird is alert by nature. When it comes to the eighth month and white dew falls, every drop makes noise as it hits the grass. At the sound of this, cranes immediately cry aloud to alert each other to move away from the spot where they have been sleeping, thinking that something harmful is approaching. [90.1564]

With this allusion Wang Ji seems not to be evoking the association of danger with the crane's calling but rather enhancing the atmosphere of the midnight scene this line depicts. Moreover, it parallels neatly with next line's "orioles sing," which reinforces the image of spring's arrival.

29. This couplet makes reference to two passages in *Zhuangzi* in which Yan Hui and Yuan Xian, two disciples of Confucius, express their contentment in life without riches and fame. See *Zhuangzi*, 28.1145 and 1139.

30. *Wenji*, 106.

31. Lu Qinli, *Tao Yuanming ji*, 40.

32. The original text reads "thirty years" (三十年). I follow editions that emend the line to "thirteen years," which do so on the assumption that a simple transposition has occurred, since Tao Qian served in office off and on for about thirteen years before retiring permanently.

33. See also Hightower, *Poetry of T'ao Ch'ien*, 50; Davis, *T'ao Yüan-ming*, 1:45; Watson, *Columbia Book of Chinese Poetry*, 129–130.

34. Lu Qinli notes that a variant reading of this line is 白雲停陰岡 ("White clouds pause on the shady ridge"; *XQHW*, 7.734).

35. *WX*, 21.1028; one of Zuo Si's contemporaries, Lu Ji (261–303), is the author of a poem similarly treating the "summoning" theme (see *WX*, 21.1029).

36. *Wenji*, 112. This poem is listed under a shorter title, "Leaning on a Staff to Search for a Recluse" (策杖尋隱士), in all three-*juan* editions. The character "*xun*" 尋 (to search) from line 1 is absent from the title in the five-*juan* editions; I have inserted it in brackets. The phrase "*fu ... de ...*" 賦 ... 得 in the long title cited here suggests that the poem is written on a prearranged topic and was composed at a social gathering as a literary exercise for a group audience. The identity of Lu Xinping, the host of this gathering, is unknown. This discovery of the full title should remind modern readers of the need to reevaluate the traditional inter-

pretation of the poem as a confession of private thoughts. There is no evidence to
indicate when the title was shortened and who was responsible for it. But the
change must have taken place long before *WYYH* was compiled, because its edi-
tors note no variant, suggesting that their base texts were all in agreement on the
later title.

37. This is a reference to the story of Yuan Hong 袁閎 of the Later Han, who
went into reclusion when he saw chaos breaking out in the world. He is said to
have wanted to go deep into the mountains but was reluctant to leave his aging
mother behind without care, so he built an earthen chamber in the courtyard of
his house and sealed himself inside. The chamber had no doors and just one win-
dow, which he opened only to take in food and water and when his mother came
to visit. He remained concealed in this chamber till his death years later. See *Hou
Han shu*, 45.1525–1526.

38. Xiaoran 孝然 refers to Jiao Xian 焦先, who lived at the end of the Later
Han. He went into reclusion when the Han court abdicated power to the Wei. At
first he lived in a thatched hut by the river, but later his hut burned down in a
brushfire, so he lived in the open elements. See his biography in Huangfu Mi's 皇
甫謐 *Gaoshi zhuan* 高士傳 (*SBBY*), 3.11b; see also *Wei shu* in *Sanguo zhi*, 11.363
n. 6. Weinian 威輦 refers to Dong Jing 董京 of Jin. A biographical sketch of him
from Wang Yin's 王隱 *Jin shu* is preserved in *Taiping yulan* 太平御覽, which
records that after the Sima clan usurped political power from the Wei and founded
the Jin dynasty, Dong Jing left the court, feigning madness. Later he disappeared
without a trace, leaving behind a poem denouncing the world's decline; see
Taiping yulan, 502.4a. The biographical sketch of Dong Jing in the *Jin shu* (com-
piled by Fang Xuanling et al. during the early Tang) focuses on his life as a home-
less recluse and does not elaborate on his leaving office; see *Jin shu*, 94.2426–2427.

39. The Zi River is also known as the Ba River 灞水 (see *Han shu*, 28A.1544),
and it is associated with the legend of Lü Shang 呂尚 (variously known as Taigong
Wang 太公望, Jiang Taigong 江太公, or Jiang Ziya 江子牙). Lü Shang was discov-
ered by King Wen of Zhou while fishing at the Ba River. Realizing that Lü Shang
possessed exceptional quality, King Wen invited him to his court to serve as a
councillor; as a consequence, Lü Shang helped King Wen establish the Zhou
empire. See Lü Shang's biography in *Shi ji*, 32.1477–1481.

40. The reference made in this line is not clear. Wang Ji's commentators
(Wang Guo'an, Kang Jinsheng, and Xia Lianbao) note only that Maoling 茂陵
(about 80 miles northwest of Chang'an) is the mausoleum town where Emperor
Wu of Han is buried, but they offer no further explanation of the significance of
this information. I have found no reference associating Emperor Wu with recluses
(implied by the net image). Under the entry "Maoling ju" in *Peiwen yunfu*, the
only citation is this very line (957.1). But besides Emperor Wu of Han, there
is another historical figure who is often associated with the name Maoling in liter-
ary tradition: Sima Xiangru 司馬相如 (179–117 B.C.), the cherished *fu* writer in
Emperor Wu's court who retired to Maoling at the end of his official career. A
Song recluse, Lin Bu 林逋 (967–1028), for example, supposedly wrote on his
deathbed: "In the past, Maoling's writings were sent for after his death; / Still I am
happy that I have never written the 'Essay on *Feng* and *Shan* Sacrifices'" (*Song shi*,

457.13432). The allusion in Lin Bu's line refers to an essay of Sima Xiangru's in which he instructs his wife, upon the occasion of his own approaching death, to give the essay to Emperor Wu in anticipation that the emperor would ask for his literary remains after he died (which was the case). Sima Xiangru's essay lavishly praises the great accomplishments of the Han, particularly Emperor Wu's, and he urges the emperor to celebrate his own accomplishments by performing the *feng* and *shan* sacrifices (封禪), a *rite de triomphe* rarely performed in history. Emperor Wu read the essay and, seven years after Sima Xiangru's death, performed the two sacrifices as recommended (see *Han shu*, 57B.2600–2609). I suspect Wang Ji too is alluding to Sima Xiangru in this line—particularly to his writing of the "Essay on *Feng* and *Shan* Sacrifices" in retirement. I am not sure, however, where *ju* 罝 (net or snare) fits into this allusion.

41. Confucius is recorded as saying: "When a state is guided in accord with the Way, a gentleman accepts a salary from the state [that is, offers his service]. When a state is led away from the Way, it is a shame for a gentleman to accept a salary from it" (*Lun yu*, 14.1).

42. See note 40.

43. Owen, *Poetry of the Early T'ang*, 65.

44. Ibid., 63.

45. *Wenji*, 77.

46. Ji Fa 姬發 (later known as King Wu of Zhou) turned against his own sovereign, Zhou 紂, the king of Yin 殷, by launching a military campaign—and moreover committed this breach of conduct during the proper period of mourning for his own deceased father (posthumously King Wen of Zhou). Thus Bo Yi and Shu Qi condemned him on both accounts; see *Shi ji*, 61.2121–2123.

47. This is the interpretation assumed by some of Wang Ji's critics. See, for example, Takagi Masakazu, "Ō Seki no denki to bungaku," 40–70; and Ogasawara Hiroe, "Ō Seki ron: Sono hito to sakuhin," 65–105.

48. *MS*, no. 167.

49. Kang Jinsheng and Xia Lianbao summarize the various interpretations of this controversial allusion in *Biannian jiaozhu*, 81 n. 5.

50. *Wenji*, 65.

51. The immediate reference probably alludes to a piece of music that Wang Ji adapted from some old tunes. Lü Cai writes in his preface to Wang Ji's collection that "he was a skilled zither player with very good taste in music. He modified some old tunes and created the 'Melody of Mountains and Waters' (山水操). His appreciative companions greatly enjoyed it" (*Wenji*, preface, 2). But the name of the tune is also a generic reference to music cherished by recluses, otherwise known as the "men of mountains and waters."

52. See the discussion of "Guyi, no. 1" in the preceding chapter.

53. *Wenji*, 85.

54. *Wenji*, 52.

55. As mentioned in Chapter 1, Wang Kangju wrote a poem refuting the traditional rationalization of the practice of reclusion, which he titled "Rebuttal to 'Summoning the Recluse.'" In the opening couplet of the poem, Wang characterizes two types of recluses: "Lesser recluses hide in the hills and marshes; / Greater

recluses hide in the court and the marketplaces." The poem goes on to argue that a man of real value and intelligence would maintain faith in the world and only a halfwit would consider hiding from it. See *WX*, 22.1030.

56. Confucius states: "They disappear in the crowds of people and hide away in the fields. Their names have faded, but their minds are set to a boundless aim. Though they may speak with their mouths, at heart they have never said a thing. At the moment, they are on a course to turn away from the world, but at heart they don't deign to follow it. They are the submergers on dry land." Guo Xiang writes in his commentary that "[submergers on dry land] refers to those who reclude among men, just as [dry land] submerges without water." See *Zhuangzi*, 25.1017–1018.

57. *Wenji*, 65.

58. This is a reference to a line in Tao Qian's "Oh, Let Me Return" (Guiqu lai ci 歸去來辭): "The three paths are already obliterated, but pine trees and chrysanthemums are still here" (Lu Qinli, *Tao Yuanming ji*, 161).

59. Ziyun refers to Yang Xiong, a Han scholar and accomplished *fu* writer. His *Han shu* biography reports that "he did not feel anxious about riches and ranks, nor did he feel depressed about being poor and humble" (*Han shu*, 57A.3514), and states that in his final years he lived in retirement, poverty-stricken and alone (*Han shu*, 57B.3585). Yang Xiong is the reputed author of a *fu* titled "Expelling Poverty" (Zhupin fu 逐貧賦) in which he depicts himself discoursing with Poverty and in the end is convinced of poverty's many virtues. For a translation and discussion of the piece see Knechtges, *Han Rhapsody*, 104–108.

60. Some editions read 倚床看婦織 (Leaning against the bed, I watch my wife weaving).

61. *Wenji*, 68.

62. The Tiered City (層城) is the legendary home of celestial gods and transcendents on Mount Kunlun. See *Shuijing zhu* 水經注 (*SBBY*), 1.1a; *Huainanzi* (*SBBY*), 4.2b.

63. This line refers to the search for the immortal islands in the Eastern Sea. See note 65.

64. Here the allusion is to a story about a certain Shi Cun 施存 of the state of Lu who was supposedly a disciple of Confucius. He spent three hundred years studying techniques for refining the Grand Elixir (*Da dan* 大丹), but in the end he simply mastered a few tricks and illusions. While he was holding office in Lingtai 靈臺, he hung a jade vase in his room that he would transform into an image of the world with the sun and the moon. He would spend his nights in this illusory world, which he called the "World in a Vase" (*hutian* 壺天). Hence people of his time called him Lord Vase (壺公). The story is originally recorded in *Lingtai zhizhong lu* 靈台治中錄 and is cited in Zhang Junfang, *Yunji qiqian*, 28.11b.

65. According to legend there are three islands in the Eastern Sea where the buildings and portals are constructed of gold and silver. It is said that one can find on these islands the immortals and the magic drug which grants immortality. Reports from seafarers claim that the buildings on the islands are visible from a distance, enveloped in clouds, but when boats draw close the islands disappear into the sea and a gust of wind pulls the boats away. See *Shi ji*, 28.1369–1370.

66. It is a conventional belief that when transcendents descend to earth, they

are preceded by nymphs playing reed pipes. The term "music players" (*lingren* 伶人) refers to these nymphs.

67. This line refers to the alchemists and magicians who fooled Emperor Wu of Han into trusting them with the pursuit of immortality. They were awarded with power and wealth but none delivered the results they promised. Some eventually were exposed as frauds and executed. See "Feng shan shu" 封禪書 in *Shi ji* (28.1384–1404) and "Jiaosi zhi" 郊祀志 in *Han shu* (25A.1215–25B.1284).

68. Wang Ji refers here to Tao Qian and probably his writing of the poetic sequence "Thirteen Poems on Reading the *Classics of Mountains and Seas*" (Du *Shanhai jing* shisan shou 讀山海經十三首). The book in question is a classic geography treatise filled with accounts of the fantastic, the mythical, and the supernatural. For the text of Tao Qian's poems see Lu Qinli, *Tao Yuanming ji*, 133–140.

69. This epithet refers to Ruan Ji, who wrote a number of poems on mythical and religious topics. He also wrote a prose piece titled "The Biography of Master Great Man" (Daren xiansheng zhuan 大人先生傳) on an imaginary mystical hero. For a discussion of Ruan Ji's literary works on mysticism and his "Daren xiansheng zhuan" see Holzman, *Poetry and Politics*, 167–226.

70. *Wenji*, 93. A variant title of this poem is "Chun ri" 春日 (Spring day), which is how it appears in Sun Xingyan's 孫星衍 reproduction of a Song three-*juan* edition, as well as in *QTS* and *Tangshi jishi*.

71. *QTS*, 43.537.

72. Adapted from Owen's translation in *Poetry of the Early T'ang*, 37.

73. As Owen observes, the third couplet is "parallel, descriptive, and using cleverly metaphorical verbs in the second position" and "would have fit comfortably in a court banquet poem" (*Poetry of the Early T'ang*, 65).

74. *Wenji*, 63.

75. *Wenji*, 46.

76. "Shimen xinying suozhu simian gaoshan huixi shilai maolin xiuzhu" 石門新營所住四面高山迴溪石瀨茂林脩竹 (*XQHW*, 2.1166).

77. *Wenji*, 67.

78. *Wenji*, 90.

79. Liang Hong 梁鴻 was a scholar of the Later Han. According to his *Hou Han shu* biography, after he graduated from the Imperial University he chose to raise pigs in the imperial hunting park, Shanglinyuan 上林苑, instead of pursuing a career in office. His neighbor's daughter, Meng Guang 孟光, was so impressed by his character that she vowed to marry no one else but him. After they got married, they retired from the world and lived on Baling Mountain 霸陵山. See *Hou Han shu*, 83.2765–2768.

80. Mr. Xu might be a reference to Xu Mai 許邁, a Jin Taoist adept whom Wang Ji mentions by name in another poem ("Youxian, no. 4" 遊仙, *Wenji*, 95). According to Xu Mai's *Jin shu* biography, after both of Xu Mai's parents passed away he sent his wife back to her own parents' home so that he could visit the famous mountains in China, learn about religious Taoism, and attempt to achieve transcendence. In 346, when he came to the Western Mountain in Lin'an 臨安 (in modern Zhejiang), he felt he had found his spiritual salvation, so he wrote to his wife terminating their marriage. He then changed his name and renounced the

profane world for the world of immortals. He later vanished without a trace, prompting many to believe he had indeed transcended to the celestial realm. See *Jin shu*, 80.2106–2107.

81. A reference to Tao Qian.

82. Xiang Ziping 向子平 is also known as Xiang Chang 向長, or Xiang Ping 向平, a renowned Eastern Han recluse who never took office. After all of his children were grown and married, he reportedly left home to travel in the five sacred mountains and was never seen again. See *Hou Han shu*, 83.2758–2759.

Chapter 4: The Recluse as Drunkard

1. See Lü Cai's preface for an account of Wang Ji's expertise in wine-related matters as well as his intemperance. In several personal letters, Wang Ji also writes openly about his drinking habits. See, for example, "Da Cishi Du Zhisong shu" 答刺史杜之松書, "Da Chushi Feng Zihua shu" 答處士馮子華書, and "Da Cheng Daoshi shu" 答程道士書 (*Wenji*, 134–135, 147–150, and 157–159 respectively).

2. *Wenji*, 52.

3. *Wenji*, 51. In all three-*juan* editions, the title of this poem reads "Chu chun" (初春).

4. A variant in the three-*juan* editions reads: 偏宜酒甕香 (It suits the fragrance from the wine vat perfectly). I follow Han Lizhou's reading in *Wenji*, which is consistent with the other two five-*juan* texts.

5. *Wenji*, 69.

6. *Wenji*, 98. The series in five-*juan* editions consists of eight quatrains as indicated in the title; only five of the eight (nos. 1, 2, 3, 6, and 7), however, are included in the three-*juan* texts, and the title of the series is changed to "Guo jiujia" 過酒家 (Stopping by the tavern). From Lü Cai's preface we learn that the poems in this group were not composed all at one time but were the "souvenirs" Wang Ji left on the walls of the taverns he frequented. Lü Cai also claims that fans of Wang Ji's tavern scribbles would seek them out, copy them down, and recite them to one another. They were quite popular and widely circulated (*Wenji*, preface, 5).

7. Liu Xie, *Wenxin diaolong*, 4.48; Yu-chung Shih, *The Literary Mind*, 67.

8. *WX*, 29.1344; Watson, *Columbia Book of Chinese Poetry*, 97.

9. *WX*, 29.1348; Watson, *Columbia Book of Chinese Poetry*, 101.

10. Dukang 杜康 is the name of the legendary inventor of wine, but later by metonymy it became a literary word for wine itself. Two poems by Cao Cao by this title are extant; the text of this one is in *WX*, 27.1281.

11. See Wang Yao, "Zhonggu wenren yu jiu," in *Zhonggu wenren shenghuo*, 44–76; see also Lu Xun, "Wei Jin fengdu ji wenzhang yu yao ji jiu zhi guanxi," 3:487–507.

12. Lu Qinli, *Tao Yuanming ji*, 55; Hightower, *Poetry of T'ao Ch'ien*, 71. For discussions of this poem see Hightower, *Poetry of T'ao Ch'ien*, 72–73; Davis, *T'ao Yüan-ming*, 1:62–64.

13. Lu Qinli, *Tao Yuanming ji*, 95; Hightower, *Poetry of T'ao Ch'ien*, 145.

14. See the entry on Tao Qian in Nienhauser, *Indiana Companion*, 766–768.

15. Lu Qinli, *Tao Yuanming ji*, 95; Hightower, *Poetry of T'ao Ch'ien*, 144.

16. Compare "Nineteen Ancient Poems, no. 15" (from *WX*, 29.1349):

A man's life span does not even stretch to one hundred,　　生年不滿百
Yet we all hold in our bosom sorrows of a thousand years.　長懷千歲憂
The days are short, and I fear the nights are long,　　　　晝短苦夜長
Why not light the candles and go for a jaunt?　　　　　　何不秉燭遊
To enjoy yourself, you should waste no time;　　　　　　為樂當及時
How can you put it off till later?　　　　　　　　　　　何能待來茲
A foolish man loves to cling to his values,　　　　　　　愚者愛惜費
But will be laughed at by later generations.　　　　　　但為後世嗤
Wang Ziqiao, the immortal,　　　　　　　　　　　　　仙人王子喬
Is impossible to wait for.　　　　　　　　　　　　　　難可與等期

17. In an initial study, "T'ao Ch'ien's 'Drinking Wine' Poems," Hightower retained the original title of the series but changed it in *Poetry of T'ao Ch'ien*, 124–157.

18. Lu Qinli, *Tao Yuanming ji*, 119; Hightower, *Poetry of T'ao Ch'ien*, 195, with a slight adjustment to line 4.

19. "Twenty Drinking Poems, no. 20" (Yinjiu shi 飲酒詩二十首), Lu Qinli, *Tao Yuanming ji*, 99; Hightower, *Poetry of T'ao Ch'ien*, 155.

20. *Wenji*, preface, 5.

21. For a discussion of the concept of *li* in early Chinese thought see Needham, "Human Laws," 3–30, and "Chinese Civilization," 194–230.

22. *Wenji*, 158.

23. *Wenji*, 97.

24. "Pine flower" (*songhua* 松花), also known as *songhuang* 松黃 (literally, "pine yellow" because of the pollen's color), refers to the small male cone of a Chinese pine tree (*Pinus sinensis*), which is used in a distilled wine for medicinal purposes; see Stuart, *Chinese Materia Medica*, 334.

25. *Shishuo xinyu*, 467; Mather, *New Account*, 309.

26. *Zhuangzi*, 31.1240; Graham, *Chuang-tzu*, 251–252.

27. *Wenji*, 117.

28. All three men, Zhang Feng, Liang Hong (of the later Han), and the legendary Laolaizi, were renowned recluses. But they are better remembered for their marriages to lofty-minded wives who encouraged them to renounce the comfort of material wealth and the glory of official fame. On Meng Guang see Chapter 3, note 79.

29. *Wenji*, 114.

30. A form of philosophical discourse (see Chapter 1).

31. One of the three legendary immortal islands in the Eastern Sea.

32. *Wenji*, 66.

33. See in particular chap. 23, "The Free and Unrestrained" (*Shishuo xinyu*, 548–576; Mather, *New Account*, 371–391).

34. *Wenji*, 98.

35. There is a variant in line 3 that may affect the meaning of the last couplet. Han Lizhou in *Wenji* reads *yu* 欲 (just about) for *wei* 未 (not yet). If we follow this reading, then *pin* 貧 (whose meaning varies from "poor" or "impoverished" to "humble," "mean," or "cheap," depending on the context) in the last line should be

interpreted as "poor" or "impoverished." In this case the translation of the last two lines should be: "My money is just about to run out; / It is all for the sake of the taverns that I am poor" (黃金消欲盡，祇為酒家貧). This reading would accentuate the self-mockery.

36. *Wenji*, 100.

37. In the Tang era there was a large population of foreign tradesmen residing in China. One of the biggest business centers for foreign settlers was the Western Market (西市) in Chang'an, where taverns were run by immigrants from Central Asia. These were popular gathering places for literati in the capital. For a discussion of foreign tavern owners and waitresses in Chang'an see Xiang Da, "Xishi hudian yu huji," in *Tangdai Chang'an yu Xiyu wenming*, 34–39; and Schafer, *Golden Peaches of Samarkand*, 7–39, especially 23.

38. *Wenji*, 59.

39. The original term is "*zhangtou qian*" 杖頭錢 (money to hang on my staff), which is an allusion to Ruan Xiu 阮脩 of the Jin. According to *Jin shu*, Ruan Xiu often walked to a wineshop with a hundred cash strung on his staff, which he would spend all in one sitting (49.1366).

40. Other than legends of their drinking, there is little historical information about these two. Although Liu Ling was a well-respected writer during his time, his only extant piece is "Ode to the Virtue of Wine" (Jiude song 酒德頌). For Liu Ling's biography see *Jin shu*, 49.1375–1376. The legends about his character are collected in *Shishuo xinyu*. Bi Zhuo in his younger days belonged to a group of libertines known as the "Eight Free Spirits" of Luoyang. When he took office as president of the Board of Civil Office, he was said to have never attended to his duties because he was drinking all the time. For his biography see *Jin shu*, 49.1381. See also *Shishuo xinyu*, 23.558; Mather, *New Account*, 378.

41. *Wenji*, 62.

42. Here I follow Sun Xingyan's text to read 浮生 (floating life) for Han's 在生 (this life). Both Luo Zhenyu's three-*juan* edition and *QTS* also read 浮生.

43. *Wenji*, 99.

44. *Shishuo xinyu*, 23.548; Mather, *New Account*, 371.

45. *Wenji*, 58.

46. *Wenji*, 61–62. This poem was discussed earlier in Chapter 1.

47. On the allusions in this couplet see Chapter 1, notes 28 and 29.

48. For a note on the textual variant in this line see Chapter 1, note 30.

49. *Wenji*, 99.

50. Han Lizhou in *Wenji* reads "*lu*" 爐, which means "stove" or some other type of wine-making vessel. I follow the three-*juan* editions and read "*lu*" 壚 (vat).

51. *Zhuangzi*, 19.674; Graham, *Chuang-tzu*, 137.

52. *Wenji*, 180. The subject of this piece resembles Liu Ling's "Jiude song" (see Lü Cai's preface); the title and form, as we shall see, suggest an imitation of Tao Qian's "Biography of Mr. Five Willows." See Lü Cai's preface for an account of Wang Ji's nickname "A-Dipper-of-Wine Scholar."

53. Han Lizhou in *Wenji* reads 天下大可見矣 (The world is big—that we can already see).

54. See, for example, Xiao Tong's "Biography of Tao Yuanming" (Tao Yuanming zhuan) in *QSG*, 3068b.

55. For the full text see *WX*, 53.2287–2293.

56. Ruan Ji's *Jin shu* biography records that Ruan Ji often drove off on his own without following any particular road. When the trail ran to an end and his cart could go no further, he would then wail bitterly and return home. See *Jin shu*, 49.1361.

57. Compare *Zhuangzi*: "The quintessence of the utmost Way (*zhidao* 至道) is deeply hidden and opaque; the apex of the utmost Way is obscure and silent" (11.390; Graham, *Chuang-tzu*, 178).

58. An entry in *Zhongshuo* records Wang Tong's dismay at his brother's "Biography of Mr. Five Dippers." The Confucian master is reported to have scolded Wang Ji: "Have you forgotten the [welfare of the] world? You indulge your heart in pleasure and violate the code of proper behavior. I will not allow you to behave like that!" See *Zhongshuo* (*SBBY*), 3.7b. Although there are questions about the authenticity of *Zhongshuo* and whether this was Wang Tong's genuine reaction or an assumed (because logical) one, the quotation reflects a common moral response to Wang Ji's promotion of intemperance as natural and spontaneous.

59. *Wenji*, 181–182.

60. Compare *Zhuangzi*, 1.24:

In the mountains of far-off Guye there lives a daemonic man, whose skin and flesh are like ice and snow, who is gentle as a virgin. He does not eat the five grains but sucks in the wind and drinks the dew; he rides that vapour of the clouds, yokes flying dragons to his chariot, and roams beyond the four seas. When the daemonic in him concentrates it keeps creatures free from plagues and makes the grain ripen every year. [Graham, *Chuang-tzu*, 46]

A similar story is found in *Liezi* (*SBBY*, 2b–3b).

61. Compare *Laozi*, 80 (*SBBY*, 23b):

Reduce the size and population of the state.
....
Even when they have ships and carts, they will have no use for them;
    and even when they have armour and weapons, they will have no
    occasion to make a show of them.
Bring it about that the people will return to the use of knotted rope,
    Will find relish in their food
    And beauty in their clothes,
    Will be content in their abode
    And happy in the way they live. [Lau, *Lao Tzu*, 142]

62. Compare the account of the Yellow Lord in *Liezi* (*SBBY*), 1a–2b; Graham, *Book of Lieh-tzu*, 34.

63. See note 60 on the daemonic man from Guye.

64. According to Sima Qian and Kong Anguo, Xi and He neglected their duties as officers in charge of observing and reporting the movements of heaven, earth, and the four seasons and indulged themselves in reckless drinking. Later they were punished for this. See *Shi ji*, 2.85.

65. Jie is the last ruler of the Xia dynasty; Zhou is the last ruler of the Shang. Both are condemned by historians and moralists for their excessive self-indulgence and extreme cruelty, which are blamed for ultimately causing the collapse of their dynasties. See *Shi ji*, 2.88, 3.105–109.

66. Compare Han Ying, *Hanshi waizhuan*: "Jie built a pool filled with wine. [It was so large that] boats could move around in it. There was also a hill made out of dregs and [from the top] it was high enough to see 10 *li* away" (in *Han Wei congshu*, 2.11b–12a). Zhou is more conventionally known for filling a pool with wine and building a hill out of dregs. See *Shi ji*, 105 and 106 n. 7.

67. Compare entries for *jiuzheng* 酒正 and *jiuren* 酒人 in the "Tianguan" 天官 section of *Zhou li* 周禮 (*Shisanjing*), 668c–670c.

68. Two notorious tyrant kings of the Zhou dynasty.

69. A utopian state that the Yellow Lord visited in his dream and where he found the ultimate Way. Upon waking from this dream, he "found himself." See *Liezi*, 2.1a–2b; Graham, *Book of Lieh-tzu*, 34–35.

70. Ibid.; *Zhuangzi*, 9.340; Graham, *Chuang-tzu*, 205.

71. See "Song Wang Xiucai xu," in Ma Qichang and Ma Maoyuan, *Han Changli wenji jiaozhu*, 257–258.

72. Cao Quan, *Wenji*, app. 1, 223–224.

73. *Wenji*, 100.

74. Owen, *Poetry of the Early T'ang*, 64.

75. Hong Xingzu, *Chuci buzhu* (*SKQS*), 7.1a–3a; Hawkes, *Ch'u Tz'u*, 90.

76. Lu Qinli, *Tao Yuanming ji*, 91–92; Hightower, *Poetry of T'ao Ch'ien*, 137.

77. *Zhuangzi*, 2.87; Graham, *Chuang-tzu*, 59.

78. *Wenji*, 57; this poem is not included in the series by the similar title "Ti jiudian loubi jueju bashou," which I have been translating "Eight Quatrains Scribbled on Tavern Walls."

Chapter 5: "You Beishan fu" and the Problem of Knowing

1. The dating of this piece is based on a remark in the poem concerning his brother Wang Tong's academy. After recalling the joyful days he spent there in the company of the learned and virtuous men studying with Wang Tong, Wang Ji writes: "Suddenly these men scattered in all directions, and two *ji* 紀 [twenty-four years] have since gone by" (*Wenji*, 5). Wang Tong's students were dispersed after his death in 617. On this evidence, the piece should be dated 641. Kang Jinsheng and Xia Lianbao come to the same conclusion in *Biannian jiaozhu*, 22. For a comprehensive treatment of the development of the *fu* genre see Xu Jie and Guo Weisne, *Zhongguo cifu fazhan shi*. For a good introduction to the study of *fu* from the Han period to the Tang see Yu Jidong, *Han Tang fu qianshuo*. For a survey of the *fu* and its place in Tang literary history see Kroll, "Significance of the *Fu*," 87–105.

2. The text of "You Beishan fu" is from *Wenji*, 1–8.

3. On the references to Wang Ji's ancestors in this passage see the discussion in Chapter 1.

4. The "Southern Mountain" (南山 or 終南山) is conventionally associated with reclusion. One of the earliest sources originates from the legend of the Four Hoary Heads of Shangshan (商山四皓), who left their service in the Qin court when they witnessed the decline of morals. After the conquest of the Qin, the Han founding emperor Liu Bang 劉邦 (r. 206–195 B.C.) invited them to serve, but they refused and were said to have gone into hiding on Mount Zhongnan (in modern Shaanxi). They were never seen again. For their biographies see *Hanshu*, 40.2033–2036; and Huangfu Mi, *Gaoshi zhuan*, 2.7a–b. Tao Qian was the first to make the association between the Southern Mountain and a life of reclusion on a farm. The Southern Mountain he denotes is not Mount Zhongnan in Shaanxi but Mount Lu (also known as Mount Zhongnan) in Jiangxi, not far from Tao's farm. In Tao's poems it is his home in retirement as well as his eternal home—his burial site.

5. See Chapter 1, notes 28 and 29, concerning the allusions in this sentence.

6. Huangfu Mi was a gentleman-in-retirement of the Western Jin period. According to his biography, though he did not start his education until he was in his twenties he quickly gained a reputation for his love of books and learning. He was repeatedly summoned by the court but chose to live out his life on his farm, dividing his time between farming and writing. It is reported too that he once argued one could take as much delight in the Ways of Yao and Shun by living in the country as one could in pursuing fame through official service (*Jin shu*, 51.1409–1418). Huangfu Mi's *Gaoshi zhuan* was very influential in Chinese recluse culture (see Berkowitz, *Patterns of Disengagement*, especially 156–160).

7. Zhongchang Tong 仲長統 (180–220) was a gentleman-in-retirement of the Later Han. In his essay "Taking Delight in My Own Ambition" (樂志論), he writes:

For living, let me have some fertile farmland and a spacious house with mountains behind and a stream in front. Ditches and ponds wind all the way through my property; bamboos and trees grow all around. The threshing ground and vegetable garden are set up in the front, an orchard is planted in back. I'll have a boat and a cart sufficient to replace my feet for the arduous task of walking and trudging so that my four limbs will surely be saved from hard work. I'll have fine dishes of delicacies to offer my parents; my wife and children will not be troubled by physical distress. When my good friends stop by for gatherings, I'll set out wine and food to entertain them. On fine occasions and auspicious days, I'll cook a lamb and a pig and present them as an offering. I'll pass my days dawdling by the vegetable beds or in the garden, going for excursions in the woods or on the plain, bathing in clear water, chasing after cool breezes, casting a hook to catch the carp swimming in the stream and shooting a dart at the geese high in the sky.... I'll ramble and roam above the common world, looking disdainfully down at the space between heaven and earth. Owing no obligation to my contemporary world, I'll be guaranteed to live out my full life span. If this is the case, then I can

soar above the sky and go beyond the cosmos. Why would I desire to enter
the gates of noble kings? [*Hou Han shu*, 49.1644]

For Zhongchang Tong's biography see *Hou Han shu*, 49.1644–1645.

8. Sun Deng 孫登 was a Jin recluse. His *Jin shu* biography describes him as a
man naturally free of anger. He had no family and lived alone in a grotto. In the
summer, he wove garments out of grass; in the winter, he let loose his hair to cover
his body. We are also told that

> when Emperor Wen 文帝 [Sima Zhao 司馬昭, 211–265] heard of [Sun Deng],
> he sent Ruan Ji to go take a look. Upon meeting [Sun Deng], Ruan Ji talked to
> him, but he did not respond. Xi Kang, too, followed Sun Deng about for three
> years, asking for his prognosis for the future, but Sun Deng never answered.
> Kang always sighed [in admiration]. [*Jin shu*, 94.2426]

See also *Shishuo xinyu*, 18.497–498; Mather, *New Account*, 332–333.

9. Wang Ba 王霸 was a recluse of the Later Han. He is also a purported
ancestor of Wang Ji, eighteen generations removed. After Wang Mang 王莽 (r.
9–22) took the throne, Wang Ba resigned from service and cut off all contact with
official circles. He spent the rest of his life as a farmer, refusing appointments from
court. Wang Ba's biography is in *Hou Han shu*, 83.2762–2763.

10. This is a reference to Tao Qian, who composed "Gui qu lai ci" 歸去來辭
(Oh, let me return!) upon leaving office. There is a variant reading of this line. All
three-*juan* versions, as well as *WYYH* and *QTW*, read 類 for 歌, and *WYYH* reads
田叟 for 田園. The editors of *WYYH* note that there is an alternative reading, 歌田
園之去來, which agrees with the five-*juan* texts, so I follow it here.

11. "Poetry is where the intent of the mind (*zhi*) goes. When in the mind, it is
intent; when set forth in words, it is poetry" (*MS*, 1.269c).

12. Ban Gu begins his preface to "*Fu* on Two Capitals" (Liangdu fu 兩都賦)
with the statement "*Fu* is a genre of the ancient songs [in the *Book of Songs*]"
(*WX*, 1.1). Ban Gu's preface is the first known statement to assert the *fu*'s legiti-
macy as a proper form of poetic expression.

13. Lu Chun, *Donggaozi ji*, postface.

14. For a discussion of the theme of this imaginary journey see Hawkes,
"Quest of the Goddess," 71–94.

15. For discussions on travel themes and motifs in Han *fu* see Knechtges,
"Journey to Morality," 162–182, and Knechtges, "Poetic Travelogue," 127–152. On
the use of the *fu* during the Han for the expression of personal aspirations and
ideals see Cao Shujuan, *Hanfu zhi xiewu yanzhi chuantong*.

16. See Chang, "Descriptions of Landscape," 105–129, and Mather, "Mystical
Ascent," 226–245. For an overview of the history of Chinese travel writing see
Strassberg, *Inscribed Landscapes*, 1–56.

17. See Lü Cai's preface. Yu Xin was a celebrated Six Dynasties poet. Wang
Ji's extant corpus lists nine *fu* pieces, but in the case of five there are only titles. In
addition to "You Beishan fu," the three other *fu* that have been preserved are "*Fu*
on the First Day of the First Month" (Yuanzheng fu 元正賦), "*Fu* on the Third

Day of the Third Month" (briefly discussed in Chapter 1), and *"Fu* on Swallows" (Yan fu 鷰賦).

18. The term *"bamei siru"* 八眉四乳 (eight eyebrows and four nipples) conventionally refers to sage-kings of high antiquity. In classical texts the sage-king Yao is always described as having *bamei*, but scholars have not agreed on its meaning. Some suggest "eyebrows that have eight tones of color" (*bacai mei* 八彩眉; see *Huainanzi* [*SBBY*], 19.6b, and Wang Chong, *Lun heng*, 3.4b, for example). Others understand it as "eyebrows shaped like the character eight" (*bazi mei* 八字眉; see *Chuxue ji*, 9.202). In the "Xiuwu xun" 脩物訓 chapter of *Huainanzi*, it is said that "King Wen had four nipples. This is what we call [the symbol of] great humane kindness" (*Huainanzi*, 19.7a). Wang Chong makes a similar statement in *Lun heng* (*SBBY*, 3.10a).

19. It was believed that a man born with a dragon face (龍顏) was destined to become the possessor of his own empire (see *Shi ji*, 8.342, for example). As for "phoenix head" 鳳頭, it is understood by many to refer to the exceptional physical features of a ruler, but I have not located a source for this term.

20. Compare *Li ji* 禮記, chap. 24, "To be sure, when the sages stand facing south, the subcelestial realm is in order"; Zheng Xuan's 鄭玄 commentary, "The reason why they stand facing south is to look [directly] at the court" (*Shisanjing*, 1440b).

21. Compare *Li ji*, chap. 9, where Confucius says: "Burying the dead in the north with the head pointing north was the ritual practice during the three ancient dynasties. This is due to [the fact that north is the realm of] darkness" (*Shisanjing*, 1302b).

22. Han Lizhou's reading in *Wenji* is 榮深情厚 (They held high honors and their compassions were deep). There are two variant readings of this line: (1) 榮深貴重 (*WYYH* and *QTW*); (2) 榮深責重 (all three-*juan* editions). Variant 1 clearly contains a graphic error, confusing 責 for 貴. Although Han's reading is plausible, I choose to follow the three-*juan* reading (variant 2) because it seems to fit the context better.

23. Most editions have 將相 (generals and ministers) for Han Lizhou's reading, 宰相 (chancellors and ministers).

24. King Zhao of Yan lived during the Warring States period. Historically he was better known as an enthusiastic pursuer of immortality than as a ruler. He is said to have sent people to sea in search of the three mythical islands: Penglai 蓬萊, Yingzhou 瀛州, and Fanghu 方壺. See *Han shu*, 25.1204. Emperor Wu of the Former Han (r. 141–87 B.C.), too, had great interest in the pursuit of immortality. His desire to live forever led him to place trust in magicians and alchemists who claimed to know how to reach immortals and obtain the drug of longevity. Encouraged by these people, he initiated special sacrifices to the hearth in hope of receiving instructions from the hearth spirits for turning cinnabar into gold. He also sent an expedition to Penglai Island in the Eastern Sea to search for immortals. See Ban Gu, "Xidu fu" 西都賦, in *WX*, 1.18; Zhang Heng, "Xijing fu" 西京賦, in *WX*, 2.60; and *Han shu*, 25A.1216–1237.

25. Tripod Lake 鼎湖 is associated with the legend of the Yellow Lord. It is said he had selected some copper from Mount Shou 首山 and cast a tripod at the

foot of Mount Jing 荊山 (in modern Henan). When he was done, a dragon appeared in the sky. It rolled down its whiskers and carried the Yellow Lord away. See *Shi ji*, 28.1394, and Liu Xiang, *Liexian zhuan*, 1.4.

26. Emperor Wu once asked his ministers, "I heard that the Yellow Lord did not die. Why then is there a tomb for him?" Someone responded, "He became an immortal and ascended to heaven. His vassals buried his gowns and caps" (*Han shu*, 25A.1233). Qiaoshan 橋山 is located in modern Shaanxi. The biography of the Yellow Lord in *Shi ji* records that "when the Yellow Lord died, he was buried on Qiaoshan"; see *Shi ji*, 1.10.

27. As recorded in *Huainanzi*, 4.2b.

28. Compare *Shuijing zhu*, "Xiang River" 湘水:

The Xiang River emerges from Beiluo Mountain in Yongchang district. It flows southeastward, passing the east side of Stone Swallow Mountain. In this mountain, there are rocks shaped like swallows, thus the name. Some of the rocks are big, some are small, just like mother swallows and baby swallows. When thunder and storms strike, then the stone swallows all start to fly, soaring and diving like real swallows. [*SBBY*, 38.6a]

29. It was a custom for people to build earthern oxen on the first day of spring to mark the beginning of the farming season. See the "Yueling" 月令 chapter in *Li ji* (*Shisanjing*, 1383c); see also *Hou Han shu*, 4.3102.

30. See note 24.

31. *WX*, 21.1022–1023.

32. Han's text reads: 任物孤遺情之直上. The three-*juan* editions, *WYYH* and *QTW*, all have 任物孤遊遺情直上, which makes much better sense. I therefore follow this reading.

33. It has always been assumed that "*wen xuan*" 文宣 here refers to Confucius, whose posthumous title Wenxuan Wang 文宣王 is well known to scholars. But this title was not awarded to Confucius until 739, more than ninety years after Wang Ji died (see *Jiu Tang shu*, 9.211). Before that, writers often referred to Confucius by his posthumous title Xuanni 宣尼 or Xuanni Gong 宣尼公, a noble title awarded to him by Emperor Ping 平帝 of the Former Han (r. 1 B.C.–A.D. 5). I therefore believe that "*wen xuan*" here refers to two people: King Wen of Zhou and Confucius. Structurally this reading parallels neatly with the pair in the line above, "*lao shi*" 老釋 (Laozi and Buddha).

34. Compare Sun Chuo, "You Tiantaishan fu" 遊天台山賦: "Of Noumenon [*li* 理], there is nothing hidden but it becomes plain" (*WX*, 11.496; Mather, "Mystical Ascent," 238).

35. This is an allusion to a passage in *Zhuangzi* reporting a conversation between Zigong 子貢, one of Confucius' disciples, and an old man in a garden. Zigong was surprised by the old man's seemingly slow and ineffective way of drawing water from the well, so he told him about a handy mechanical device that could draw water more quickly. Upon hearing this, the old man laughed and said: "Those who have clever mechanical devices inevitably have a clever plan for them. Those who have clever plans inevitably have clever hearts. If one holds a clever

heart in his bosom, then he will not equip himself with purity. If one does not equip himself with purity, then his mind won't be stable. If his mind is not stable, the Way will not bear it" (*Zhuangzi*, 12.444–445; Graham, *Chuang-tzu*, 186–187).

36. This is an allusion to a passage in *Zhuangzi*: One day Zhuangzi was walking in a garden when he came across a rare bird. Just as he was about to shoot it with a slingshot, he noticed that the bird was preying on a mantis which was stalking a cicada which for its part was enjoying the shade it had found. Each one of these creatures was so absorbed in the target in front of it that it was completely oblivious to the danger behind. Zhuangzi put down his slingshot and was about to leave when the gardener came and accused him of theft. Zhuangzi returned home and did not come back to the courtyard for three months. See *Zhuangzi*, 20.758.

37. This is an allusion to the story in the *Mahāparinirvāna Sūtra* that gives an account of Gautama Buddha's six years of austerities.

38. In *Zhuangzi* it is said that the giant Peng "beats the whirlwind and rises 90,000 *li*" (1.6); see Chapter 2, note 10, for an earlier reference to this bird.

39. Both the Dark Palace 玄宮 and the Purple Capital 紫都 refer to the celestial realm occupied by the immortals and transcendents.

40. Some editors read *"qing xi"* 青溪 as a proper name, but I have found no evidence to support this reading.

41. In Xi Kang's *Jin Shu* biography, we find this account of a "sacred scroll":

Xi Kang once was wandering in the mountains and marshes to gather herbs. He was enjoying himself so much that he was in a trance and forgot to return home.... When he came to the mountains of Ji commandery ... Kang also encountered Wang Lie. Together they went into the mountains.... In a stone grotto, Lie saw a roll of scripture written on white silk. He then called for Xi Kang to come and get it, but the scripture immediately disappeared. Lie sighed saying, "Shuye [that is, Xi Kang] has a very extraordinary mind and intent yet he never encounters his opportunity. This is fate!" [49.1370]

Wang Ji seems to be suggesting that he fared better than Xi Kang in that immortals revealed to him spiritual writings whereas they hid them from Xi Kang.

42. In *Shuyi ji* 述異記, there is a story about an encounter between a woodcutter of the Jin period by the name Wang Zhi 王質 and two transcendents. Wang Zhi was cutting wood in the mountains when he came across two young boys playing chess. One of the boys gave Wang Zhi something that looked like the pit of a date. He ate it and no longer felt hungry, so he put his axe next to him and sat down to watch the boys play chess. In what seemed only moments later when the game was over, Wang Zhi discovered that so much mortal time had passed that the handle of his axe had already rotted away. See Ren Fang, *Shuyi ji*, 113a–b.

43. Han's edition reads 靈應 for 靈蹤.

44. "Purple chamber" 紫房 in this context refers to a Taoist alchemical kiln in which elixirs are prepared. I have translated *"tan"* 壇 as "pedestal" because, given the context of this section, it most likely refers to the base upon which an alchemical kiln and cauldron would be placed, rather than a ritual altar. For examples of

these terms used in reference to elixir making see Wu Wu, *Danfan xuzhi*, 19:57a–61b.

45. Li Daoyuan in *Shuijing zhu* (1.1a) provides the following description of Mount Kunlun: "Kunlun Mountain has three tiers. The bottom one is called Fantong 樊桐, also referred to as Bantong 板桐. The middle one is called Xuanpu 玄圃, also referred to as Langfeng 閬風. The top one is called Cengcheng 層城, also referred to as Tianting 天庭. These are the places where celestial gods and immortals live."

46. Compare "Piqiu gong zhuan" 披裘公傳 (Biography of the man who wears fur) in Huangfu Mi, *Gaoshi zhuan* (*SBBY*), 1.4b.

47. Li Shan 李善 (d. 689) cites the *Shizhou ji* 十洲記 account of the mushroom fields as follows:

Bell Mountain [Zhongshan 鍾山] is in the Northern Sea. There are tens of thousands of terrestrial immortals who live there. They plow fields to grow mushrooms and keep track of the acreage. [See Li Shan's note to Bao Zhao's 鮑照 "*Fu* on the Dancing Cranes" [舞鶴賦], *WX*, 14.632]

48. This is an imaginary utopian society described in Tao Qian's "Tale of Peach Blossom Spring" (Taohua yuan ji 桃花源記).

49. The Great Gulf refers to Bohai 渤海 (alternatively Canghai 滄海, the Great Sea). In the "Biography of Wang Yuan" 王遠傳 there is an account of Wang Yuan's reunion with a transcendent, Magu 麻姑 ("Dame Hemp"), who emphasizes how long it had been since they last met by claiming that the Great Sea had turned into mulberry fields three times. See Ge Hong, *Shenxian zhuan*, 7.4a.

50. Wang Jia 王嘉 records the following in *Shiyi ji* 拾遺記:

The western part of Mount Kunlun is called Xumi Mountain 須彌山. It is located directly under the Seven Stars [of the North Dipper] and emerges from the green sea. There are nine tiers on the mountain.... On the third tier,... there is one kind of apple that grows in winter and the color is like green jade. If one washes it with well water and eats it, his bones will become soft and flexible and he can leap into the Great Void. [*Shiyi ji*, 10.221]

51. Huan Tan 桓譚 lists five types of *shenren* 神人 (divine person) in *Xinlun* 新論, and he terms the second type *yinlun* 隱淪 (the hidden and evanescent). See *QSG*, 15.550b.

52. The "Highest Prime" refers to the beginning of time.

53. The "Greatest Clarity" refers to the realm of transcendents.

54. I follow the reading in all other editions: 耘 for 移 and 蒔 for 時.

55. The identity of this Hejian 河間 is unclear. Some readers suggest that he is Liu De 劉德, the son of Emperor Jing 景帝 of the Han (r. 157–142 B.C.), based on the fact that Liu De's noble title was Hejian Xianwang 河間獻王 (Prince Xian of the Yellow River region; see Kang Jinsheng and Xia Lianbao, *Biannian jiaozhu*, 34 n. 17). But Liu De was better known in history as an accomplished Confucian scholar, and there is no historical evidence to suggest that he was interested in

practicing transcendental Taoism. Another possibility is that Wang Ji is referring to Heshang Gong 河上公 (Old Man by the River), whose real name and historical identity are unknown. According to Ge Hong, Heshang Gong was a recluse from the period of Emperor Wen 文帝 of the Former Han (r. 180–157 B.C.) who lived on the bank of the Yellow River (see *Shenxian zhuan*, 3.1a–b). In intellectual history, Heshang Gong was regarded as an authority on the interpretation of *Laozi*. (A commentary on *Laozi* was attributed to him.) Traditions of mystical culture, however, portray him as a divine being. Alternatively, Wang Ji could be referring to Xuansu 玄俗, a probably legendary medicine seller said to have lived during the Han period. (His name, literally "the Mysterious Commoner," suggests he is fictional.) According to Liu Xiang, Xuansu cast no shadow even when he stood in the sun (a sign he was an immortal) and his medicine was said to have wondrous effects. Supposedly because he claimed to be a native of the Yellow River region (Hejian), he was also known as Hejian or Hejianren. See *Liexian zhuan*, 2.62.

56. Huainan refers to Liu An, commonly known by his noble title Prince of Huainan 淮南王. Credited with writing *Huainanzi* and the prototype of "Summoning the Recluse," he is also known for his keen interest in pursuing immortality. His biography in *Shenxian zhuan* reports that he transcended to the world of immortals together with his eight ministers. See *Shenxian zhuan*, 4.1a–5a. I have taken the first of two variant readings of this line: (1) 無靈受 (lacks the acumen to receive [instruction]); (2) 無虛受 (lacks the capacity of emptiness to receive), which is a term from the *Book of Changes*, hexagram 31. The compilers of *WYYH* note that one of the editions they used had the first reading. The Li Chan 李檉 five-*juan* edition follows the first reading but notes that all other received editions have the second reading. Han Lizhou suggests that 虛 in variant 2 is a scribal error and that the correct reading should be as in variant 1 (see *Wenji*, 14 n. 68).

57. The Winnowing Basket (*ji* 箕) is Sagittarius; the Dipper (*dou* 斗) is Ursa Major. Because Sagittarius is positioned south of Ursa Major, the two are often paired as "the Southern Winnowing Basket and the Northern Dipper" (南箕北斗) for the purpose of parallelism.

58. In legend Woquan 偓佺 was an immortal and contemporary of Yao who spent his time collecting herbs in the mountains. Once he offered Yao some pine nuts, but Yao was too busy to eat them. Those who ate his pine nuts all lived two or three hundred years. See *Liexian zhuan*, 1.5. Magu was a legendary immortal; her story is in *Shenxian zhuan*, 7.3a–5b (see also note 49 in this chapter).

59. Green Dragon (Qing long 青龍), or the Year Star (Sui xing 歲星), corresponds to Jupiter. Black Ox (Xuan niu 玄牛), or the Lunar Lodging of the Ox (Niu xiu 牛宿), corresponds to Capricorn. On an ancient Chinese zodiac chart, we find that the dragon occupies the Eastern Palace (Cang long 蒼龍) and dominates morning hours (*chen* 辰) whereas the ox occupies the Northern Palace (Xuan wu 玄武) and dominates night hours (*chou* 丑). The significance of the heavenly stems *jia* 甲 and *yi* 乙, which Wang Ji attaches to the terrestrial branches *chen* and *chou* in the text, is unclear. Although it is easy to explain the significance of *jia* in the first line—since it is associated with the direction east and the color green (*qing* 青)—*yi* has nothing to do with the direction north or the color black. I suspect that *jia* and *yi* simply indicate order of sequence, as we would say "first and next" (and

in any case I would reject the far-fetched allegorical interpretation of You Xinli in "Wang Ji ji qi zuopin," 176–177). I follow Han's reading of this line. All three-*juan* editions read: 青龍就食於甲辰. If we follow Han's text, the meaning will be as I have translated, taking *jiuyang* as "providing material support as well as physical attendance." If we follow the three-*juan* reading, however, the line should be rendered "the Green Dragon feeds at Jiachen," taking *jiushi* as "eating food." The *WYYH* compilers, while accepting the latter reading, do note that one of the earlier editions reads 就養 for 就食. It is conceivable that later editions were based on a text with a defective character. If the top portion of 養 is damaged, then all one would see is the bottom graph 食.

60. Presumably Wang Ji is referring to those who are said to have attained immortality.

61. That is, "transcendents."

62. "Imbibing the Nine Blossoms" is one of the exercises for achieving longevity. As "Chang xuan" 暢玄 of the "Inner Chapters" in *Baopuzi* (1.3a) informs us: "Swallow the Nine Blossoms at the edge of clouds and chew Six Pneuma at the Cinnabar Aurora."

63. "The Three Splendors" are *jing* 精, *qi* 氣, and *shen* 神 (essence, vitality, and spirit). This is also a term for one of the meditation practices, referring to the stage when all three "spirits" congeal and become one vital force in the brain, at which point one will attain transcendence. See, for example, Zhang Boduan's preface to *Jindan sibai zi* in *Dao zang*, 24:161a.

64. Han's edition reads 攬 for 擥 in all other texts.

65. Compare Zhang Hua 張華 (232–300), "Jiaoliao fu" 鷦鷯賦 (*Fu* on a wren; *WX*, 13.618):

Brambles are not too shabby for him;	匪陋荊棘
Angelica and thoroughwort are not too luxurious for him.	匪榮菖蘭
When he moves his wings, he is happy;	動翼而逸
When he settles on his feet, he is content.	投足而安
He trusts fate and follows the noumenon;	委命順理
He worries about nothing in the world.	與物無患

66. The Vermilion Wall refers to one of the peaks of Mount Tiantai (in modern Zhejiang). The Dark Garden is also known as Langfeng on Mount Kunlun. See note 45 and see *Huainanzi*, 4.2b.

67. Liu Xiang, a classics scholar and bibliographer of the Former Han, was the compiler of *Liexian zhuan*. Ge Hong devoted a whole chapter in his *Baopuzi* to techniques for making elixirs and prescribing them. See the "Inner Chapters" of *Baopuzi*, 4.21b–35b.

68. The term "Three Clarities" is a collective reference to the transcendental realms Highest Clarity (*Shang qing* 上清), Grand Clarity (*Tai qing* 太清), and Jade Clarity (*Yu qing* 玉清). For a comprehensive explanation of terminology in religious Taoist literature see Schafer, *Mirages*, 16–25.

69. Jiang Yuanxu was a Han recluse. He is mentioned, by the name Jiang Xu

蔣詡 in Yang Zhen's 楊震 *Hou Han shu* biography, which records that he went into hiding in A.D. 7 in order to avoid a court summons. It is said that when living in seclusion, Jiang blocked his gate with brambles, spending his time walking on the three paths he cut through the bamboo grove on his property (54.1759).

70. In his "Biography of Mr. Five Willows," Tao Qian introduces himself with these words: "I do not know the origin of this gentleman, nor am I very clear about his family name or his studio name. There are five willow trees next to his house, and that's how he acquired his sobriquet" (Lu Qinli, *Tao Yuanming ji*, 6.175).

71. Junping refers to the Han recluse Zhuang Zun 莊遵 (first century B.C.). He is also known as Yan Zun 嚴遵, a name altered in order to avoid the taboo on Emperor Ming's 明帝 personal name. In order to support himself, Yan set up a shop in the marketplace of Chengdu to tell fortunes. Each day, after he had made a hundred *qian*, an amount enough to sustain himself, he closed shop and gave lectures on *Laozi*. See *Han shu*, 72.3075.

72. On Zizhen (Zheng Pu 鄭樸) see Chapter 3, note 27.

73. *QTW* reads 天下之無事 (nothing is happening in the world).

74. I follow Han's text in its reading of 受 for 度 in the three-*juan* editions.

75. On the "pine flower" see Chapter 4, note 24.

76. "Phoenix feet" refers to the feet that support the zither; "dragon lips" refers to the front part at the head of the zither (termed "forehead"), which looks like paired crescent moons.

77. See Liu An, "Zhao yinshi," in Hong Xingzu, *Chuci buzhu*, 2.90; Hawkes, *Ch'u Tz'u*, 244–245.

78. Xu You is a legendary recluse from high antiquity. When Yao heard about his great reputation, he offered Xu You the rule of the kingdom; but Xu You refused to be persuaded. He washed his ears in the stream and went into hiding. See *Gaoshi zhuan*, 1.2b–3a.

79. Zhang Chao refers to the Later Han recluse Zhang Kai 張楷 (also known as Gongchao 公超). He lived in the mountains outside Hongnong 弘農 (modern Shaanxi) but attracted so many followers that the valley where he was hiding soon became as crowded as a marketplace. Later the site was known as Gongchao Shi 公超市 (Gongchao's Market). See *Hou Han shu*, 36.1242.

80. The works reportedly compiled by Wang Tong include *Xu shi* 續詩 (Continuation of the *Book of Songs*), *Xu shu* 續書 (Continuation of the *Book of Documents*), and *Yuan jing* 元經 (Primal classics—a work modeled after the *Spring and Autumn Annals*), as well as the *Li lun* 禮論 (Discussions on rites), *Yue lun* 樂論 (Discussions on music), and *Zan yi* 讚易 (Comments on the *Book of Changes*). See Du Yan, "Wenzhongzi shijia," *QTW* (23a). For a discussion of the authenticity problems of these works see Wechsler, "Confucian Teacher," 250–259.

81. This refers to the famous classics scholar Zheng Xuan 鄭玄 (127–200) of the Later Han, who studied the classics with Ma Rong 馬融 for over ten years before returning home to open his own school. For his biography see *Hou Han shu*, 35.1207–1213.

82. This refers to Bing Yuan 邴原 (third century), another classics scholar of the Later Han. He came from the same region as Zheng Xuan, and he too

operated a school. For this reason he and Zheng Xuan were repectfully referred to by their contemporaries as the "School of Zheng and Bing Qingzhou." See *Wei shu*, 11.351 n. 2. Han's text reads 安國 for 根矩. For his discussion of the alternative reading see *Wenji*, 17 n. 110.

83. These trees are *qi* 杞 (*Salix cheilophilia* or *Salix purpurea*) and *zi* 梓 (*Catalpa bungei* or *Catalpa ovata*).

84. Ni Hill is situated in the southeastern suburb of Qufu 曲阜 in modern Shangdong province, the birthplace of Confucius. See "Kongzi shijia" 孔子世家 in *Shi ji*, 47.1905.

85. These are the names of two rivers that wrap around Qufu. Confucius' school was located in this area. Han Lizhou reads 泗涘 (by the water of Si River) for 洙泗.

86. "Wang Kongzi" literally means "Wang, the Confucius." The next two intertextual commentaries are also Wang Ji's own.

87. The term "circular grove" is often used to refer to *taixue* 太學 (imperial college).

88. The earliest known reference to Queli is found in a memorial submitted to the throne by Mei Fu 梅福 (fl. first century B.C.), urging the emperor to honor Confucius' descendants as the legitimate scions of the Yin 殷. In this memorial Mei Fu writes: "Now, Zhongni's temple does not extend outside Queli. The descendants of the Kong clan were not excused from registering their residents. Treating the sage with sacrificial offerings for a common man is not the intent of the Great Heaven." On the first statement in this passage, the Tang commentator Yan Shigu 顏師古 (581–645) notes: "Queli is the old home of Confucius. [Mei] is saying that aside from this place, there is no other place that performs ritual sacrifices to Confucius." And on the second, Yan writes: "[This is to say that] they are registered as common men." See *Han shu*, 67.2925–2926.

89. A.k.a. Zilu, one of Confucius' disciples.

90. A.k.a. Zhuangzi.

91. Compare *Lun yu*, 7.15: "The Master said, 'In the eating of coarse rice and the drinking of water, the using of one's elbow for a pillow, joy is to be found. Wealth and rank attained through immoral means have as much to do with me as passing clouds'"; Lau, *Analects*, 88.

92. See note 78 on the image of a recluse washing his ears.

93. This line makes reference to the following story in *Zhuangzi*: "Zang and Gu went out herding together and both lost their sheep. When Zang was asked how he lost his sheep, he said he was holding a book reading. When Gu was asked, he said he was playing chess. These two men were doing different things, but the fact that they lost their sheep was the same" (8.307). Sun Xinyan's and Luo Zhenyu's editions read 驅牛 (herd cattle) for 驅羊.

94. These two lines refer to two hexagrams in the *Book of Changes*. Both advise self-preservation in unfavorable situations. The first line refers to hexagram 56 (Wilhelm, *I Ching*, 216–219 and 674–679) and the second line refers to hexagram 36 (139–142 and 564–569).

95. This alludes to the singing of a phoenix in *MS*, no. 252. Zheng Xuan's commentary on this stanza reads:

In the case where a phoenix sings on the mountain ridge, it is because by looking down from high above it can observe where there is a good place to gather and perch. By analogy, worthy men wait for the indication of a ruler's righteous conduct before they move, soar, and then gather. In the case where a dryandra tree grows, this represents the emerging of a wise ruler. As for the fact that it grows in the early sun, it implies warmth and gentleness, which is also an indication of the moral capacity of the ruler. [*Shisanjing*, 547a]

96. In the fourteenth year of Duke Ai 哀公 of Lu (482 B.C.), news came that a unicorn was captured in the western suburb of the capital of Lu. According to *Shiji*, upon hearing this news Confucius lamented, "Our Great Way is coming to an end," and he made the event his last entry in the *Spring and Autumn Annals (Chunqiu)* that he was compiling (47.1942).

97. There are three different readings of this line among various editions: (1) the five-*juan* editions read: 知何所榮; (2) all three-*juan* editions as well as *WYYH* and *QTW* read: 我何所營; (3) the compilers of *WYYH* note that one of the editions they saw read: 知何所營. Similarly, the surviving portion of the manuscript discovered in the Dunhuang caves reads: 知何營. It is difficult to make much sense out of the second version. Either the first or third reading seems plausible. I choose to follow the third because the Dunhuang manuscript confirms the variant noted by the editors of *WYYH* and it was discovered so late that it had the least opportunity for corruption.

98. There are two problems with this line. First, all three-*juan* editions and *WYYH* have the character *yu* 余 (I) at the beginning of the line. But the passage describes Wang Tong's death, so it is quite safe to conclude that "*yu*" was mistakenly added by a scribe. Second, different editions variously give "forty-two years of age," "thirty-three years of age," or "thirty-two years of age." According to "Wenzhongzi shijia," Wang Tong was born in the fourth year of the Kaihuang era 開皇四年 (584) and had his capping ceremony (traditionally held on one's twenty-*sui* birthday) in the third year of Renshou 仁壽三年 (603). On the basis of these two dates, by the year 617 Wang Tong should have been thirty-four *sui* 歲 by Chinese count.

99. For a study of Tang *huaigu* poems see Frankel, "Contemplation of the Past," 345–365.

100. According to *Shanxi tongzhi* 山西通志, citing an older gazetteer, Guye Mountain is about 35 *li* northeast of Hejin district 河津 and the Fen River runs south of the town. The same source also records a Donggao Village on the east side of the town. See *Shanxi tongzhi*, 55.40a. As for the significance of Guye Mountain in these lines, see Chapter 4, note 60, as well as the following passage in *Zhuangzi*: "Yao brought order to the people in the world and stability to the govenment within the seas. But when he went to visit the Four Masters [Wang Ni 王倪, Nieque 齧缺, Piyi 披衣, and Xu You] faraway on Guye Mountain north of the Fen River, he was in such a trance that he forgot all about his empire" (1.30).

101. Lu Qinli, *Tao Yuanming ji*, 89.

102. This alludes to the story of a Jin scholar by the name Sun Kang 孫康, who came from a poor family that could not afford to buy lamp oil. In winter, Sun

Kang used the reflection from the snow on the ground for his reading light. See *Chuxue ji*, 2.28.

103. This alludes to the story of Che Yin 車胤, another Jin scholar from a poor family, who collected fireflies in the summer to serve as his reading light at night. See his biography in *Jin shu*, 83.2177.

104. Laolaizi had a reputation for being a filial son. When he was seventy years old, he would still put on brightly colored clothes and mimic infants to make his parents laugh. See *YWLJ*, 20.369. Huang Xiang 黃香 (fl. A.D. 84) of the Later Han was a classic model of filial piety. His mother died when he was only nine years old, and he took over the responsibility of caring for his father. In the summer he cooled down his father's bed with a fan; in winter he warmed it up with his own body heat. See Ban Gu, *Dongguan Han ji*, 19.6a–b.

105. In ancient times, a young man took his capping ceremony at the coming of age. For the first period after his initiation, he wore a cap made of black cloth. See "Yuzao" 玉藻, *Li ji* (*Shisanjing*, 1476c).

106. The identity of these two men is unclear. It has been suggested that they are Lu Su 魯肅 (*zi*, Zijing 子敬, died at age 46) and Guan Lu 管輅 (*zi*, Gongming 公明, died at age 48), both of the Three Kingdoms period. But judging from the context, it seems that Wang Ji is relating them to his own family affairs. I suspect they are Wang Ji's siblings.

107. Hexagram 3 in the *Book of Changes* casts the image of difficulty at the beginning. The judgment advises a man in such situations to hold back and undertake nothing in order to avoid bringing disaster upon himself. See Wilhelm, *I Ching*, 16–20 and 398–405.

108. These are two recluses from the Spring and Autumn period. See *Lun yu*, 18.6.

109. Concerning Bo Yi and Shu Qi see Chapter 3, note 46.

110. Hexagram 33 encourages one to "cheerfully retreat" When he sees the way ahead clear and he himself is free of doubt, so that he will be led to the good; Wilhelm, *I Ching*, 129–132 and 550–554. Kang Jinsheng and Xia Lianbao suggest that "the man from North Sea" refers to Zheng Xuan, who was a native of Beihai (North Sea) in Shandong. Zheng Xuan spent most of his life teaching and writing about the classics. During the final years of the Former Han, when the court was infested with power struggles between different cliques, Zheng Xuan shut himself behind his door to write commentaries and refused to have anything to do with the official circle. See *Hou Han shu*, 35.1207–1213.

111. On the Southern Mountain see note 4 in this chapter.

112. Feng Jingtong 馮敬通 is Feng Yan 馮衍 (fl. first century A.D.), an eccentric scholar of the Later Han. When he was slandered in court, he wrote "Xian zhi fu" 顯志賦 (*Fu* displaying my ambition) to express his feelings. In the piece, composed in a fashion that Hellmut Wilhelm characterizes as "the scholar's frustration" ("Scholar's Frustration," 310–319), the speaker complains that he is caught in a bad time when values are turned upside down and his worthy qualities are not recognized. For Feng Yan's biography and the text of his "Xian zhi fu" see *Hou Han shu*, 28A.962–28B.1003.

113. Zhao Yuanshu is Zhao Yi 趙壹 (ca. 130–ca. 185), another eccentric writer

of the Later Han. His arrogant manner frequently got him in trouble with the authorities, we are told, and he died a bitter man. His surviving *fu* are regarded as good examples of Later Han satire; the best known is "Ci shi ji xie fu" 刺世疾邪賦 (*Fu* satirizing the world and denouncing the crooked). For Zhao Yi's biography and the text of this piece see *Hou Han shu*, 80B.2628–2635.

114. The term "time-to-return" (*danggui* 當歸) is the popular name for honeywort (*Cryptotaenia canadensis*), a medicinal plant used to stimulate women's generative organs and make them "revert" to their husbands so that their chances of bearing children will increase (Stuart, *Chinese Materia Medica*, 133). "Lofty ambition" (*yuanzhi* 遠志) refers to milkwort (*Polygala sibirica*). The medicinal power comes from the root of the plant, which is believed to enhance one's mental and physical powers, strengthen one's will and character, as well as improve one's memory and understanding (Stuart, *Chinese Materia Medica*, 338–339). Chinese poets often evoke the names of these two plants, as Wang Ji does here, to pun on their literary meaning—*danggui* "time to return" or "ought to return" (that is, return to official service) and *yuanzhi* "lofty ambition" (meaning "to preserve one's moral integrity").

115. Han Lizhou reads: *si* 似 (seem; resemble), but I follow the reading in the three-*juan* editions, *WYYH* and *QTW*: *si* 巳 (the sixth terrestrial stem; to give rise to).

116. See also Wang Ji's own annotation after line 284.

117. Three-*juan* texts and *WYYH* read: 舊知出處絕塵埃 (My old friends retreat to seclusion, cut off contact with the dusty world). In later editions of Wang Ji's collection, there is an eight-line poem with the title "Beishan" that is almost identical to this section, beginning with this line and reading: 舊知山裏絕塵埃. It is quite likely that the "poem" is an excerpt from the *fu* later mistaken for an independent piece. Whatever the case, it supports the five-*juan* reading.

118. Ziping is the courtesy name of Xiang Chang 向長, a Later Han recluse who retired from office after his children were married. See *Hou Han shu*, 83.2758.

119. Zhongshu is the courtesy name of Min Gong 閔貢, of the Later Han, who reputedly regarded taking office as too much of a burden and chose to live in reclusion and poverty. See *Hou Han shu*, 53.1740.

120. This line alludes to a passage in the "Zhi beiyou" 知北遊 chapter of *Zhuangzi* (22.813). Nieque 齧缺 asked Piyi 被衣 about the Way. But before Piyi had finished explaining, Nieque fell asleep, manifesting through his own action (or rather inaction) the proper attainment of the Way that Piyi was speaking of. Piyi was very pleased and walked away singing:

> Body like a withered corpse,
> mind like dead ashes,
> true in the realness of knowledge,
> not one to go searching for reasons,
> dim dim, dark dark,
> mindless, you cannot consult with him:
> what kind of man is this! [Watson, *Chuang Tzu*, 237]

121. *Yuanhe junxian tu zhi* (306) records:

Baodu Mountain (Baodu Shan 抱犢山) is 60 *li* north of Cheng district in Jin prefecture. The cliffs stand 1,000 *ren* high and the top of the mountain is wide. There are rivers running through it. This mountain is over 300 *li* away from the sea. On a clear day, the sea is in plain sight. In the past, there was a recluse who carried his calf to the mountain and farmed there. Thus the mountain acquired its name.

122. Kang Jinsheng and Xia Lianbao suggest that this is an allusion to Lei Cizong 雷次宗 (fifth century). According to Lei's biography in *Song shu*, in order to entice Lei Cizong out of reclusion Emperor Wen of Song built a lecture hall for him at the foot of Rooster Cage Mountain (Jilong Shan 雞籠山), also known as Rooster Crowing Mountain) in the northwestern part of Nanjing. The lecture hall was named Summoning the Recluse Hall (Zhaoyin Guan 招隱館). See *Song shu*, 93.2292–2294.

123. Compare *Zhuangzi*, 1.22: "When a wren builds its nest in deep woods, it occupies no more than one branch. When a mole drinks at the river, it takes no more than a bellyful."

124. In medieval China, high-ranking court officials wore purple robes; thus the term is used in this couplet to indicate power and merit in court. The Elixir of Return (還丹), also referred to as "the Great Elixir of Nine Returns" (九轉還丹), is the most refined of the various elixirs. It is claimed that consuming it guarantees a person transcendence to heaven and transformation into an immortal. See Ge Hong's chapter on "Golden Elixirs" in the "Inner Chapters" of *Baopuzi*.

125. When Zou Yan was imprisoned after a false accusation, the story goes, frost descended on the earth in the middle of the summer and nothing would grow. Zou Yan played his reed pipe, which turned the earth warm and crops flourished in abundance. See *Liezi* (*SBBY*), 5.5b.

126. Xi Kang, it is said, dug a pool around a big willow tree on his property, and in summers he wrought iron under the tree. See *Ji shu*, 49.1372.

127. Dong Feng 董奉 was a recluse from the Three Kingdoms period who lived in the mountains and practiced medicine. He never charged his patients but asked them to plant apricot trees in his garden for payment. He often sat under these trees to meditate, and legend has it that he later became a transcendent. See *Shenxian zhuan*, 6.9b–12b.

128. In *Shishuo xinyu* there is an anecdote about Sun Chuo discussing Zuo Si's and Ban Gu's *fu* on capitals. He compared these works to "the drumming and piping for the Five Classics"; see 4.203; Mather, *New Account*, 135. In another anecdote from the same source, Sun Chuo showed his "*Fu* on Roaming in Tiantai Mountains" to Fan Qi and made the following statement: "Try throwing it on the ground; it will surely resound like metal bells and stone chimes" (4.205; 137). The term has since been used to praise the quality of a literary piece.

129. "Pellets and balls" refers to a poem's polished form. In the biography of Wang Yun 王筠 (481–549), a renowned poet of the Liang dynasty, there is a passage recording Shen Yue's praise of Wang's highly polished poetic style: "Xie Tiao

had always said, 'A good poem is smooth and refined, turning like pellets.' Recently I have seen several poems [by Wang Yun] and only then did I know how true [Xie's statement] is." See *Nan shi*, 22.609–610.

130. Luo Zhenyu notes that 醉 (drunk) in most editions is a graphic error and suggests that the text should read 晬 (one year of age / young and tender look). Kang Jinsheng and Xia Lianbao identify Minghe as Xun Yin 荀隱 (*zi*, Minghe), a young talent of the Jin period. On Xun Yin see *Jin shu*, 54.1482.

131. Boluan is the Han hermit Liang Hong. See *Hou Han shu*, 83.2765–2768.

132. There are two variant readings of this line. Han's text and *QTW* read: 逐食 (search for food). Sun and Luo editions read: 逐日 (chase sunlight). I follow the former.

133. "Eight thick-browed noblemen" refers to the eight ministers in Liu An's court, supposed to have ascended to heaven together with Liu An. See note 56.

134. *Shuo yuan* (*SBBY*), 7.3a–4a.

135. *Laozi*, 1.1a.

136. *Zhuangzi*, 2.72–73; Watson, *Chuang Tzu*, 39.

137. Lu Qinli, *Tao Yuanming ji*, 89; Hightower, *Poetry of T'ao Ch'ien*, 130. It is widely accepted that the last two lines in Tao Qian's poem explicate another passage from *Zhuangzi*, chap. 26, where Zhuangzi says: "The point of words lies in the meaning. Once the meaning is comprehended, then one can forget about the words." One of Tao Qian's commentators, Gu Zhi 古直, identifies the passage in *Zhuangzi* cited above (see previous note) as the source of the allusion, and Hightower agrees. The passages make the same point: the ultimate comprehension of the truth needs no words. Wang Ji, however, is making an argument on the broader issue of "knowing the Way."

Conclusion

1. See also Cao Xun, "Wang Ji mingxia de Wu Shaowei shi," 174. Editors of two modern critical editions—Han Lizhou of the five-*juan* edition and Kang Jinsheng and Xia Lianbao of the three-*juan* edition—acknowledge that the poem was erroneously ascribed to Wang Ji but nevertheless were reluctant to remove it from Wang Ji's collection. Instead Han Lizhou preserves the poem in the section "Addendum" (Bu yi 補遺; *Wenji*, 207–208), while Kang and Xia list it under "Poems with Questionable Attributions" (Cunyi shi 存疑詩; *Biannian jiaozhu*; 135–140).

2. These include You Xinli, "Wang Ji yinianlu," 149–185; Han Lizhou, "Wang Ji shiwen xinian kao," 64–73. The most misguided project, as we shall see, is Kang Jinsheng and Xia Lianbao's *Wang Ji ji biannian jiaozhu*, which presumes to arrange the entire three-*juan* collection in chronological order.

3. *Wenji*, preface, 2.

4. See my discussion of this poem in Chapter 2, where I point out that the little evidence we do have of its composition date suggests it was written during the early Tang.

5. Kang and Xia, *Biannian jiaozhu*, 77 n. 1.

6. *Wenji*, 112 n. 6.

7. Li Chan 李樅, five-*juan* edition.

8. Cao Quan 曹荃 and Huang Ruheng 黃汝亨, three-*juan* editions.

9. Lin Yunfeng 林雲鳳, Sun Xingyan, Luo Zhenyu 羅振玉, *SBCKXB* three-*juan* editions, as well as *QTS* and *Tang shi jishi*.

10. Both Stuart and Read identify *shizhu* as *Dianthus chinensis*, or common Chinese pink; see Stuart, *Chinese Materia Medica*, 149; Read, *Chinese Medicinal Plants*, no. 547.

11. *Wenji*, 70.

12. See Bo Juyi, "Jiuri zuiyin" 九日醉吟 (Chanting in drunkenness on the ninth day of the ninth month), "Zuiyin Xiansheng zhuan" 醉吟先生傳 (Biography of Mr. Chanting-in-Drunkenness), and "Zuiyin Xiansheng muzhiming" 醉吟先生墓誌銘 (Tomb inscription for Mr. Chanting-in-Drunkenness) in Gu Xuejie, *Bo Juyi ji*, 17.367, 70.1485–1486, and 71.1503–1504 respectively.

13. Su Shi, *Su Dongpo ji xuji*, in *Su Dongpo ji*, 33:12.12–13.

14. Su Shi, *Su Dongpo houji*, in *Su Dongpo ji*, 2:9.21–22.

15. See Egan, *Word, Image, and Deed*; Fuller, *Road to the East Slope* (subtitled *The Development of Su Shi's Poetic Voice*).

Bibliography

❀

Primary Sources

EDITIONS OF WANG JI'S COLLECTED WORKS

Han Lizhou 韓理洲, ed. *Wang Wugong wenji (wujuanben huijiao)* 王無功文集 (五卷本會校). *5-juan* edition originally compiled by Lü Cai 呂才 (600–665). Shanghai: Shanghai guji chubanshe, 1987.

Jian Youyi 簡有儀, ed. and comm. *Donggaozi ji jiaoshi* 東皋子集校注. *3 juan*. M.A. thesis, Furen University, Taipei, 1970.

Kang Jinsheng 康金聲 and Xia Lianbao 夏連保, ed. and comm. *Wang Ji ji biannian jiaozhu* 王績集編年校注. *3 juan*. Taiyuan: Shanxi renmin chubanshe, 1992.

Lu Chun 陸淳 (d. 805), ed. *Donggaozi ji* 東皋子集. *3 juan*. *SKQS* edition. 1781 reproduction of an edition produced during the Chongshen 崇禎 era (1628–1644).

———. *SBCK xubian* edition. Facsimile of the Tieqin tongjian lou 鐵琴銅劍樓 collection of Zhao Qimei's 趙綺美 1609 manuscript.

Sun Xingyan 孫星衍 (1753–1818), ed. *Wang Wugong wenji* 王無功文集. *3 juan*. *Congshu jicheng* 叢書集成 edition. Critical edition based on a Qing transcription of a Song edition of Lu Chun's *Donggaozi ji*.

———. 1906 Luoshi Tangfeng lou 羅氏唐風樓 reproduction of Sun Xingyan's edition reedited by Luo Zhenyu 羅振玉 (1866–1940).

Wang Guo'an 王國安, ed. and comm. *Wang Ji shi zhu* 王績詩注. Shanghai: Shanghai guji chubanshe, 1981.

OTHER PRIMARY SOURCES

Ban Gu 班固 (32–92), comp. *Dongguan Han ji* 東觀漢記. *SBBY*.

Bei Qi shu 北齊書. Comp. Li Boyao 李百藥 (565–648). Reprint, Beijing: Zhonghua shuju, 1972.

Bei shi 北史. Comp. Li Yanshou 李延壽 (fl. 629). Reprint, Beijing: Zhonghua shuju, 1974.

Cai Yong 蔡邕 (133–192). *Cai Zhonglang ji waiji* 蔡中郎集外集. *SBBY*.

———. *Qin cao* 琴操 *Shaowu Xushi congshu* 邵武徐氏叢書.

Chen Hongchi 陳鴻墀, comp. *Quan Tang wen jishi* 全唐文紀事. Reprint, Shanghai: Shanghai guji chubanshe, 1987.

Chuxue ji 初學記. Comp. Xu Jian 徐堅 (659–729) et al. Reprint, Beijing: Zhonghua shuju, 1962.

Dai Mingyang 戴明揚, ed. and comm. *Xi Kang ji* 嵇康集. Beijing: Renmin wenxue chubanshe, 1962.

Dao zang 道藏. Shanghai: Shanghai shudian chubanshe; Beijing: Wenwu chubanshe; Tianjin: Tianjin guji chubanshe, 1988.

Du Yan 杜淹 (d. 628). "Wenzhongzi shijia" 文中子世家. *Quan Tang Wen*. 135.18b–23a.

Du Yu 杜預 (222–284), ed. and comm. *Chunqiu jing zhuan jijie* 春秋經傳集解. 2 vols. Reprint, Shanghai: Shanghai guji chubanshe, 1986.

Ge Hong 葛洪 (ca. 280–ca. 340). *Baopuzi* 抱扑子. Reprint, Shanghai: Shanghai guji chubanshe, 1990.

———. *Shenxian zhuan* 神仙傳. *Han Wei congshu* 漢魏叢書.

Gu Xuejie 顧學頡, ed. *Bo Juyi ji* 白居易集. Beijing: Zhonghua shuju, 1985.

Guo Shaoyu 郭紹虞, comp. *Qing shihua xubian* 清詩話續編. Ed. Fu Shousun 富壽蓀. Shanghai: Shanghai guji chubanshe, 1983.

Han shu 漢書. Comp. Ban Gu. Reprint, Beijing: Zhonghua shuju, 1962.

Han Ying 韓嬰 (1st century B.C.). *Hanshi waizhuan* 韓詩外傳. *Han Wei congshu*.

Hong Xingzu 洪興祖 (1070–1135), comm. *Chuci buzhu* 楚辭補注. *SKQS*.

Hou Han shu 後漢書. Comp. Fan Ye 范曄 (398–446). Reprint, Beijing: Zhonghua shuju, 1963.

Huan Tan 桓譚 (ca. 43 B.C.–A.D. 28). *Xinlun* 新論. *Quan Hou Han wen* 全後漢文, *juan* 13–15. *Quan Shanggu Sandai Qin Han Sanguo Liuchao wen*.

Huangfu Mi 皇甫謐 (215–282). *Gaoshi zhuan* 高士傳. *SBBY*.

Ji Yougong 計有功 (*jinshi*, 1121), comp. *Tangshi jishi* 唐詩紀事. Ed. and comm. Wang Zhongyong 王仲鏞. *Tangshi jishi jiaojian* 唐詩紀事校箋. Chengdu: Bashu shushe, 1989.

Jiaozheng Songben Guangyun 校正宋本廣韻. Comp. Chen Pengnian 陳彭年 (961–1017) et al. Reprint, Taipei: Yiwen yinshuguan, 1986.

Jin shu 晉書. Comp. Fang Xuanling 房玄齡 (578–648) et al. Reprint, Beijing: Zhonghua shuju, 1974.

Jiu Tang shu 舊唐書. Comp. Liu Xu 劉昫 (887–946) et al. Reprint, Beijing: Zhonghua shuju, 1975.

Laozi Dao De jing 老子道德經. Comm. Wang Bi 王弼 (226–249). *SBBY*.

Li Daoyuan 酈道元 (d. 526). *Shui jing zhu* 水經注. *SBBY*.

Li ji 禮記. *Li ji zhengyi* 正義. Comm. Kong Yingda 孔穎達 (574–648). *Shisanjing zhushu*.

Li Jifu 李吉甫 (9th century). *Yuanhe junxian tu zhi* 元和郡縣圖志. 2 vols. Reprint, Beijing: Zhonghua shuju, 1983.

Li Zhijun 李志鈞 et al., eds. *Ruan Ji ji* 阮籍集. Shanghai: Shanghai guji chubanshe, 1978.

Liezi 列子. *SBBY*.

Liu An 劉安 (179–122 B.C.). *Huainanzi* 淮南子. *SBBY*.

Liu Jingshu 劉敬叔 (fl. 468). *Yi yuan* 異苑. *Xuejin taoyuan* 學津討源.

Liu Xiang 劉向 (79–8 B.C.). *Liexian zhuan* 列仙傳. *Congshu jicheng*.

———. *Shuo yuan* 說苑. *SBBY*.

Liu Xie 劉勰 (ca. 465–ca. 522). *Wenxin diaolong* 文心雕龍. Ed. and comm. Zhou Zhenfu 周振甫. *Wenxin diaolong zhushi* 文心雕龍注釋. Taipei: Liren shuju, 1984.

Lu Deming 陸德明 (550–630). *Jingdian shiwen* 經典釋文. Reprint, Beijing: Zhonghua shuju, 1983.

Lu Qinli 逯欽立, comp. *Xian Qin Han Wei Jin Nanbeichao shi* 先秦漢魏晉南北朝詩. 3 vols. Reprint, Beijing: Zhonghua shuju, 1983.

———, ed. and comm. *Tao Yuanming ji* 陶淵明集. Hong Kong: Zhonghua shuju, 1987.

Lun yu 論語. *Lun yu zhushu* 注疏. Ed. and comm. He Yan 何晏 (d. 249). Subcomm. Xin Bin 邢昺 (931–1010). *Shisanjing zhushu*.

Ma Qichang 馬其昶 (1855–1930), comp., and Ma Maoyuan 馬茂元 [Ma Tongbo 馬通伯], ed. and comm. *Han Changli wenji jiaozhu* 韓昌黎文集校注. Shanghai: Zhonghua shuju, 1957.

Nan Qi shu 南齊書. Comp. Xiao Zixian 蕭子顯 (489–537). Reprint, Beijing: Zhonghua shuju, 1972.

Nan shi 南史. Comp. Li Yanshou 李延壽 (fl. 618–676). Reprint, Beijing: Zhonghua shuju, 1975.

Peiwen yunfu 佩文韻府. Comp. Zhang Yushu 張玉書 (1642–1711) et al. Reprint, Shanghai: Shanghai shudian, 1983.

Quan Shanggu Sandai Qin Han Sanguo Liuchao wen 全上古三代秦漢三國六朝文. Comp. Yan Kejun 嚴可均 (1762–1843). Reprint, Beijing: Zhonghua shuju, 1958.

Quan Tang shi 全唐詩. Comp. and ed. Peng Dingqiu 彭定求 (1645–1719) et al. Reprint, Beijing: Zhonghua shuju, 1960.

Quan Tang wen 全唐文. Comp. and ed. Dong Gao 董誥 (1740–1818) et al. Reprint, Beijing: Zhonghua shuju, 1983.

Ren Fang 任昉 (460–508), comp. *Shuyi ji* 述異記. *Han Wei congshu*.

Sanguo zhi 三國志. Comp. Chen Shou 陳壽 (233–297). Reprint, Beijing: Zhonghua shuju, 1962.

Shang shu 尚書. *Shangshu zhengyu* 尚書正義. Comm. Kong Yingda. *Shisanjing zhushu*.

Shanxi tongzhi 三西通志. Comp. Wang Xuan 王軒 (1823–1887) et al. Reprint, Beijing: Zhonghua shuju, 1990.

Shi ji 史記. Comp. Sima Qian 司馬遷 (145–ca. 86 B.C.). Reprint, Beijing: Zhonghua shuju, 1959.

Shijing 詩經. *Maoshi zhengyi* 毛詩正義. Comm. Kong Yingda. *Shisanjing zhushu*.

Shisanjing zhushu 十三經注疏. Ed. Ruan Yuan 阮元 (1764–1849). Reprint, Beijing: Zhonghua shuju, 1979.

Shishuo xinyu 世說新語. Comp. Liu Yiqing 劉義慶 (403–444). Ed. and comm. Yang Yong 楊勇. *Shishuo xinyu jiaojian* 世說新語校箋. Taipei: Zhengwen shuju, 1988.

Song shi 宋史. Comp. Tuo Tuo 脫脫 (1313–1355) et al. Reprint, Beijing: Zhongua shuju, 1977.

Song shu 宋書. Comp. Shen Yue 沈約 (441–513). Reprint, Beijing: Zhonghua shuju, 1974.

Su Shi 蘇軾 (1036–1101). *Su Dongpo ji* 蘇東坡集. Shanghai: Shangwu yinshuguan, 1958.

Sui shu 隋書. Comp. Wei Zheng 魏徵 (580–643) et al. Reprint, Beijing: Zhonghua shuju, 1973.

Taiping guangji 太平廣記. Comp. Li Fang 李昉 (925–996) et al. Reprint, Beijing Zhonghua shuju, 1961.

Taiping yulan 太平御覽. Comp. Li Fang et al. Reprint, Beijing: Beijing Zhonghua shuju, 1960.

Tang huiyao 唐會要. Comp. Wang Pu 王溥 (922–982). Reprint, Beijing: Zhonghua shuju, 1955.

Tangwen cui 唐文粹. Comp. Yao Xuan 姚鉉 (968–1020). *SBCK*.

Wang Bijiang 汪辟疆, ed. *Tangren xiaoshuo* 唐人小說. Reprint, Shanghai: Shanghai guji chubanshe, 1978.

Wang Chong 王充 (A.D. 27–ca. 100). *Lun heng* 論衡. *SBBY*.

Wang Jia 王嘉 (d. 390). *Shiyi ji* 拾遺記. Reprint, Beijing: Zhonghua shuju, 1981.

Wang Shumin 王叔岷, ed. and comm. *Zhuangzi jiaoquan* 莊子校詮. Taipei: Zhongyang yanjiuyuan lishi yuyan yanjiusuo, 1988.

Wang Tong 王通 (584?–617). *Wenzhongzi zhongshuo* 文中子中說. Ed. and comm. Ruan Yi 阮逸 (fl. ca. 1022–1063). *SBBY*.

Wei shu 魏書. Comp. Wei Shou 魏收 (505–572) et al. Beijing: Zhonghua shuju, 1974.

Wen xuan 文選. Comp. Xiao Tong 蕭統 (501–531). Comm. Li Shan 李善 (d. 689). 5 vols. Taipei: Wenjin chubanshe, 1987.

Weng Fanggang 翁方綱 (1733–1818). *Shizhou shihua* 石洲詩話. *Qing shihua xubian*. Comp. Guo Shaoyu.

Wenyuan yinghua 文苑英華. Comp. Li Fang 李昉 et al. Reprint, Beijing: Zhonghua shuju, 1966.

Wu Jun 吳均 (469–520). *Xu Qi Xie ji* 續齊諧記. *Han Wei congshu*.

Wu Wu 吳悮 (12th century). *Danfan xuzhi* 丹房須知. *Dao zang*.

Xin Tang shu 新唐書. Comp. Ouyang Xiu 歐陽修 (1007–1072) et al. Reprint, Beijing: Zhonghua shuju, 1975.

Xin Wenfang 辛文房 (fl. ca. 1300), comp. *Tang caizi zhuan* 唐才子傳. Reprint, Shanghai: Zhonghua shuju, 1965.

Yan Zhitui 顏之推 (531–591). *Yanshi jiaxun* 顏氏家訓. Ed. Zhou Fagao 周法高. Taipei: Zhongyang yanjiuyan lishi yuyan yanjiusuo, 1960.

Yang Bojun 楊伯峻, ed. and comm. *Chunqiu Zuozhuan zhu* 春秋左傳注. Beijing: Zhonghua shuju, 1982.

Yijing 易經. *Zhou yi zhengyi* 周易正義. Comm. Kong Yingda. *Shisanjing zhushu*.

Yiwen leiju 藝文類聚. Comp. Ouyang Xun 歐陽詢 (557–641). Reprint, Shanghai: Shanghai guji chubanshe, 1965.

Zhang Boduan 張伯端 (987–1082). *Jindan sibai zi* 金丹四百字. *Dao zang*.

Zhang Junfang 張君房, comp. *Yunji qiqian* 雲笈七籤. *SBCK*.

Zhao Youwen 趙幼文, ed. and comm. *Cao Zhi ji jiaozhu* 曹植集校注. Beijing: Renmin wenxue chubanshe, 1984.

Zhou li 周禮. *Zhou li zhushu* 注疏. Comm. Zheng Xuan 鄭玄 (127–200). Subcomm. Jia Gongyan 賈公彥 (fl. 650). *Shisanjing zhushu*.

Zhou shu 周書. Comp. Linghu Defen 令狐德棻 (583–666) et al. Reprint, Beijing: Zhonghua shuju, 1971.

Zhu Xi 朱熹 (1130–1200). *Zhu Wengong wenji* 朱文公文集. Reprint, Taipei: Guangwen chubanshe, 1971.

Secondary Sources and Translations

Bailey, L. H., and E. I. Bailey. *Hortus Third: A Concise Dictionary of Plants Cultivated in the United States and Canada*. Revised by the staff of the Liberty Hyde Bailey Hortorium. London: Collier MacMillan, 1976.

Berkowitz, Alan J. *Patterns of Disengagement: The Practice and Portrayal of Reclusion in Early Medieval China*. Stanford: Stanford University Press, 2000.

Bingham, Woodbridge. *The Founding of the T'ang Dynasty: The Fall of the Sui and Rise of the T'ang*. 2nd ed. New York: Octagon Books, 1975.

Bodde, Derk. *Festivals in Classical China*. Princeton: Princeton University Press, 1975.

Bol, Peter. *"This Culture of Ours": Intellectual Transitions in T'ang and Sung China*. Stanford: Stanford University Press, 1992.

Cao Shujuan 曹淑娟. *Hanfu zhi xiewu yanzhi chuantong* 漢賦之寫物言志傳統. Taipei: Wenjin chubanshe, 1987.

Cao Xun 曹汛. "Wang Ji mingxia de Wu Shaowei shi" 王績名下的吳少微詩. *Zhonghua wenshi luncong* 中華文史論叢 (April 1984): 174.

Cen Zhongmian 岑仲勉. *Sui Tang shi* 隋唐史. Rev. ed. 2 vols. Beijing: Zhonghua shuju, 1982.

Chan, Wing-tsit. *A Source Book in Chinese Philosophy*. Princeton: Princeton University Press, 1963.

Chang, Kang-i Sun. "Descriptions of Landscape in Early Six Dynasties Poetry." In *The Vitality of the Lyric Voice*, ed. Shuen-fu Lin and Stephen Owen. Princeton: Princeton University Press, 1986.

Chen Yinke 陳寅恪. *Sui Tang zhidu yuanyuan lüelun gao* 隋唐制度淵源略論稿. Reprint, Shanghai: Shanghai guji chubanshe, 1982.

———. *Tangdai zhengzhishi shulun gao* 唐代政治史述論稿. Reprint, Shanghai: Shanghai guji chubanshe, 1982.

Davis, Albert Richard. *T'ao Yüan-ming, A.D. 365–421: His Works and Their Meaning*. 2 vols. Cambridge: Cambridge University Press, 1983.

Egan, Ronald. *Word, Image, and Deed in the Life of Su Shi*. Cambridge, Mass.: Harvard University Press, 1994.

Feng Chengji 馮承基. "Guanyu Wang Wugong de jixiang kaozheng" 關於王無功的幾項攷證. *Youshi xuebao* 幼獅學報 10 (1959).

Feng Youlan 馮友蘭 [Fung Yu-lan]. *History of Chinese Philosophy*. Trans. Derk Bodde. Princeton: Princeton University Press, 1953.

———. *Zhongguo zhexue shi* 中國哲學史. Reprint, Hong Kong: Sanlian shuju, 1992.

Frankel, Hans. "Fifteen Poems by Ts'ao Chih: An Attempt at a New Approach." *Journal of the American Oriental Society* 84 (1964): 1–14.

———. "The Contemplation of the Past in T'ang Poetry." In *Perspectives on the T'ang*, ed. Arthur Wright and Denis Twitchett. New Haven: Yale University Press, 1973.

Fu Xuancong 傅璇琮. "Tangdai shiren kaolüe" 唐代詩人攷略. *Wenshi* 文史 8 (1980): 159–163.

Fuller, Michael A. *The Road to the East Slope: The Development of Su Shi's Poetic Voice.* Stanford: Stanford University Press, 1990.

Gao Guangfu 高光復. "Lüelun Wang Ji de zongdan ji qi shi de pingdan" 略論王績的縱誕及其詩的平淡. *Jiamusi shizhuan xuebao (Shehui kexue ban)* 佳木斯師專學報(社會科學版) 1 (1985): 35–40.

Graham, A. C. *The Book of Lieh-tzu.* London: John Murray, 1960.

———. *Chuang-tzu: The Seven Inner Chapters and Other Writings from the Book Chuang-tzu.* London: Allen & Unwin, 1981.

Griffiths, Mark, ed. *New Royal Horticultural Society Dictionary of Gardening.* London: Macmillan, 1992.

Gu Yanwu 顧炎武 (1613–1682). *Ri zhi lu jishi* 日知錄. Ed. and comm. Huang Rucheng 黃汝成. Reprint, Changsha: Yuelu shushe, 1994.

Han Lizhou 韓理洲. "Wang Ji shiwen xinian kao" 王績詩文系年考. *Shanxi daxue xuebao (zhe she ke)* 山西大學學報(哲社版) 2 (1983): 64–73.

———. "Wang Ji shengping qiushi" 王績生平求是. *Wenshi* 文史 18 (1983): 177–188.

———. "Lun Wang Ji de shi" 論王績的詩. *Xibei shifan xueyuan xuebao (she ke)* 西北師範學院學報(社科) 1 (1984): 78–83.

———. "'Gujing ji' shi Sui Tang zhi ji de Wang Du suozuo xinzheng" 古鏡記是隋唐之際的王度所作新證. *Xueshu yuekan* 學術月刊 6 (1987): 43–49.

Hawkes, David. *Ch'u Tz'u: The Songs of the South.* Oxford: Clarendon Press, 1959.

———. "The Quest of the Goddess." *Asia Major*, n.s. 13 (1967): 71–94. Reprint, *Studies in Chinese Literary Genres*, ed. Cyril Birch. Berkeley: University of California Press, 1974.

Henricks, Robert G. *Lao-tzu: Te-tao ching: A New Translation Based on the Recently Discovered Ma-wang-tui Texts.* New York: Ballantine Books, 1989.

Hightower, James Robert. "T'ao Ch'ien's 'Drinking Wine' Poems." In *Wenlin: Studies in the Chinese Humanities*, vol. 1, ed. Chow Tse-tsung. Madison: University of Wisconsin Press, 1968.

———. *The Poetry of T'ao Ch'ien.* Oxford: Clarendon Press, 1970.

Holcombe, Charles. *In the Shadow of the Han: Literati Thought and Society at the Beginning of the Southern Dynasties.* Honolulu: University of Hawai'i Press, 1994.

Holzman, Donald. *Poetry and Politics: The Life and Works of Juan Chi, A.D. 210–263.* Cambridge: Cambridge University Press, 1976.

Hsiao, K. C. [Xiao Gongquan]. *A History of Chinese Political Thought.* Vol. 1: *From the Beginnings to the Sixth Century A.D.* Trans. Frank Mote. Princeton: Princeton University Press, 1979.

Hucker, Charles O. *A Dictionary of Official Titles in Imperial China*. Stanford: Stanford University Press, 1985.

Imaba Masami 今場正美. "Ōseki no 'Koyi' roku shu ni tsuite" 王績の古意六首 について. *Gakurin* 學林 11 (1988): 27–39.

Ji Yun 紀昀 et al., eds. *Siku quanshu zongmu tiyao* 四庫全書總目提要. Reprint, Shanghai: Shangwu yinshuguan, 1933.

Jia Jinhua 賈晉華. "Wang Ji yu Wei Jin fengdu" 王績與魏晉風度. In *Tangdai wenxue yanjiu* 唐代文學研究, ed. Zhongguo Tangdai wenxue xuehui and Xibei daxue zhongwenxi. Guilin: Guangxi shifan daxue chubanshe, 1990.

Jiang Xingyu 蔣星煜. *Zhongguo yinshi yu wenhua* 中國隱士與文化. Shanghai: Zhonghua shuju, 1947.

Knechtges, David R. *The Han Rhapsody: A Study of the Fu of Yang Hsiung (53 B.C.–A.D. 18)*. Cambridge: Cambridge University Press, 1976.

———. "A Journey to Morality: Chang Heng's *The Rhapsody on Pondering the Mystery*." In *Essays in Commemoration of the Golden Jubilee of the Fung Ping Shan Library (1932–1982)*, ed. Chan Ping-leung. Hong Kong: Fung Ping Shan Library, Hong Kong University, 1982.

———. *Wen xuan, or Selections of Refined Literature*. Vol. 1: *Rhapsodies on Metropolises and Capitals*. Princeton: Princeton University Press, 1982.

———. *Wen xuan, or Selections of Refined Literature*. Vol. 2: *Rhapsodies on Sacrifices, Hunting, Travel, Sightseeing, Palaces and Halls, Rivers and Seas*. Princeton: Princeton University Press, 1987.

———. "Poetic Travelogue in the Early Han." *Proceedings of the 2nd International Conference on Sinology, Section on Literature*. Taipei: Academica Sinica, 1989.

Kong Fan 孔繁. *Wei Jin xuanxue he wenxue* 魏晉玄學和文學. Beijing: Zhongguo shehui kexue chubanshe, 1987.

———. *Wei Jin xuantan* 魏晉玄談. Shenyang: Liaoning jiaoyu chubanshe, 1991.

Kroll, Paul W. "Notes on Three Taoist Figures of the T'ang Dynasty." *Society for the Study of Chinese Religions Bulletin* 9 (1981): 19–41.

———. "The Significance of the *Fu* in the History of T'ang Poetry." *T'ang Studies* 18/19 (2000–2001): 87–105.

Lau, D. C. *Lao Tzu: Tao Te Ching*. Harmondsworth: Penguin, 1963.

———. *Confucius: The Analects*. Harmondsworth: Penguin, 1979.

Lin, Shuen-fu, and Stephen Owen, eds. *The Vitality of the Lyric Voice: Shih Poetry from the Late Han to T'ang*. Princeton: Princeton University Press, 1986.

Liu Xiangfei 劉翔飛. "Tangren yinyi fengqi ji qi yingxiang" 唐人隱逸風氣及其影響. M.A. thesis, Taiwan National University, 1978.

Lu Kanru 陸侃如 and Feng Yuanjun 馮沅君. *Zhongguo shishi* 中國詩史. 3 vols. Beijing: Zuojia chubanshe, 1956.

Lu Xun 魯迅. "Wei Jin fengdu ji wenzhang yu yao ji jiu zhi guanxi" 魏晉風度及文章與藥酒之關係. *Eryi ji* 而已集. In *Lu Xun quanji* 魯迅全集, vol. 3. Reprint, Beijing: Renmin wenxue chubanshe, 1973.

Lü Simian 呂思勉. *Sui Tang Wudai shi* 隋唐五代史. 2 vols. Shanghai: Zhonghua shuju, 1959.

Mather, Richard B. "The Mystical Ascent of the T'ien-t'ai Mountains." *Monumenta Serica* 20 (1961): 226–245.

———. "The Controversy over Conformity and Naturalness During the Six Dynasties." *History of Religions* 9 (1969–1970): 160–180.

———. *Shih-shuo hsin-yü: A New Account of Tales of the World, by Liu I-ching with commentary by Liu Chün.* Minneapolis: University of Minnesota Press, 1976.

McMullen, David. *State and Scholars in T'ang China.* Cambridge: Cambridge University Press, 1988.

Moriya Mitsuo 守屋美都雄. *Rikuchō monbatsu no ichi kenkyū* 六朝門閥の一研究. Tokyo: Nippon shuppan kyōdō kabushiki kaisha, 1951.

Mou Runsun 牟潤孫. "Tangchu nanbei xueren lunxue zhi yiqu ji qi yingxiang" 唐初南北學人論學之異趣及其影響. *Xianggang zhongwen daxue zhongguo wenhua yanjiusuo xuebao* 香港中文大學中國文化研究所學報 1 (1968): 51–88.

Needham, Joseph. "Human Laws and Laws of Nature in China and the West (I)." *Journal of the History of Ideas* 12 (1951): 3–30.

———. "Chinese Civilization and the Laws of Nature (II)." *Journal of the History of Ideas* 12 (1951): 194–230.

———. "Corrigenda to Part II." *Journal of the History of Ideas* 12 (1951): 628–629.

Nienhauser, William H., Jr., ed. *The Indiana Companion to Traditional Chinese Literature.* Bloomington: Indiana University Press, 1986.

Ogasawara Hiroe 小笠原博慧. "Ō Seki ron: Sono hito to sakuhin" 王績論：その人と作品. In *Shūchaku to tentan no bungaku* 執着と恬淡の文學. Chūgoku bungaku no sekai 中國文學の世界 4. Ed. Chūgoku koten kenkyūsha 中國古典文學研究社. Tokyo: Kasama shoin, 1980.

Ōno Jitsunosuke 大野實之助. "Ō Seki to sono shifū" 王績とその詩風. *Chūgoku koten kenkyū* 中國古典研究 18 (1971): 64–92.

Owen, Stephen. *The Poetry of the Early T'ang.* New Haven: Yale University Press, 1977.

———. *Traditional Chinese Poetry and Poetics: Omen of the World.* Madison: University of Wisconsin Press, 1985.

———. *Readings in Chinese Literary Thought.* Cambridge, Mass.: Harvard University Press, 1992.

Read, B. E. *Chinese Medicinal Plants from the Pen Ts'ao Kang Mu, A.D. 1596.* Peking: Peking National History Bulletin, 1936; reprint, Taipei Southern Materials Center, 1982.

Schafer, Edward H. *The Golden Peaches of Samarkand: A Study of T'ang Exotics.* Berkeley: University of California Press, 1963.

———. *Mirages on the Sea of Time: The Taoist Poetry of Ts'ao T'ang.* Berkeley: University of California Press, 1985.

Shih, Vincent Yu-chung. *The Literary Mind and the Carving of Dragons: A Study of Thought and Pattern in Chinese Literature.* Reprint, Hong Kong: Chinese University Press, 1983.

Somers, Robert M. "Time, Space, and Structure in the Consolidation of the T'ang Dynasty (A.D. 617–700)." *Journal of Asian Studies* 65 (1986): 971–994.

Strassberg, Richard E. *Inscribed Landscapes: Travel Writing from Imperial China*. Berkeley: University of California Press, 1994.

Stuart, G. A. *Chinese Materia Medica: Vegetable Kingdom*. Revision of 1st ed. by Frederick Porter Smith. Shanghai: American Presbyterian Mission Press, 1911; reprint, Taipei: Southern Materials Center, 1987.

Sun Wang 孫望. *Wosou zagao* 蝸叟雜稿. Shanghai: Shanghai guji chubanshe, 1982.

Takagi Masakazu 高木正一. "Ō Seki no denki to bungaku" 王績の傳記と文學. *Ritsumeikan bungaku* 立命館文學 124 (1955): 40–70.

Tu Wei-ming. "Profound Learning, Personal Knowledge, and Poetic Vision." In *The Vitality of the Lyric Voice*, ed. Shuen-fu Lin and Stephen Owen. Princeton: Princeton University Press, 1986.

Twitchett, Denis, ed. *The Cambridge History of China*. Vol. 3: *Sui and T'ang China, 589–906*, pt. 1. Cambridge: Cambridge University Press, 1979.

Waley, Arthur. *The Book of Songs: The Ancient Chinese Classic of Poetry*. Reprint, New York: Grove Press, 1960.

Wang Yao 王瑤. *Zhonggu wenren shenghuo* 中古文人生活. Hong Kong: Zhongliu chubanshe, 1973.

Wang Zhongmin 王重民. "Dunhuang ben 'Donggaozi ji' canjuan ba" 敦煌本東皋子集殘卷跋. *Jinling xuebao* 金陵學報 5 (1935): 359–362.

Warner, Ding Xiang. "Wang Tong and the Compilation of the *Zhongshuo*: A New Evaluation of the Source Materials and Points of Controversy." *Journal of the American Oriental Society* 121 (2001): 370–390.

Watson, Burton. *Chuang Tzu: Basic Writings*. New York: Columbia University Press, 1964.

———. *The Columbia Book of Chinese Poetry: From Early Times to the Thirteenth Century*. New York: Columbia University Press, 1984.

Wechsler, Howard J. *Mirror to the Son of Heaven: Wei Cheng at the Court of T'ang T'ai-tsung*. New Haven: Yale University Press, 1974.

———. "The Confucian Teacher Wang T'ung (584?–617): One Thousand Years of Controversy." *T'oung Pao* 58 (1977): 225–272.

———. *Offerings of Jade and Silk: Ritual and Symbol in the Legitimation of the T'ang Dynasty*. New Haven: Yale University Press, 1985.

Wilhelm, Hellmut. "The Scholar's Frustration: Notes on a Type of 'Fu.'" In *Chinese Thought and Institutions*, ed. John K. Fairbank. Chicago: University of Chicago Press, 1957.

Wilhelm, Hellmut, and David Knechtges. "T'ang T'ai-tsung's Poetry." *T'ang Studies* 5 (1987): 1–23.

Wilhelm, Richard. *The I Ching or Book of Changes*. Trans. Cary Baynes. Princeton: Princeton University Press, 1967.

Wright, Arthur F. *The Sui Dynasty*. New York: Knopf, 1978.

Wright, Arthur F., and Denis Twitchett, eds. *Perspectives on the T'ang*. New Haven: Yale University Press, 1973.

Xiang Da 向達. *Tangdai Chang'an yu Xiyu wenming* 唐代長安與西域文明. Beijing: Sanlian shudian, 1957.

Xiao Gongquan [K. C. Hsiao] 蕭公權. *Zhongguo zhengzhi sixiangshi* 中國政治思想史. Taipei: Zhonghua wenhua chuban shiye weiyuanhui, 1954.

Xu Jie 許結 and Guo Weisne 郭維森. *Zhongguo cifu fazhan shi* 中國辭賦發展史. Nanjing: Jiangsu jiaoyu chubanshe, 1996.

Xu Zong 許總. *Tangshi shi* 唐詩史. 2 vols. Nanjing: Jiangsu jiaoyu chubanshe, 1994.

Ye Qingbing 葉慶炳. "Wang Ji yanjiu" 王績研究. *Renwen xuebao* 人文學報 9 (1970): 167–189.

Yin Xieli 尹協理 and Wei Ming 魏明. *Wang Tong lun* 王通論. Beijing: Zhongguo shehui kexue chubanshe, 1984.

You Xinli 游信利. "Wang Ji yinianlu" 王績疑年錄. *Zhonghua xueyuan* 中華學苑 8 (1971): 149–185.

———. "Wang Ji ji qi zuopin" 王績及其作品. *Zhonghua xueyuan* 中華學苑 9 (1972): 151–177.

Yu Jidong 俞紀東. *Han Tang fu qianshuo* 漢唐賦淺說. Shanghai: Dongfang chuban zhongxin, 1999.

Yu, Pauline. *The Poetry of Wang Wei: New Translations and Commentary*. Bloomington: Indiana University Press, 1980.

Zhang Daxin 張大新 and Zhang Bai'ang 張百昂. "Wang Ji sanyin sanshi bubian" 王績三隱三仕補辨. In *Tangdai wenxue yanjiu* 唐代文學研究, ed. Zhongguo Tangdai wenxue xuehui and Xibei daxue zhongwenxi. Guilin: Guangxi shifan daxue chubanshe, 1990.

Zhang Mingfei 張明非. *Tangyin lunsou* 唐音論藪. Guilin: Guangxi shifan daxue chubanshe, 1993.

Zhang Xihou 張錫厚. "Guanyu 'Wang Ji ji' de liuchuan yu wujuanben de faxian" 關於王績集的流傳與五卷本的發現. *Zhongguo gudian wenxue luncong* 中國古典文學論叢 1 (1984): 70–95.

———. "Lun Wang Ji de shiwen ji qi wenxue chengjiu" 論王績的詩文及其文學成就. *Wenxue yichan* 文學遺產 2 (1984): 116–126.

———. "Wang Ji shengping bianxi ji qi sixiang xinzheng" 王績生平辨析及其思想新證. *Xueshu yuekan* 學術月刊 5 (1984): 71–75.

———. "Yingdang quanmian pingjia Wang Ji de tijiu yongyin shi" 應當全面評價王績的題酒詠隱詩. *Tangdai wenxue luncong* 唐代文學論叢 7 (1986): 22–27.

Zheng Zhenduo 鄭振鐸. *Chatuben Zhongguo wenxueshi* 插圖本中國文學史. Beijing: Beiping pushe chubanshe, 1932.

Index

❀

Index of Titles in English

Titles of poems not written by Wang Ji are in italics, with the author's name in brackets. For two poems that share the same title, their first lines are also provided. Initial articles are omitted.

At Night in the Mountains, 70

Before Getting Married, in the
    Mountains, I State My Intent, 99
Beginning of Spring, 90
Being Recommended to Court, I
    Answer the Summons and Bid
    Farewell to Old Friends in My
    Home Village, 20
Biography of Mr. Five Dippers, 105

Chinese Pink by My Steps, 150

Declining a Summons, Pleading Illness,
    72–73
Drifting My Boat on the River, 50
Drinking Alone, 102
Drinking Alone in the Rainy Season
    [Tao Qian], 93–94

Early Spring, 83
Eight Quatrains Scribbled on Tavern
    Walls, no. 1, 101; no. 2, 91; no. 3,
    104; no. 5, 102; no. 6, 109; no. 7,
    101
Expressing My Feelings [Wei Zheng],
    44–45

Expressing My Innermost Thoughts,
    48–49
Extempore Chant Made Up on My
    Return to Eastern Creek at Night,
    85
Extempore Chant Written After I Was
    Drunk, 103

Fu on Roaming the Northern
    Mountains/You Beishan fu, in
    sections throughout Chapter 5
Fu on the Third Day of the Third
    Month, 18 (from preface), 19
    (excerpt)

Gazing on the Wilds, 77

In Spring, in the Garden, After Feeling
    Exhilerated, 90–91
In the Capital, Homesick for My Old
    Garden, I See My Fellow Villager
    and Inquire, 22
In the Garden on a Spring Night, 80
In the Village in Spring, After Drinking,
    98
Instant Record of My Thoughts on a
    Spring Morning, 54

Index of Titles in Chinese

❋

Titles are arranged alphabetically in the order of their pinyin pronunciation and then in the order of their tones. For poems that share the same title, their first lines are also provided. The name of the author for poems not written by Wang Ji is given in brackets.

About the Author

❀

Ding Xiang Warner is assistant professor of Chinese literature in the Department of Asian Studies at Cornell University.

Production Notes for Warner/A WILD DEER AMID
SOARING PHOENIXES

Cover and Interior designed by Santos Barbasa Jr. in New Caledonia,
with display type in Trump.

Composition by Asco Typesetters, Hong Kong.
Printing and binding by The Maple-Vail Book Manufacturing Group.

Printed on 50# TCF paper, 440 ppi.